COUNTRYSIDE LAW

COUNTRYSIDE LAW

by

J. F. GARNER,

and

B. L. JONES

SECOND EDITION

SHAW & SONS Ltd.,
Shaway House,
London DA1 4BZ

1991

First published	–	–	–	*June 1987*
Second Edition	–			*June 1991*
Second Edition with supplement		–	–	*January 1993*

ISBN 0 7219 1061 0

A CIP catalogue record for this book is available from
the British Library

Printed in Great Britain by
Bell and Bain Ltd., Glasgow

CONTENTS

[v]

CHAPTER 1

PROTECTION AND ENJOYMENT OF THE COUNTRYSIDE

INTRODUCTION

Although this book is principally about the law it is not directed primarily at lawyers, although it is hoped that it will be of interest to them. The book has been written for the "lay" reader who is interested generally in the protection and enjoyment of the countryside, and who would like some knowledge of the main areas of the law of England and Wales which relate to those matters. The book does not cover the laws of Scotland and Northern Ireland, which in numerous respects differ from those in England and Wales.

In stating the law we have tried to avoid lawyers' jargon so far as possible; and where this has not proved possible we have sought to explain terms so as to render the text comprehensible. In a book of this size we have, naturally, not been able to give completely comprehensive accounts of all the branches of law described. We have tried, however, to avoid giving over-simplified summaries of the rules. To have done so would have been to mislead the reader. Moreover, much of the interest of the law lies in its intricacies, so long as the reasons for those intricacies are explained.

In addition to providing an account of legal rules and principles, an attempt has been made briefly to describe and assess the changes which have occurred to, and the threats which face, our countryside; by which term we refer not only to the physical landscape itself but also its flora and fauna. Fuller accounts of these matters may be found else-

[1]

where:[1] our aim has been simply to provide sufficient information to show the need for the law as an instrument to
help protect the countryside from harm, and to help to
assess the adequacy of the laws which exist. In this last
connection it should be noted that, to be effective, laws need
to be both appropriate in form and also to be adequately
enforced. We shall, therefore, include discussion of the legal
powers and duties of central and local government, and
also of a number of other public bodies with specific legal
functions in relation to the countryside. In other words we
shall try to avoid simply providing a bare account of rules
of law, and seek to give some idea of the effectiveness of
the rules in practice.

Scope of the Book

In substance this book covers a wide range of matters. We
have interpreted our title, *Countryside Law*, as extending
beyond simply a discussion of those laws which aim at the
protection of scenic amenity, fauna and flora, and as including also laws which promote access to and enjoyment of the
countryside by the now predominantly town dwelling public.
Thus, we include not only rules about habitat and species
protection, planning restrictions and pollution controls; we
also give accounts of the laws relating to public rights of
way, rights of access to open country, and rights in respect
of common land.

Conflicts

Of course, these twin aims of "protection" and of "promotion of enjoyment" of the countryside overlap and conflict. They **overlap** in the sense that little enjoyment is likely
to be gained by members of the public rambling along a
right of way through a landscape denuded of hedgerows,
trees, wild flowers and birds, and polluted in its air and
water. The aims **conflict** in that dangers exist of harm being
done to the countryside by its being opened up for public

---

[1] See, for example, M. Shoard, *The Theft of the Countryside* (1980); R. Mabey,
The Common Ground (1980); Pye-Smith and Rose, *Crisis and Conservation*
(1984); B. Green, *Countryside Conservation* (2nd ed 1985); N. V. Moore, *The
Bird of Time: the science and politics of nature conservation* (1987).

enjoyment. Ready access from the cities necessitates major roads and motorways, and sadly the presence of visitors means litter, the picking of wild flowers, the disturbance of animal and bird life, as well as a demand for car parks, caravan sites, cafés and hotels. Even visitors who mean well and behave well may do harm unintentionally. In some locations mere pressure of visiting numbers causes problems. As Oscar Wilde wrote in his *Ballad of Reading Gaol:* ".... each man kills the thing he loves."

Development of Countryside Law

To a large extent "countryside law" is a twentieth century phenomenon. The first glimmerings were to be seen in legislation relating to commons in the 1860s and 1870s,[1] the creation of the National Trust in 1895[2] and, perhaps, in the publication in 1901 of Ebenezer Howard's *"Garden Cities of Tomorrow"*;[3] but little more happened until after the mass trespass on Kinder Scout in Derbyshire by members of the embryonic Ramblers Association in 1932, which made the Access to Mountains Act of 1939 virtually inevitable. Then, after the war, came the *Hobhouse Report*[4] of 1947 and the important National Parks and Access to the Countryside Act 1949, creating the National Parks Commission (later to be known as the Countryside Commission) and making legal provision for the establishment of national parks, areas of outstanding natural beauty, nature reserves and sites of special scientific interest. The Countryside Act of 1968 provided for country parks, but it was not until the conservation and environmental movements of the 1970s, inspired in part by the example of the United States,[5] had awakened public opinion, that the Wildlife and Countryside Act 1981, the foundation of much of the modern law, was passed.

---

[1] Metropolitan Commons Act 1866; Commons Act 1876. See further, below, p. 161.

[2] See, below, p. 151.

[3] See, below, p. 53.

[4] *Footpaths and Access to the Countryside* (Cmd 7207).

[5] In particular by the National Environmental Policy Act of the U.S. Congress of 1969.

Common Law and Statute

In another sense, however, countryside law is as old as the common law of England. By "common law" is meant the principles of law developed by the judges through their decisions in particular cases — a process of legal development which continues to this day. From early times the common law was much concerned with the land itself, and this until comparatively recently meant the open countryside and its agriculture. Many of the intricate rules of land law, the law of estates and tenures, the relations between landlord and tenant, the law of fixtures and the law of waste, developed in and for an agricultural community living and working in the countryside. However, since the industrial revolution of the eighteenth and nineteenth centuries, and the mechanisation of transport in the twentieth century, conditions in, and the demands made of, the countryside have changed dramatically. Today, while agriculture remains an important part of the nation's economy, the countryside has become of considerable importance as the nation's recreation ground. The Peak District, for example, annually provides open air recreation and exercise for some 20 million people from Manchester, Birmingham and the Black Country, and the East Midlands, while the grasslands and moors of the Lake District are annually being eroded by the boots of thousands of tourists and walkers. The modern problem, therefore, is to reconcile the various and often conflicting claims of farmers, tourists, and conservationists. A principal means of reconciling, or at least achieving some compromise between, these differing interests is through the machinery of the law, and accordingly the law of the countryside is now more concerned with such matters than with the traditional law of property.

In achieving these various objectives the judge-made principles of common law are now of rather less importance than the detailed provisions of statutes passed by Parliament, and of regulations made under statutory authority by the central ministries and other bodies. Nevertheless, we shall need to consider certain branches of the judge-made common law at appropriate points. For example, we shall consider the

law of nuisance as part of our discussion of pollution control,[1] the laws of trespass and nuisance in our discussion of
public rights of way,[2] and the rules as to rights of common
in our chapter on common land.[3] As regards **statutory** protection of the countryside we shall be most concerned with
the provisions of the National Parks and Access to the
Countryside Act 1949, the Wildlife and Countryside Act
1981, the Planning Acts of 1990 (reenacting earlier legislation dating from 1947 and incorporating amendments since
that date), the Water Act 1989 and the Environmental Protection Act 1990.

As we shall see, even in relation to statute law the role
of the judges is important. Where provisions are ambiguous
or unclear it may be necessary for a judge to interpret the
legislation to decide a case. That interpretation will establish
a precedent defining the meaning of the provision.

In addition to these "domestic" sources of countryside
law there is also a body of law which derives either from
international treaties to which the UK is a party, or from
the environmental law and policy of the European Community. As regards the former, it is important to note that
treaty obligations do not in themselves give rise to any
enforceable rights in the English courts; nor do they confer
powers on government to take action which would otherwise
be unlawful. The consequence is that when an international
obligation is entered into by the UK government it is necessary for the government to consider whether the law as
it stands is sufficient to ensure compliance with the new
obligations; or whether new legislation needs to be passed
through Parliament. An example of the former situation is
the way in which the UK has protected certain wetland sites
of internationally important habitat value for wildfowl by
means of agreements entered into with site owners (in some
cases bodies such as the RSPB or county conservation trusts,
or by means of orders under the pre-existing legislation
providing for the creation or designation of nature reserves

---

[1] Chapter 7.
[2] Chapter 3.
[3] Chapter 5.

or sites of special scientific importance (SSSIs). An example where special legislation has been necessary is in relation to our obligations under the Convention on Trade in Endangered Species (CITES).

The situation is a rather different in relation to European Community obligations. Such obligations, in the sphere of the environment, generally take the form of "directives". Where these satisfy certain tests as to certainty and clarity they have "direct effect" within member states. This means that, at any rate in relation to a dispute with an agency of the state, an individual may call in aid the provisions of the relevant directive, and a court will give judgement on the basis that the directive forms a part of English law. Indeed, the doctrine of the **primacy** of EC law requires the court to give effect to the directive even where there is later contradictory legislation emanating from the Westminster parliament. Even where a directive does not have direct effect (*eg* because it is insufficiently precise for a court to apply) there exists an obligation under EC law for the member state to legislate so as to achieve the aims and objectives of the directive. Some discretion is therefore left to the state as to the precise manner of implementation. Nevertheless, in one way or another the directive must be implemented. In addition to such **formal implementation** it is also necessary for states to ensure that the legislation is appropriately **enforced** if it is to comply with its obligations.

When the Common Market was established in 1958, and throughout the whole of the 1960's, environmental considerations were not regarded as a part of its remit. More recently, however, it has been appreciated that such considerations need to be addressed as an aspect of the living standards of citizens within the Community, and also because differences in environmental laws and enforcement policies between member states can distort the fundamental Community aim of creating a single competitive market. A company in one country which has to comply with a strict pollution control regime is at a competitive disadvantage in comparison with a company in another country with more lax standards of law or enforcement. For these reasons a very considerable number of directives have emanated from the EC over the last 20 years and many of these have had important consequences in terms of new legislation from Westminster (*eg* environmentally sensitive areas), delegated legislation from government departments (*eg* environmental impact assessment in relation to major development projects), or simply in terms of the standards imposed under pre-existing legislation (*eg* in relation to quality obligations in relation to drinking and bathing water purity). In addition to these numerous environmental directives the Community has recently agreed that environmental considerations should be taken into consideration in relation to the formation and development of all aspects of EC policy. It will therefore be relevant to the ways in which policies on such matters as agriculture, transport, energy, and regional aid are developed and implemented. The frequency with which all these subjects and issues are referred to in the press and on the broadcasting media is clear testimony to the great significance of the European Community today in environmental matters.

ADMINISTRATION

To administer and enforce this mass of legislation it has been necessary to establish new specialised agencies as well as simply conferring powers and duties on the ordinary, pre-existing, agencies of central and local government.

Central Government

Taking first the pre-existing agencies, the **central government** is responsible for the drafting of new legislation and steering such measures through Parliament; and for making regulations and other forms of subordinate legislation which may be needed to implement provisions contained in statutes that have previously been passed by Parliament. The central government departments have numerous important powers in relation to the matters we shall discuss. These include powers to license otherwise prohibited activities (such as those, described in chapter 6, on the protection of birds, animals and plants); to decide appeals from decisions of local authorities or other bodies (for example, appeals against refusals of planning permission); to confirm or reject orders which such bodies seek to make (such as compulsory purchase orders, or footpath closure or diversion orders); and to make grants or loans from the central exchequer for statutorily authorised purposes. The most important ministry in relation to conservation of the countryside is the Department of the Environment, and in relation to Welsh matters, the Welsh Office. Nevertheless, other Departments' activities have a bearing on the rural environment, most notably perhaps the Ministry of Agriculture, Fisheries and Food (MAFF), and the Department of Transport.

In order to co-ordinate environmental policy as between the various central departments there has recently been established a standing committee of Cabinet Ministers. The Environment White Paper of autumn 1990 has stated that this committee is to be retained, and that a minister in each central department will be nominated as having responsibility for environmental aspects of the policies and the running of that department.

Local Authorities

Legislation has also conferred a large number of important functions on the numerous multi-purpose **local authorities.** Such authorities, outside London, are of three kinds: parish councils (of which there are several thousand), district councils (of which there are some 450 in England and Wales), and county councils (44 in England and Wales).

Most of the local government functions with which we shall be concerned are the responsibility of the **district councils.** It is they, for example, who are the planning authorities responsible for virtually all planning matters, (although the county councils have been responsible for the preparation of development plans, and are responsible for decisions in respect of "minerals"—mining, quarrying, sand and gravel extraction). The main functions of the **county councils,** from our point of view, are as highway authorities and in relation to the registration of commons. As regards the **parish councils**, which exist in all rural areas, we may note that although their powers are of a rather limited nature they do represent the organ of local government most minutely concerned with the countryside. They constitute the most localised form of decision-making, and may help foster local pride and civic responsibility in relation to their areas. The powers of these councils include the installation of bus shelters and seats in public places;[1] they may accept responsibility for the control of litter;[2] they may acquire unenclosed or waste land and make it available for public use as an open space;[3] and they may take steps to safeguard public rights of way.[4] A further function of parish councils is to respond to the district council's notification to them of planning applications in their areas. Such notification is obligatory where the parish council has informed the district council that it wishes to be so notified; though the parish council may choose to confine the notification requirement to particular kinds of planning application only. The district council is not obliged to accept the views of the parish council in relation to applications, but this arrangement can result in a degree of public participation in planning decisions, and may be of value in ensuring that more fully informed decisions are taken.

Each parish council must, at least once a year, hold a parish meeting, attendance at which is open to all local government electors in the parish.[5] Parishes having less than 200 inhabitants do not have to have a parish council. There must, nevertheless, still be a parish meeting. The expenses of parish councils are met by demands (called "precepts") which they serve on their district councils; this is then collected by district councils as part of the community charge.

In Wales the parish councils are known as **community councils** but the difference is one of name only; they have the same powers as their English counterparts. Similarly, in some small towns in England parish councils may exist under

---

[1] Local Government (Miscellaneous Provisions) Act 1953 s. 4; Parish Councils Act 1957 s. 1.
[2] Litter Act 1983 ss. 5, 6.
[3] Open Spaces Act 1906 ss. 9, 10.
[4] Highways Act 1980 s. 130.
[5] Local Government Act 1972 ss. 9–17.

the name of "town" council; again their powers are not different, though the council's chairman and vice-chairman become known as "town mayor" and "deputy town mayor" respectively!

Water Authorities

In addition to the multi-purpose local authorities there were, until 1989, 10 regional water authorities in England and Wales, each covering one or more river basins. Their boundaries were different from those of local authorities, being drawn so that "integrated river basin management" could be achieved. Regulated by the Water Resources Act 1963, and the Water Acts of 1973 and 1983, they were statutory corporations whose members were appointed by the Secretary of State. The authorities levied their own rates and were responsible for the collection and conservation of water, for its supply to domestic, commercial and industrial users, for the collection, treatment and discharge of sewage, and for the prevention of pollution of inland, estuarine and coastal waters.

Many changes to the structure of the water industry were, however, made in the Water Act 1989. This Act provided for the assets and functions of the water authorities to be divided between

(i) successor, privatised, water supply companies and sewerage companies. These have inherited the utility (water supply and sewerage) functions of the former water authorities, and perform these functions under the superintendence of a Director General of Water Services and the Water Services Office;

(ii) a new national public body – the National Rivers Authority (NRA) – which has inherited functions related to river and coastal pollution control, land drainage and flood defence, water resource management (eg abstraction from rivers, drought orders), fisheries and navigation.

This separation of functions between the new commercially orientated water supply and sewerage companies and the new national regulatory and enforcement agency marks a considerable improvement on earlier government proposals under which all the functions, except for land drainage, were to have been conferred on the privatised companies. The likelihood of privately owned companies performing adequately the sort of functions now conferred on the NRA (including monitoring their own activities and taking action where necessary) was generally felt to be slim; and indeed this very combination of all the various "water" functions in the existing public sector water authorities was by the 1980s being regarded with some disfavour. Accordingly the revised scheme to be found in the 1989 Act, separating commercial activities from those of a regulatory/enforcement nature is to be welcomed from an environmental point of view.

Of course, mere institutional independence is insufficient. The NRA must be adequately resourced to be able to perform properly its various functions, and it must display the will to impose adequately stringent pollution standards and to back this up with a reasonably vigorous enforcement policy. The former water authorities had been much criticised for failures in both these latter respects. In its first year the NRA has generally appeared to observers to be adopting a more potent pollution control stance than had been seen before. Problems as to the level of its resources do however exist: a matter to which it has itself adverted.

Although this separation of functions has received a general welcome the privatisation legislation did in various other respects give rise to much concern amongst environmental and amenity groups. In particular, it was feared that access by members of the public to reservoirs and surrounding catchment land might be curtailed by the new companies. Over the years the former water authorities had moderated earlier more restrictive attitudes that such public access was a threat to water purity, and many such areas had become of very considerable recreational value. A high proportion of reservoirs had been made open for fishing, sailing, sail-boarding and canoeing; the surrounding land commonly being open for walking, horse-riding or birdwatching. The very great significance of this land for these purposes is shown by the fact that of some 440,000 acres owned by the former water authorities, some 180,000 falls within national parks, areas of outstanding natural beauty or are sites of special scientific interest. Amenity groups feared that such public use of this prime scenic and recreational land would be restricted as the new commercially oriented water companies sought to generate income by selling off any such land which might be considered surplus to wants, and might decide to charge for access to other remaining land.

This controversy resulted in the inclusion in the Water Act, as eventually enacted, of a number of provisions designed to impose environmental obligations on the new privatised companies. For example, it is provided (in section 8) that ministers and the companies should in the exercise of their functions **take into account** the effects of their actions on the beauty or amenity of any rural or urban area (and its flora, fauna, features and buildings), **have regard to** the desirability of protecting and conserving buildings, sites and objects of archaeological or historic interest, and **exercise their powers** so as to further the conservation and enhancement of natural beauty and the conservation of flora, fauna and geological or physiological features of special interest. More specifically, the section goes on to impose duties to

(a) have regard to the desirability of preserving for the public any freedom of access to areas of woodland, mountains, moor, heath, down, cliff, or foreshore and other places of natural beauty;

(b) have regard to the desirability of maintaining the availability to the public of any facility for visiting or inspecting any building, site or object of archaeological, architectural or historic interest; and

(c) take into account any effect which any proposals would have on any such freedom of access or on the availability of any such facility.

Further, the NRA is required to "such extent as it considers desirable" generally to promote

(a) the conservation and enhancement of the natural beauty and amenity of inland and coastal waters and land associated with such waters;

(b) the conservation of flora and fauna which are dependent on the aquatic environment; and

(c) the use of such waters and land for recreational purposes.

The value of such very general duties as these in legislation has sometimes been doubted. The duties are rarely absolute; they are commonly subject to compatibility with other, primary, objectives or duties contained in the Act. They are usually couched in rather limited terms—"to have regard to", "to take into account", "so far as it considers desirable". Moreover, it is often not clear what follows from failure to comply with such duties.

In the particular context of the Water Act 1989 these problems have been addressed in two ways. The Act makes provision for its terms to be "fleshed out", so as to provide clearer guidance as to obligations imposed, by the promulgation of Codes of Practice. Such Codes are intended to give "practical guidance" as to "desirable practice". Prior to issuing a Code the Secretary of State is required to have consulted a wide variety of public bodies, including the Countryside Commission and the Nature Conservancy Council. A Code on Conservation, Access and Recreation was issued in 1989 (S.I. 1989/1152).

As regards enforcement of general statements of environmental obligation, the 1989 Act includes these obligations amongst a list of duties which are enforceable by ways of a special procedure under section 20. Under this section the Secretary of State can make enforcement orders against water companies not complying with certain of the obligations imposed under the Act. It will therefore be appropriate for those aggrieved to draw the attention of the Secretary of State to any failures to comply with the various environmental duties described above. The Secretary has a duty to serve an enforcement order on any company in contravention of its obligations. This duty does not apply, however, to cases of trivial contravention, to cases where an "undertaking" had been given by the company that it is going to comply with obligations, and to cases where the duties were not complied with because of the primacy of other more fundamental duties in the Act. In these three situations the Secretary of State retains a power to invoke the enforcement order mechanism but is not under a duty to do so.

The enforcement order served on the water company will state what is required to comply with its terms. Failing such compliance the Secretary of State may go to court to obtain an injunction to reinforce his order; in an extreme case a special administration order can be sought under which the court will appoint an administrator to take over the running of the company.

Even apart from these specific provisions, it may be argued that such statements in legislation are of importance. They demonstrate the significance attached by the legislature to environmental matters, they constitute a range of items to be borne in mind as a matter of routine, and provide very clear foundation for environmental "objectors" or campaigning groups to have their views heard and taken into account.

Whatever the value of the provisions described above, they were by themselves inadequate to assuage the fears expressed above of loss of amenity land as a result of sales by the new companies. The Act seeks to deal with this problem by providing specifically (section 152) that sales of land by the new companies shall require ministerial consent. In determining applications for consent the Secretary of State is, at least in relation to land in national parks, areas of outstanding natural beauty, the Broads and sites of special scientific importance, obliged to comply with the general environmental duties described above. Consent may be given conditionally. Such conditions may include the obligation first to offer the land on stated terms to a specified person or body (*eg* a conservation body) at market price; and where the land falls within an area such as that just described (*ie* national park etc) the consent may contain a condition of having to consult with the Countryside Commission or the Nature Conservancy Council (as appropriate) and to enter into such management agreements with those bodies as the Secretary of State may require. The Act further empowers companies intending to sell land to enter into a covenant with the Secretary of State accepting obligations with respect to public freedom of access to the land or to the use or management of the land. Any such agreement or convenant will then be binding on any purchasers of the land and their successors in title (section 152 (7)).

Forestry Commission

Another public body with functions which are of considerable significance to the countryside is the Forestry Commission. This body was established, by statute, in 1919 to ensure that an adequate supply of timber would be available for national needs; the long period of time between planting and felling making this an unsuitable matter to entrust to free enterprise response to supply and demand. The Commission is the largest landowner in the United Kingdom, and has powers of compulsory acquisition for forestry purposes. Its own holdings amount to some 2.9 million acres, and it advises private owners as to the management of a further million acres. Fuller information about the activities and environmental responsibilities of the Forestry Commission may be found in Chapter 4. At this stage, however, we may note that since 1982 the Government has been extending its "privatisation" policy to forestry. This has been partly an application of principle: the view that forestry should not be a government or public sector activity. And partly an attempt to secure a limitation on general public expenditure, the Forestry Commission traditionally being a loss-making concern. Accordingly, the Commission is selling woodland plantations to the private sector. Some 300,000 acres were so sold during the 1980s and present instructions are for the Commission to dispose of a further 250,000 acres during the 1990s.

Conservation and amenity groups have expressed much concern both at the very fact of such sales, and also at some of the particular sales which have taken place. Indeed, on a number of occasions voluntary organisations have made "rescue" purchases of tracts of woodland which they have considered to be of important wildlife habitat value. Since such purchases have often been made with the assistance of government grants (through, for example, the National Heritage Memorial Fund or the Nature Conservancy Council) there has been criticism that such sales have simply constituted the recycling of public money.

Even where the woodland transferred to private ownership is not itself perceived to be under threat, problems exist where the new private owner is less willing to permit public access that had formerly been the case when owned by the Forestry Commission. A policy of incorporating public access obligations into such sales of land was recommended by the House of Commons agriculture committee in January 1990, but action to adopt this practice is still awaited.

SPECIALISED AGENCIES

In addition to the conferment of statutory functions of environmental significance on the institutions described above, there have also been created a number of specialised agencies whose responsibilities are focussed exclusively on the protection of, or promotion of enjoyment of, the countryside. Two such bodies have been of particular significance: the Countryside Commission and the Nature Conservancy Council.

Following implementation of what proved to be a particularly controversial part of the Environmental Protection Act 1990, the Nature Conservancy Council's functions are now performed by separate national Councils in England and Scotland. In Wales a new body has been created, the Countryside Council for Wales, and that body exercises in that country the functions formerly performed by both the NCC and Countryside Commission.[1]

In the opinion of the NCC and most other conservation organisations this dismemberment of the NCC will be harmful to the cause of nature conservation. It will be damaging to the NCC's scientific competence, will diminish its international standing as an independent conservation adviser, and will have adverse effects on its overall efficiency.

Opponents of the changes asserted that this was the price the NCC was to pay for its very active opposition to afforestation plans in respect of the blanket bog Flow country in the Caithness and Sutherland areas of Scotland; plans which initially had seemed to meet with the approval of the Secretary of State for Scotland. However, concerted campaigning by a range of environmental organisations, including the NCC, in due course led to changes in the proposed drainage and planting so as to protect at least the more sensitive zones. During the passage through Parliament of the Environmental Protection Bill it was commonly asserted by opponents that the measure was designed to reduce the influence of the NCC by breaking it up into several "country" bodies, in Scotland and Wales losing also its identity as separate from the rather differently orientated Countryside Commissions.

The Government explanation of the change was rather different. In its view it was desirable to split the NCC into national bodies in order to ensure that it was properly atuned to the differing needs and requirements of each of the particular countries. Critics argued, however, that this objective could be achieved by other means; for example by furthering the regional organisation of what, they argued, should remain a truly national institution.

Opposition to the proposals in the bill were more intense than the Government had anticipated, and in due course the bill was amended in the hope of producing an acceptable compromise. As finally enacted the Act provides for the

---

[1] As from 1992 it is planned that a new body, Scottish Natural Heritage, shall be established to perform these combined functions in Scotland: Natural Heritage (Scotland) Bill 1990/91.

establishment of a joint committee, with a small secretarial and technical staff, which is intended to assist coordination of the activity of the new bodies, and which will be able to speak, as a body with a distinguished personnel, with considerable authority on issues of importance in and to Great Britain as a whole.

We shall now examine the history and functions of the Countryside Commission and the NCC, remembering as we do so that the NCC now exists as separate bodies for England and Scotland,[1] and that in Wales its functions have been merged with those of the Countryside Commission in the new Countryside Council for Wales.

Countryside Commission

The Countryside Commission, originally known as the National Parks Commission, was established by the National Parks and Access to the Countryside Act 1949 and was reconstituted under its present name by the Countryside Act 1968. Members of its governing body, headed by a Chairman and Deputy Chairman, are appointed by the Secretary of State for the Environment and are dismissable by him; and it receives annually an exchequer grant included in the moneys voted by Parliament for the Department of the Environment. Whether these arrangements are those best suited to ensuring an independent approach to its task has been, for some critics, a matter of doubt. Although its annual grant is the largest given to any such body, far exceeding that of the Nature Conservancy Council, it has for long regarded its finances as inadequate to fulfil properly its many tasks and reponsibilities.

The functions of the Commission were originally confined to the designation of National Parks, the supervision of their management by, in most cases, the local county planning authorities, and the designation of Areas of Outstanding Natural Beauty. However, its functions were considerably extended by the Countryside Act of 1968. Its principal objectives are now to seek the preservation and enhance-

---

[1] But see fn 1 p. 17 above.

ment of the landscape beauty of the countryside, and to encourage the development and improvement of facilities for informal recreation and access to the countryside by members of the public. It is not itself a land-owning body and possesses few direct executive powers. It seeks to achieve its aims by a wide variety of means. It tenders much advice on countryside matters to organs of central and local government and also to private individuals and groups. As we shall see later in this book, there are numerous situations in which ministers or local authorities are required to consult with the Countryside Commission prior to taking some action or a decision. Much advice is given to farmers and other landowners as to good conservation practice by the appointment, with grant-aid from the Countryside Commission, of countryside advisers. The Commission has aimed to have one such appointment for each county by 1990. This advice is organised either by county councils or by local Farming and Wildlife Advisory Groups. Advice is also given to voluntary groups at the most local levels to assist them in monitoring, conserving and promoting the enjoyment of their particular areas. In addition, the Commission has developed strategic policies for particular areas; such as, for example, its proposals for the future of the economically depressed upland regions, and its policies for securing appropriate kinds of industrial and commercial development in rural areas. These policies are then given publicity in the Commission's Reports and other publications. They also influence the Commission in its important role as a "pressure group", lobbying on behalf of the countryside against any detrimental activities of governmental bodies as well as of private individuals and concerns. As a pressure group it monitors the operation of legislation and indicates whether changes are needed. Examples of this include its work in reviewing the effectiveness of the Wildlife and Countryside Act 1981, and its concern for reform of the inadequate laws concerning the rights of access to, and the management of, commons. Moreover, it may, sometimes, play a valuable role during the passage of legislation through Parliament. In this connection, it expressed at an early stage its concern at the originally published arrangements for the privatisation of the water authorities. When revised legislation was brought before Parliament in due course the Commission lobbied strongly for the environmental and public access provisions described earlier.

In addition to lobbying in relation to legislation, the Commission also is willing, when it feels appropriate, to take a public stance on matters of government policy. It was active in the, admittedly unsuccessful, campaign to prevent a bypass being constructed through the Dartmoor National Park so as to ease pressure of traffic in Okehampton. It has made clear its concern to ensure that the adverse environmental impact of the channel tunnel scheme (and high speed rail link through Kent) is kept to a minimum. Its concern was probably instrumental in the level of investment planned by British Rail to safeguard and reduce the impact on the Kent countryside. The Commission has also consistently set itself against any easing by government of the development constraints which have operated over the metropolitan green belt.

The Commission also plays a key role in the designation of various kinds or area—National Parks, Areas of Outstanding Natural Beauty, Environmentally Sensitive Areas, and Long Distance Footpaths.[1] Lastly, it does valuable work on a local basis by making grants and loans to persons (other than public bodies) in respect of projects designed in the opinion of the Commission to improve or enhance the beauty of the countryside. Thus, it may pay sums to a farmer towards the cost of planting trees and hedges, or improving the state of footpaths across his land. In some cases management agreements may be entered into. These may involve payments to a landowner in return for his agreement as to how he will farm or otherwise use his land. Such agreements have not been easy to negotiate but are of considerable potential value. In relation to both grant-aid and management agreements an overriding limitation on the Commission's activities has been the inadequacy of its resources both in terms of manpower and in money.

---

[1] Each of these designations is considered further in Chapters 3 and 4.

Nature Conservancy Council

Equally concerned with the countryside, though from a slightly different standpoint, has been the Nature Conservancy Council. This body was originally created by Royal Charter in 1946 as the Nature Conservancy, and was put on a statutory basis with a change of name by the Nature Conservancy Council Act 1973. Like the Countryside Commission the NCC's members are all appointed and dismissible by the Secretary of State for the Environment.

The NCC has among its principal functions the establishment, maintenance and management of National Nature Reserves and Marine Nature Reserves; the initiation, by service of the appropriate notices, of the procedure for the designation of SSSIs (Sites of Special Scientific Interest);[1] and the giving of advice on nature conservation matters to the Secretary of State, local authorities and to private individuals. In many instances legislation requires the Secretary of State to consult the NCC prior to taking action — eg the listing of new species of birds or animals for protection under Part I of the Wildlife and Countryside Act 1981.[2] The NCC also has duties to commission and support, by financial means or otherwise, the carrying out of research into matters which it considers relevant to nature conservation. The NCC's functions possess also an international dimension. It is the principal body responsible for ensuring UK compliance with international environmental treaty obligations, and for collecting and supplying statistical and other information on such matters. Thus, for example, it identifies and seeks government designation and protection for wetland sites of habitat importance for waterfowl (Ramsar Convention), and also Special Protection Areas under the European Community Wild Birds Directive.

It will be apparent from what has been stated about the Countryside Commission and the NCC that their activities overlap. Accordingly they co-operate closely with each other in their work. In Wales this overlap has been recog-

---

[1] See further on Reserves and SSSIs, Chapter 4.
[2] See further, Chapter 6.

nised and the institutions are now merged as the Countryside Council for Wales.

Nevertheless, there are clear differences in the general approaches and objectives of the two institutions. Thus, while the Countryside Commission is concerned to preserve and enhance the beauties of the countryside and make it accessible to the public, the NCC is more concerned with nature conservation, which is not necessarily confined to the countryside and is also not confined to visual amenity. The Commission concentrates on the interests of the public in recreation and enjoyment of the countryside, while the NCC has a stronger emphasis on the scientific approach, and many of the areas of land managed by, or under the protection of, the NCC are not open to the general public at all.

THE OUTLOOK

In the chapters which follow much will be said of the very great changes which have taken place in our countryside during the post-war period. The loss of hedgerows and broadleaved woodlands, the drainage of wetlands for arable cultivation, the ploughing of moorland and heath for coniferous afforestation, and the shift in many areas from pasture to cereal production has much altered, visually, many areas of our countryside, and has proved harmful to many plants and animals by the destruction of their habitats. It has been estimated that in this post-war period Britain has lost around 125,000 miles of hedgerows, nearly all its flower-filled hay meadows, and over half its heathland, marsh, downland and natural woodland. In addition, some 50,000 acres of countryside are lost each year for residential, commercial and other development.

However, although complacency is by no means yet appropriate, some hopeful signs for the future may be detected. The over-production of cereals has now been recognised and it was announced in 1988 that farm capital grants which encouraged increasing production would be ended in favour of a grant system related more to conservation objectives. Further, a "set-aside" scheme by which farmers would receive payments for taking land out of agriculture production has been introduced. Those who, in addition, take positive steps to manage the set-aside land for conservation or recreational purposes may receive additional payments under the Countryside Premium Scheme.

In addition, it is evident that all of the main political parties are anxious to promote a strong environmental image. Increasingly, during the 1980s, legislation passed through Parliament has contained provisions designed to provide some safeguard to the environment. The general environmental provisions of the Water Act 1989 have already been considered. A slightly earlier example was the Agriculture Act 1986. This requires that in discharging any functions connected with agriculture in relation to any land the minister shall, so far as is consistent with the proper and efficient discharge of those functions, have regard to and endeavour to achieve a reasonable balance between a number of stated considerations. These are the promotion and maintenance of a stable and efficient agricultural industry, the economic and social interests of rural areas, the conservation and enhancement of the natural beauty and amenity of the countryside (including its flora and fauna and geological, physiographical and archaeological features), and the promotion of the enjoyment of the countryside by the public.[1]

Most recently, the provisions of the Environmental Protection Act 1990 should secure better integrated, and hence more effective, pollution control in respect of the polluting activities of those industrial processes most potentially harmful to the environment, should substantially improve upon the formerly rather unsatisfactory arrangements for controlling the disposal of waste, will streamline procedures for taking action against certain defined statutory nuisances, and contain more stringent provisions to deal with the problem of litter. All these matters will be considered more fully

---

[1] Agriculture Act 1986 s. 17. Note also s. 1: assistance from the MAFF to be available for projects having conservation objectives. See also, the Electricity Act 1989, Schedule 9.

later in this book. The benefits which will accrue from this important legislation are likely to depend on the resources available to the enforcing and implementing agencies. Some concern has already been expressed on this matter. Her Majesty's Inspectorate of Pollution, the NRA, and the local authorities with new waste regulatory authority functions and new litter abatement functions have all indicated concern at their capacity to perform effectively these important responsibilities.

Finally, it is appropriate to mention the White Paper of October 1990 (*"This Common Inheritance"*) in which the government has outlined its policies for what it calls "Britain's Environmental Strategy". Although regarded as a rather disappointing document in terms of global environmental problems (greenhouse effect, ozone-layer depletion) it deals with a number of domestic matters of some importance to this book, and its terms will be noted where appropriate. The Labour Party has produced a document of its own (*"An Earthly Chance"*) indicating a generally more radical programme, albeit, of course, from the luxury of opposition. Whichever party governs through the 1990s the agenda for action has been set, and public expectations are likely to be high.

CHAPTER 2

PLANNING

INTRODUCTION

In this chapter we shall examine some aspects of the law and practice relating to town and country planning. Broadly speaking, the capacity of local planning authorities, the district and to a lesser extent the county councils, to protect and promote the countryside through the exercise of their planning powers arises in two ways. On the one hand they have been required to produce "development plans". This has required them to survey the present and future needs of their areas as a whole and to decide how best to accommodate the competing demands for residential, industrial and commercial development, for mineral extraction, and for recreation and leisure; whilst not being wasteful of agricultural land and seeking also to preserve and promote the visual amenity of the urban and rural landscape. Much work has gone into the production of these "blueprints" for a well-planned future. However, the realisation of the blue prints is not an easy matter: predictions and forecasts may prove to have been faulty or may be falsified by subsequent events, and in a relatively free rather than authoritarian society there are few positive powers of compulsion of individuals and businesses in order to achieve the planned future. Nevertheless, such planning is essential, not only to provide a background against which the merits of individual applications for planning permission may be assessed, but also in order that local government (and central government) can anticipate likely needs for the various kinds of public services—roads, schools, water supply and so on. This is obvious enough in the urban context; but the same is true also in respect of the countryside. In particular, the very great increase since the 1950s in the ability, because of increased leisure-time and mobility, of the residents of towns to visit and enjoy the countryside has required central and local government to plan carefully how to accommodate such recreational use.

The other means by which local planning authorities may protect and preserve the countryside is by the way in which they exercise their powers of development control; in other words, their decisions, case by case, in relation to applications for planning permission. Although we have referred to the importance of planning authorities having a broad plan to guide them as to how to reconcile future needs, it is their actual decisions in response to applications for planning permission which are of most significance. Accordingly, the plan of this chapter will be to begin by outlining the main features of the **development control** system (*i.e.* the need for, and decision-making in respect of, planning permission) and thereafter to consider the law relating to the preparation of **development plans**. This ordering of the subject-matter reflects the relative importance of the two topics, and should minimise the danger that would otherwise exist of exaggerating the significance of development plans as they affect actual development control decisions.

DEVELOPMENT CONTROL

Origins

The modern system of land use planning in England and Wales can be traced back at least to an Act of Parliament of 1909[1]; though there were harbingers of the statutory system to be seen before this time in the controls that could be exercised by landlords over their tenants through covenants in leases, and also by the insertion of restrictive covenants on the outright sale of land. Thus, a landowner leasing land to a developer might impose covenants in the long-term building lease, and these covenants would bind the sub-lessees to whom the developer let the buildings. The famous Royal Crescent in Bath, the Bedford Estate in

---

[1] Housing, Town Planning etc. Act 1909.

Bloomsbury, and parts of the Calthorp Estate in Edgbaston, Birmingham were effected and regulated by this means. It was only, however, in the middle of the nineteenth century that the law came to recognise the power of a vendor on the outright sale of land (sale of the freehold) to impose restrictive covenants as to the use which might be made of the land sold, for the benefit of retained adjoining land. Such restrictive covenants were enforceable by and against successors in title to both the land affected (the "servient tenement") and the land benefitted (the "dominant tenement"). And early this century this principle was extended to the concept of the "building scheme", whereby a builder of a new development might impose identical conditions on each purchaser of a plot, and on completion of the development these restrictions would be mutually enforceable by each of the plot owners.

Control over land use by restrictive covenants was, however, wholly dependent on private initiative and was inevitably very much localised in operation. For comprehensive control over the use of land it was necessary for governmental statutory powers to be established. Although a start was made by the 1909 Act, referred to above, the first application of statutory controls to the **countryside** came in 1932[1], and the system which remains the basis of the present law was introduced by the Town and Country Planning Act 1947. This Act, together with later legislation, was first consolidated in the Town and Country Planning Act 1971; this and later legislation has recently been consolidated in the Town and Country Planning Act 1990, the Planning (Listed Buildings and Conservation Areas) Act 1990, and the Planning (Hazardous Substances) Act 1990.

Need For Planning Permission

The most outstanding feature of the system dating from 1947 was, and remains, the "nationalisation" of the right to develop land[2]. Since that time no owner or occupier has been able lawfully to develop his land unless either he has

---

[1] Town and Country Planning Act 1932.
[2] For the meaning of "development" see below, p. 29.

B

obtained planning permission from his local district council, or the proposed development falls within one of a number of exemptions contained in the statute[1] or in regulations made under the statute. The meaning of the term "development" will be considered in some detail below. As regards the exemptions, the most important provisions are to be found in the Town and Country Planning (Use Classes) Order 1987[2], which excludes certain defined changes of use of land from the need for planning permission; and in the Town and Country Planning General Development Order 1988, which lists certain operations on land as being ones in respect of which planning permission may be deemed to have been obtained.

It should be noted that refusal of planning permission attracts no right to compensation. Another way of looking at the matter, therefore, is that the grant of planning permission is very often something of very considerable significance in terms of the value of the land in question. This is commonly called "planning gain". Given the benefits that may accrue from a grant of planning permission it is not surprising that local authorities may seek to attach some price to this favour. Planning agreements, sanctioned by the planning legislation, are quite commonly negotiated between local authorities and major developers under which permission is granted on condition that the developer makes an appropriate contribution towards "infrastructure". This might comprise road junctions or additional sewage arrangements necessitated by the proposed development. Some concern has been expressed that local authorities have overstepped the mark and have sought to extract planning gain contributions in respect of matters not really associated with the proposed development at all. It is expected that central government guidance will soon clarify the limits of these arrangements. Nevertheless, it is now appreciated that environmental works may very properly be the subject of such agreements. If the planned development may have some deleterious effect on the environment it may be that

---

[1] Numerous exemptions are set out in s. 55(2) of the TCPA 1990.
[2] S.1 1987/764.

remedial or other works can minimise the harm or compensate for the damage entirely. Environmental considerations should therefore always be considered in connection with such planning agreements.

Meaning of "development"

It is clearly of fundamental importance to know what is meant by the term "development". The legislation defines this concept, and there are two limbs to the definition. Development may take place either by "the carrying out of building, engineering, mining or other operations in, on, over or under land", or by the "making of any material change of use of any buildings or other land"

"Building Operations"

The meaning of the first part of this definition, "building or other operations", has not caused a great deal of difficulty in practice. Two matters are, however, worth mention. First, the control of mining and quarrying was never very satisfactory under the ordinary planning legislation. Accordingly, revised arrangements were introduced by the Town and Country Planning (Minerals) Act 1981. These are of some considerable importance in terms of control over countryside land use, and will be considered further later[1]. Secondly, and rather surprisingly, it has not been clear whether the demolition of a building constitutes "development". Although it might be thought that this involves a building or an engineering operation, it appears that the approach of the Ministry has been that, by itself, demolition does not constitute development. Though if it is intended to rebuild, or use the land thereafter for a different purpose, planning permission **will** be needed. Special rules do apply, however, as we shall see to protect listed buildings[2] and buildings in conservation areas[3]; but no clear control over demolition exists in other situations.

In recent years some attention has focused on an alleged

---

[1] See, below, p. 43
[2] See, below, p. 50.
[3] See, below, p. 52.

practice of some developers, wanting to develop sites on which presently exist buildings of architectural or other value. It is claimed that instead of seeking planning permission at the outset for their whole project, they demolish buildings first and then seek permission to develop the cleared site. Whatever the merits of the new development compared with the old they will now be in a position to argue that their proposals are to be preferred to leaving the land vacant. In response to this problem a private member's bill was introduced into parliament in 1989 with the aim of making demolition an activity which would in itself require planning permission. The bill did not attract government support and so failed to pass. Instead the government issued a consultation paper to seek further views as to the extent of this problem and suggesting alternative approaches to its resolution. The point may, however, have been resolved by judicial decision and without need for legislation. In February 1991 the High Court ruled that demolition did indeed amount to developement[1]

"Material Change of Use"

Rather more difficulty has arisen as regards the scope of the second part of the definition: "material change of use". The courts have made clear that the term "material" means material in the planning sense[2], so that it is the likely effects of a change of use on local amenity which determine its materiality, and have stressed that whether or not a change is material in any particular case is essentially a matter of "fact and degree" rather than a matter of "law", thereby restricting the scope of review by the courts in determining planning appeals[3].

As regards the words "change of use" the courts have held that this may occur by the **intensification** of an existing use[4]. The distinction to be drawn appears to be between

---

[1] *Cambridgeshire City Council* v *Secretary of State for the Environment*, (*The Times*, 20 Feb. 1991).

[2] See, *e.g. Marshall v Nottingham Corporation* [1960] 1 WLR 707.

[3] See further, below, p. 36.

[4] *Brooks and Burton Ltd. v Secretary of State for the Environment* [1977] 1 WLR 294.

mere intensification of an existing use, which will not amount to a "change of use", and intensification which is such as to render appropriate a different description of the use to which the land is being put[1]. The difference necessary is, perhaps, that of a "private residence which is let occasionally" becoming a "holiday home"; or a "field with a caravan in it" becoming a "caravan site"; or a "field with a rusty car in it" becoming a "scrap-heap". The courts have also held that a use may be **abandoned**, with the consequence that resumption of that former use may amount to a change of use requiring planning permission[2]. However, clear evidence is necessary to show that a use has indeed been abandoned rather than simply having ceased with some intention to recommence; and this is particularly the case where the use in question is one which is by its nature intermittent or seasonal. Evidence may, however, be direct or indirect. Thus, for example, the period of time during which there has been non-use may, in an appropriate case, lead to an inference or abandonment. It should be noted, however, that **mere** cessation or abandonment of a use without any subsequent resumption does not amount to a change of use. Otherwise, by refusing planning permission for abandonment a local planning authority could compel continuation of a use!

In recent years the case law has been much concerned with the question of the determination of the "planning unit" within which to assess whether there has been a material change of use. To take a simple example—is there a change of use when a use which was formerly carried on in one part of a person's land is transferred to another part? If the land is regarded as a single unit the answer will be "no". If, however, the land is regarded as separate adjoining units, albeit in common ownership, the answer may be the opposite. The approach of the courts has, broadly, been as follows. The starting-point has been to assume that the **unit of occupation as a whole** is the appropriate planning unit

---

[1] *Royal London Borough of Kensington and Chelsea v Secretary of State for the Environment* [1981] JPL 50.

[2] *Hartley v Minister of Housing and Local Government* [1970] 1 QB 413.

unless or until it appears that some smaller unit is appropriate. Where the land occupied is used for a single main "use" together with other incidental or ancillary uses, the fact that these other uses take place at particular defined locations (*e.g.* certain buildings or fields) does not by itself warrant division of the area into separate planning units. Equally, it is still generally appropriate to consider the land as a single unit where there are several activities carried on without any being merely incidental or ancillary to the others in situations where the different activities are not confined rigidly to distinct areas of the land. However, where several unrelated activities are carried on in clearly distinct areas it may be appropriate to regard each as a separate planning unit[1].

Agriculture and Forestry

As explained earlier, it is not **all** proposed development, as defined above, which requires planning permission. A number of important exceptions to this obligation exist. From our point of view the most significant of these exemptions are those which relate to agriculture and forestry. The legislation provides that change of use of land, or buildings, from an existing use to use for the purpose of agriculture or forestry (including afforestation) does not amount to development[2]; nor does any change from one kind of agriculture or forestry use to a different kind[3]. The very wide scope of this exemption from planning control is emphasised by the Act's definition of agriculture as including:

> "horticulture, fruit growing, seed growing, dairy farming, the breeding and keeping of livestock (including any creature kept for the production of food, wool, skins or fur, or for the purpose of its use in the farming of land), the use of land as grazing land, meadow land, osier land, market gardens and nursery grounds and the use of land

---

[1] *Burdle v Secretary of State for the Environment* [1972] 1 WLR 1207.

[2] T.C.P.A. 1990, s. 55(2)(e), as interpreted in *McKellen v Minister of Housing and Local Government* (1966) 188 E.G. 683.

[3] *Crowborough Parish Council v Secretary of State for the Environment* [1981] JPL 281.

for woodlands where that use is ancillary to the farming of the land for other agricultural purposes".

It therefore follows that changes in the course of husbandry between pasture and arable, woodland and open meadow, and many other changes of use concerned with agriculture are all outside the system of planning control. Moreover, the policy of exclusion of agricultural matters from planning control is further evidenced by the fact that many building and other operations concerned with agriculture are covered by the General Development Order (Part 6), and as such do not require express planning permission. This exemption applies only to agricultural land of more than one acre, and applies to building or other operations which are "requisite for the use of that land for the purposes of agriculture", subject to certain limitations relating to area covered, height and adjacency to roads. The building or alteration of **dwellings** is expressly excluded from the Order, but the provisions would cover a wide range of other matters such as the construction of barns, glass-houses, and other agricultural buildings, the erection of fences, the removal of hedges, the filling in of dips in land to ease ploughing and cropping, and the filling in of ponds.

The policy of excluding agriculture and forestry from planning control has become increasingly controversial in recent years. The alteration of the agricultural landscape to secure greater efficiency in farming, most marked in eastern England, has had important consequences both for the visual attractiveness of the landscape, and also in terms of habitat protection for flora and fauna. The uncontrolled drainage of wetlands, the removal of hedgerows and copses to maximise field areas and facilitate use of modern machinery, the change in husbandry between arable and pasture as and when subsidy changes have altered their relative attractiveness, the block-planting of conifers in ways which mask the contours of valleys and hills, and other such matters have all given rise to much concern. Pleas that the agriculture and forestry exemptions be removed, or be made more limited, have been voiced on many occasions; but governments have resisted such demands, preferring to seek

to protect the environment from agricultural and forestry
damage in other ways than by giving a licensing power to
planning authorities. Many of the alternative safeguards will
be considered later in this book: see, for example, discussion
of Sites of Special Scientific Interest, Nature Reserves,
Environmentally Sensitive Areas, management agreements
entered into between landowners and public authorities such
as the Countryside Commission or local authorities,
environmental obligations attached to government grants
(*eg* the Countryside Premium Scheme), duties in relation to
the environment imposed by statute on the Forestry Commission and other public bodies, Tree Preservation Orders
and Conservation Areas. Such methods of protection are
of undeniable value, but are considered by many to be
inadequate or ill-suited to protection of the ordinary, as
distinct from the more especially valuable or beautiful,
countryside. Moreover, some government policies on agriculture have seemed to be in conflict with conservation objectives. The spectre of grant-aided removal of hedgerows and
woodlands and drainage of wetlands has attracted much
criticism from conservationists, including publicly-funded
bodies such as the Countryside Commission and the Nature
Conservancy Council. The outlook appears, however, not
unduly gloomy. The trust in farmers to preserve and protect
the landscape and countryside may in the first three post-war
decades have been misplaced; but environmental knowledge
and consciousness seems to be growing, and not least
amongst the farming community. This, allied with problems
of overproduction and the consequent need to encourage
the "set aside" of land or the "extensification" of production
gives cause for some optimism. Moreover, as we shall see
progress is being made to link agricultural grant and subsidy
policies to agricultural practices which maintain and improve
the natural environment rather than harm it.

Some changes in planning law are, however, likely in
relation to the erection of agricultural buildings. The 1990
environment White Paper noted that modern farm buildings
are commonly now of a scale and design more akin to
industrial developments than to the traditional style of barn.

Given that such modern buildings are prone to blend poorly into the landscape some degree of development control is needed. The announced intention of government is to consult about a proposal, not to require farmers to seek planning permission as such for the erection of such buildings, but to confer powers on planning authorities to control their siting, design and external appearance. This would be to extend to the whole country controls which have existed for some years in some, and since 1986 in all, of the National Parks. A further proposed change is to restrict the exemption from planning permission to agricultural land of 5 hectares in area instead of the current .4 hectares.

Procedure

So far in this Chapter we have considered the circumstances in which planning permission is or is not needed. Assuming that planning permission **is** required for an owner or occupier's proposed actions, the procedure is that he must make out a written application supported by plans of the site and send it, with the prescribed fee, to his local district council. His application will be acknowledged and a decision be given within two months, unless he agrees to an extension of that time.

Although all "development" has since the 1947 Act required local governmental planning permission it has recently been reaffirmed that a presumption should always exist in favour of the grant of permission. This presumption should only be displaced where the proposed development would cause "demonstrable harm to interests of acknowledged importance"[1].

A planning authority granting planning permission may do so either unconditionally or "subject to such conditions as they think fit". The courts have, however, imposed certain limits on this power to attach conditions. In particular, a condition must have been imposed for a planning purpose and not for an ulterior purpose; and the condition must fairly and reasonably relate to the development permitted

---

[1] See *eg* White Paper—*Lifting the Burden* (1985) and PPGI.

by the planning permission. Accordingly, a condition in a planning permission for a caravan site which required the implementation of a rent control scheme was held invalid as not relating to amenity and being for a planning purpose[1]. Any refusal of permission, or attachment of conditions to permission, must be accompanied by reasons. If his application is refused, or if he regards conditions that may have been attached to a grant of planning permission as unacceptable, he has the right to appeal to the Secretary of State[2]. Such appeals are in most cases determined by inspectors, appointed by the Secretary of State, who reach their decisions, in simple cases, after consideration of the papers and an informal visit to the site; and, in more important cases, following the holding of a local public inquiry. Since the early 1980s the policy has been to restrict cases where the decision is taken by the Secretary of State, rather than by the inspector, to cases involving clear issues of regional or national, and not just local, policy. Examples of the former have included the application by the National Coal Board to mine the Vale of Belvoir, and the application by the British Airports Authority to develop Stansted. Inspectors are normally civil servants on the staff of the Department of the Environment who, though familiar with ministry policies on planning matters, regard themselves as independent and impartial as between the local authority and the appellant. If the appellant is unsuccessful in this appeal he may exercise a further right of appeal to the High Court. However, a significant limitation to this appellate function of the courts needs to be stressed. In hearing such appeals the court is confined, in this context, to determining whether the planning authority or the Minister has erred **in law** (or as to a matter of procedure); the court is not concerned with issues of fact or planning merits. In other words the courts take the view that provided the decision-maker has understood correctly the legal principles applicable, his actual decision, reached in applying those principles to the facts, is not challengeable by appeal to the Courts. The court will not interfere simply on the grounds that it might

---

[1] *Mixnam's Properties Ltd v Chertsey UDC* [1965] AC 735.
[2] T.C.P.A. 1990, s. 78(1).

itself have come to a different conclusion. The application of a legal rule to facts is in such cases labelled a "matter of fact and degree" rather than a matter of "law". The role of the courts is therefore a limited one, confined to situations where reasons for a decision disclose a clear misunderstanding or misinterpretation of the applicable rules, and also to cases where although no such **express** mis-statement is apparent, nevertheless the decision reached on the evidence is so unreasonable as to permit an **inference** that the law applicable has been misunderstood[1]. The significance of this is that it makes the Ministry and not the courts the final arbiter of issues of planning merits; and an understanding of Ministry policy on particular planning issues is essential to an informed knowledge of planning law. To this end the Department of the Environment's Planning Policy Guidance notes (PPG), its circulars giving guidance to planning authorities, and summaries of decisions[2] reached on planning appeals are of considerable importance.

A further point to note in connection with planning appeals is that where planning permission has been **refused** by the planning authority, and the would-be developer appeals against that refusal, there will be an opportunity for local objectors to state their views to the inspector before the appeal is decided. In contrast, local objectors may have less opportunity to make known their views in cases where the local planning authority are minded to **grant** planning permission. No neighbour, or other affected person, has any right of appeal against a **grant** of planning permission. Accordingly, residents and amenity groups need to be vigilant as to planning applications (*e.g.* by keeping watch over the public register of applications), so as to be able to make known their views to the local planning authority **before** it reaches its decision. In this connection an alert parish council may exert a valuable influence. Such councils, which exist in all rural areas, have a right to be informed about pro-

---

[1] See, for example, *Bendles Motors Ltd. v Bristol Corporation* [1963] 1 WLR 247.

[2] To be found in, for example, the Journal of Planning and Environmental Law, the Estates Gazette, and Planning Appeals. D.O.E. PPGs and Circulars are included in the Encyclopaedia of Planning Law.

posals for development within their areas[1], thus ensuring
opportunity to make their objections known to the district
council before any decision is taken.

DEVELOPMENT PLANS

In order to assist planning authorities in their numerous
decisions as to planning permission, and also to try to secure
some degree of consistency and predictability in relation to
those planning decisions, the planning legislation provides
for such decisions to be taken against the back-drop of a
development plan for the area. Such plans have been drawn
up (and revised) by a process involving survey of existing
land use, forecast of future needs, production of draft proposals as to optimum future land use, consultation, and
public inquiry into objections, prior to eventual approval.
At present, outside London and the metropolitan urban
areas, a development plan consists of two parts: a structure
plan and a number of local plans. The former is essentially
a written statement supported by diagrams, outlining the
county planning authority's general policies in respect of
future development in the area, including measures for the
improvement of the physical environment and the management of traffic. Local plans, the responsibility of district
councils, supplement the structure plan. They consist of
maps with accompanying text. They usually do not cover
the whole county area, but give detailed information as to
planning policy in relation to particular areas. Most urban
areas will, however, be covered. Moreover, there may be
more than one local plan dealing with any single area; each
will then deal with a particular topic, such as communi-
cations, educational or recreational facilities, or tourism.

This system has not, however, worked entirely satisfactorily. As regards local plans a problem has existed that not
all districts have produced plans covering the whole district
area, and some have still not produced final district plans
at all. Legislation is anticipated to make it mandatory for
district councils to produce fully district-wide local plans,

---

[1] Local Government Act 1972, Schedule 16, para. 20.

and a stream-lined process for the creation and adoption of such plans is to be provided. As regards the county councils, proposals published in 1989 indicated an intention to abolish the county structure plan as a part of the development plan, providing instead for "national" and "regional" planning guidance and "county planning policy" to be afforded to districts to assist their formulation of their local "unitary" development plan. This change would follow the introduction of such unitary development plans in the London and metropolitan urban areas in the mid 1980s. The national, regional and county input would ensure that the detailed local plans could satisfactorily deal with planning issues which need to be addressed from a broader geographical standpoint. During 1990, however, this proposal was changed and the present intention is that counties should continue to produce structure plans but that these should be slimmer than hitherto, concentrating only on certain key, strategic, issues. These are to include the scale and broad location of housing, industrial and commercial development, the rural economy, highways and other transport questions, mineral working, green-belt and conservation issues, waste disposal and land reclamation arrangements. Local plans will have to be consistent with structure plans, and structure plans will have to be consistent with national and regional guidance emanating, following consultation, from the central ministry. However, it will not as a matter of course be necessary for the Secretary of State to approve each structure plan. A system of self-adoption will operate.

The development plan process is an aspect of what is usually referred to as "positive planning", in comparison with the "restrictive planning" development control process. The former is concerned with identifying for an area its needs, determining where and how best to accommodate those needs, and promoting actual development, which may be by private enterprise or the public sector. The latter concept, "restrictive planning", refers to the case by case handling of individual development applications in order to prevent development of an inappropriate nature in inappropriate places.

The two aspects, positive and restrictive, are not, however, entirely separate. When determining applications for planning permission the local planning authority is required[1] to have regard to the provisions of the development plan (*ie* both the rather general structure plan and the more detailed local plan), and also to any other material considerations. So far as the development plan is concerned this does not mean that the authority has to follow its provisions slavishly; but if it proposes to depart to any substantial extent from the policies there set out it must first advertise its proposals, take into account any representations it may receive in response from members of the public, consult with the county council, and in some circumstances refer the matter to the Secretary of State who may decide that it is an appropriate case in which to exercise his power to "call in" the planning application for determination by himself[2]. Accordingly, the development plan constitutes a guide to would-be developers as to the likely decision of the planning authority as to the grant or refusal of planning permission. It is, however, a guide only. The fact that a developer's intentions may be fully consistent with the plan does not absolve him from the need to obtain planning permission; nor does it guarantee him such permission. Equally, the fact that a proposal is inconsistent with the plan does not debar the authority from departing from it and granting permission. Moreover, many development plans, not having been recently revised, are somewhat out of date and so provide an increasingly unreliable guide to the local planning authority's current policies.

In accordance with the statutory obligation to take all material considerations into account it appears that there has always existed a duty positively to consider the likely environmental implications of any application for planning consent, and to take such considerations into account in determining whether an application can be approved provided certain "environmental" or "amenity" conditions are attached to the grant of permission. This duty to have regard

---

[1] T.C.P.A. 1990, s. 70(2).
[2] T.C.P.A. 1990 s. 77. See further, below, p. 43.

to the environment has, however, been bolstered recently by the addition in certain circumstances of an obligation to go through a more formal process of "environmental impact assessment" (EIA) before planning approval is granted. The origin of this duty is a directive from the EC which has been incorporated into English law by a statutory instrument effective from mid 1988. This instrument lists a range of kinds of development projects in respect of which the process of EIA is either mandatory in all cases (Annex 1), or in respect of which the local planning authority is required to consider whether the characteristics of that proposed development (*ie* its likely environmental effects) require EIA. (Annex 11). In relation to the latter, it might be complained, the authority is therefore only under the obligation in circumstances where it considers it ought to be under the obligation! The lists of projects within the annexes are quite lengthy, especially the list in Annex 11. Annex 1 includes such matters as crude oil refineries, thermal power stations, radioactive waste storage or disposal installations, construction of motorways and "express" roads, and waste disposal installations for the incineration, treatment or landfill of toxic and dangerous waste.

Where EIA is required it involves consideration of the effects of the proposed development on —

— human beings, fauna and flora,
— soil, water, air, climate and the landscape,
— the inter-action between the factors above,
— material assets and the cultural heritage.

Information is required to be supplied by the developer about the proposed development, and about measures proposed to avoid, reduce or remedy adverse environmental effects. A non-technical summary of this information must also be provided! This information is available to the public. The planning authority must then consult bodies with relevant environmental responsibilities and the public are invited to comment. All the information and views are then to be taken into account in coming to a decision.

The statutory EIA procedure is to be welcomed but its

significance should not be exaggerated. In the first place the highly-developed planning controls which have existed in the UK since the last war already provided, at least implicitly, for such considerations to be taken into account; albeit not in such a formally prescribed way and not always at the pre-decision stage. Often such matters would only have been aired fully at a public inquiry following refusal of permission. It follows that in the past where permission has been granted by the planning authority (and objectors then have no rights of appeal) such considerations may not have been rigorously examined. Secondly, it must be remembered that the number of projects where EIA is always required is likely to be quite small. These are the big development projects which in recent years have tended to generate a good deal of local, and often national, controversy; and in respect of which considerable amounts of environmental information has been made available to the decision-makers, both from the developers and from official and voluntary amenity, conservation and environmental groups. The real significance of the measure will depend on the policy of authorities in exercising their discretion as to Annex 11 projects; and also the way in which it may help engender an attitude in industry and elsewhere that some form of environmental assessment should become a matter of "habit" before companies take important decisions of many kinds. Already the initials "EIA" have acquired a common usage well beyond the statutory context just described.

In addition to this, the "material considerations" which should be taken into account in determining planning applications will include any advice from the Secretary of State, issued from time to time in the form of Planning Policy Guidance notes, replacing the earlier system of circulars, which is relevant to the application in hand. The planning authority will also take into account the policies of the Secretary of State which are evident from reported planning appeals. In these ways central government policy pervades planning control in a way which extends beyond the mere fact of the right of appeal to the Secretary of State. Chief

Planning Officers in each planning authority will be familiar with the policies on particular matters which are applied by the Ministry, and will take decisions, or advise their planning committees, accordingly. Central government influence may in some cases be more direct still. The Secretary of State may decide to "call in" an application for decision by himself[1]. This is, however, likely to be done only in cases raising important questions of regional or national significance. The procedure has been used in recent years in order to exert some central influence over the siting of out-of-town hypermarkets, and also in relation to applications to work minerals. This latter matter is of more than just local significance because to decide whether or not to permit quarrying in a scenic area requires information not only as to the likely impact on that area, but also about the national need for the mineral in question and its alternative availability. Where the "call in" procedure is implemented the Secretary of State first convenes a local public inquiry before one of his inspectors, and then makes his decision in the light of the inspector's report and recommendations. It may be noted that the "call in" procedure thus ensures an opportunity for opponents to register formally their objection, an opportunity which might not have arisen had the matter not been called in and the planning authority been minded to grant planning permission[2].

ENFORCEMENT

The preparation of development plans and the requirement of obtaining planning permission would be meaningless in the absence of adequate means of **enforcement** of planning controls. Consequently, the legislation provides that the planning authority may issue an enforcement notice in any case of breach of planning control. By "breach of planning control" is meant the carrying out of development without planning permission where such permission is required by law; or failure to observe conditions imposed on the grant of permission.

---

[1] T.C.P.A. 1990, s. 77.
[2] See, further, above, p. 37.

A copy of an enforcement notice must be served on every owner or occupier, of the land affected. The notice will require cessation of the offending operations or change of use, as the case may be, and probably require return or reversion to the *status quo ante*. In the case of breach of planning control by failure to comply with a planning condition the notice will require compliance with that condition. If the enforcement notice which has been served is not complied with within the time stated in the notice, any person failing to comply with its terms may be prosecuted for an offence before the local magistrates. It is the failure to comply with the enforcement notice which constitutes the offence; it is not, in general, an offence simply to act in breach of planning control. In the case of breach of control by unauthorised building operations a failure to comply with an enforcement notice may be followed by the local planning authority exercising its powers to enter onto the land in question and pull down the offending building, and the planning authority may recover its reasonable expenses in so acting from the person in default, suing him in the courts if necessary.

The legislation does, however, impose a time limit within which planning authorities must act if they wish to issue enforcement notices. This time limit obliges authorities to issue such notices not more than four years after the breach of planning control which is complained of. However, this time limit only applies in relation to "operations" type development and not to unauthorised changes of use. An unauthorised change of use may be the subject of an enforcement notice notwithstanding that it may have continued for more than four years, except in two cases: where the unauthorised use commenced before 1964, or where the change of use is of a building to a single dwelling house.

Instead of waiting to be prosecuted, a person served with a copy of an enforcement notice may prefer to try to protect his position by appealing against its terms to the Secretary of State. On such an appeal the appellant may argue that what he has done, or is doing, does not amount to development, or that he does not need planning permission for the development because of the General Development Order or the Use Classes Order. It is also possible on an appeal against an enforcement notice to argue that although planning permission was necessary it ought, had it been applied for, to have been granted, and accordingly that it is not appropriate for the planning authority to have issued an enforcement notice. Similarly, where an enforcement notice relates to alleged breach of a condition attached to a planning permission it is possible on an appeal to the Secretary of State to argue that such a planning condition should not have been imposed in the first place.

Any such appeal to the Secretary of State will be dealt with in manner similar to that on an appeal against a **refusal** of planning permission: that is, by an inspector, appointed by the Secretary of State, and the inspector will usually take the decision himself. There is a further right of appeal on a point of law (and **not** on an issue of planning merits) from the decision of the Secretary of State (or more usually his inspector) to the High Court.

During the period in which an appeal against an enforcement notice is being dealt with the "development" which is the subject-matter of the notice may, quite lawfully, continue. No offence is committed, and no enforcement action may take place, until after the appeal has been finally determined. There is, however, a power to issue a "stop notice". Such a notice will bring into play criminal penalties if development continues pending the appeal being heard. Local authorities must, however, act with some circumspection in issuing "stop notices". If the appeal against the enforcement notice proves successful the planning authority will be liable to give compensation for any losses suffered in complying with the stop-notice.

In recent years some concern has been expressed at the inability of planning authorities to take quick and effective action to deal with breaches of the planning legislation. Following a detailed consideration of this matter it was announced in late 1990 that legislation would be introduced to strengthen the power of the authorities by—

making it easier for court injunctions to be obtained to prevent actual or threatened breaches of planning control;

providing better and quicker means of obtaining information about suspected breaches of control; and

providing for the imposition of much higher fines on those found guilty of enforcement offences.

RURAL PLANNING ISSUES

Urban Sprawl

A very major concern during the post-war period has been to preserve the rural landscape from urban sprawl. The uncontrolled suburban development which was such a marked feature of the inter-war period, became after the war, subject to a degree of planning constraint, the new emphasis being placed on New Towns rather than the enlargement of existing urban areas. The "green belts" policy will be considered later, but quite apart from this specific device there has, in the post-war years, been a very deliberate policy of trying to contain development within the perimeters of cities and towns, with restriction of new building to "infill" sites. At any rate in the immediate post-war period this policy was not of great hardship to developers owing to the need to reconstruct areas of towns destroyed by war-time blitz and the consequent ready availability of sites.

As well as trying to contain urban sprawl in the general sense, there has also been a policy against ribbon development[1], with its particular evil of securing the coalescence of formerly separate and distinct towns. Although not all would agree, these policies have been pursued with some measure of success. The extent of loss of agricultural land to industrial and residential development has been less than would otherwise have been the case; and there have been preserved, within a few miles of even the grimiest and drabbest of our cities, areas of easily accessible and relatively unspoilt countryside. Furthermore, the continuation of the

---

[1] Restriction of Ribbon Development Act 1935.

"infill" policy may be of help in engendering inner-city redevelopment. There are, as always, contrary arguments. Some, for instance, would point to the high price of, consequentially scarce, development land and also to the resulting high density of communal city living.

As applied to **rural** areas, these general policies have sought to restrict sporadic development to that which is necessary to sustain agriculture. Even development for such purposes (*ie* new farm dwellings) is restricted whenever possible to existing towns and villages. Moreover, expansion of villages to satisfy commuter demand has been a matter that has been closely watched. In some cases planning permission for dwellings has been granted subject to the condition that the building be for agricultural workers exclusively, though such conditions are notoriously difficult to enforce.

In addition to, and supporting, these general policies of containment there has been an especially strong policy of development restraint in relation to a number of particularly highly valued parts of the countryside. These areas include the National Parks, Areas of Outstanding Natural Beauty, Green-Belts, Sites of Special Scientific Interest and Areas of High Landscape Value. Such areas, along with uplands little suited to development projects, total well over half of the total area of England and Wales. The onus on the developer, which may be difficult in any rural area, becomes greater still in such areas.

Industry and Employment

Although these policies are to be welcomed, and many conservationists would call for them to be applied more strongly, there are associated difficulties and dangers. What policy should be adopted, for example, about the establishment of industry in rural areas? It is too easy to suggest blanket exclusion. As agriculture employs fewer and fewer workers the evil of rural depopulation has emerged; and a landscape of derelict farm labourers' cottages is scarcely likely to be thought an attractive one. Maybe the buildings will all be bought up and "prettified" by commuters; but a village deserted by day, or all week, is not the kind of rural village that visitors to the countryside wish to find. Ultimately, we may need to accept that if industry brings employment, and if employment sustains the population and economy of the countryside's villages, then some degree of landscape harm may be a price worth paying. Much, of course, will depend on the nature of the industry in question; and in this connection the Department of the Environment issued a circular in 1980 pointing out that much industry today is not smoky and noisy as of old, but clean and "hi-tech". Accordingly, it was likely that there would be no serious planning objections to the establishment of such industrial or commercial concerns in residential areas or rural areas. The circular specifically mentions the suitability of disused agricultural buildings for fledgling small businesses. In this connection the activities of the Council for Small Industries in Rural Areas (COSIRA) and the Development Corporation in converting old buildings to new uses are of significance. An example of this has been the conversion of the disused railway station at Bakewell in Derbyshire to offices and a laboratory.

Recreation and Leisure

This leads us to a similar issue: to what extent are we willing to sacrifice features of the landscape in order that people may visit and enjoy the countryside? Where is the balance to be drawn between fast access roads to the most scenic areas, and the preservation of the landscape, together with its flora and fauna, in the areas which may be spoiled in constructing those roads. When visitors arrive in the countryside they wish to be able to park their cars. Car parks are therefore needed. Visitors wish to be able to stay overnight, or for a holiday. Provision is therefore needed for hotels, caravan sites and camping sites. Policies of total exclusion of things such as these may be appropriate for certain prime landscape areas, but generally the task is one of skilfully siting and landscaping such development so that it is as unobtrusive as is possible. A caravan site on a coastal promontory is an eye-sore; if sited in an incline and masked by trees it may offend relatively few people and provide moderately priced accommodation for many.

The issue of caravan sites has in fact been a matter in respect of which additional legislative controls have been provided by Parliament. Problems arose during the 1950s from the proliferation of sites, in many cases unauthorised, both for residential and holiday caravanning. Concern focussed not only on the despoilment of the landscape which was resulting from inappropriately prominent sites, but also focused on the lack of proper services and equipment at many sites. The latter public health problem was in large part a result of the common practice of planning authorities granting planning permission for such use on a temporary basis only.

In 1960, therefore, caravan sites became subject to legislative requirements which operate alongside, and in addition to, ordinary planning controls. The Caravan Sites and Control of Development Act 1960 provides that caravan sites, whether residential or for holiday use, must be licensed by the local authority. A local authority may restrict use of a site to holiday rather than residential caravanning by use of appropriate planning conditions: for example, a condition limiting use of the site to the summer season, and perhaps also requiring removal of the caravans at the end of each season. The 1960 Act also confers powers on local authorities to **establish** caravan sites. In one context a duty exists to exercise this power. Under the Caravan Sites Act 1968 local authorities are required to provide adequate sites for gypsies residing in or resorting to their areas. Despite this legislative obligation, progress in the provision of sites has been slow[1]. The problem is largely that of opposition to proposed sites by local residents. The cost of establishing sites is no longer a problem for local authorities; since 1979 the entire capital cost has been borne by central government[2].

---

[1] See the Cripps Report: *Accommodation for Gypsies — A Report on the Working of the Caravan Sites Act 1968.* (HMSO).
[2] D.O.E. Circular 11/79.

SPECIAL CONTROLS

Advertisements

The legislation also provides a number of **special** controls in relation to certain matters. Thus, there are provisions which subject the display of advertisements (a term which is widely defined[1]) to local authority consent. Application for consent is necessary except in relation to exempted classes of advertisement and a category of advertisement in respect of which consent is **deemed** to have been obtained, but in respect of which the local planning authority may order discontinuance. The planning authority's decision, if it be to refuse consent, must be taken on grounds of amenity or public safety. Against refusal of consent, or a discontinuance order, appeal lies to the Secretary of State. A person who displays an advertisement without consent (where this is required) or in defiance of a discontinuance order commits a criminal offence. Such controls are valuable in allowing local authorities to prevent despoliation of the countryside by large numbers of, often gigantic, hoardings as is characteristic of many other countries. Moreover, it helps secure road safety by permitting the prevention of a multitude of commercial signs at cross-roads and roundabouts. Control over advertisements may be made even greater if a district planning authority, with ministerial consent, declares an area to be one of special control. In such event most of the normal exemptions from control, referred to above, cease to apply. Over a third of England and Wales is now in this special control category, including nearly all areas of open countryside.

Listed Buildings

Also subject to special controls under the planning legislation are buildings of "special architectural or historic" interest. Insofar as the attractiveness of our countryside is enhanced by the older buildings to be found within it, it is

---

[1] ". . . any word, letter, model, sign, placard, board, notice . . . in the nature of, and employed wholly or partly for the purposes of advertisement, announcement or direction . . . ". Town and Country Planning (Control of Advertisements) Regulations 1984, r. (1); T.C.P.A. 1990, s. 336.

appropriate for special restrictions to apply to them. The Act provides for the listing, by the Secretary of State, of buildings which are to be subject to this special control. There is no right of appeal against such listing. Categories of building suitable for listing are described in Circular 8/87. Where a building is listed it becomes an offence for any person to alter, extend or demolish the building so as to affect its character as a building of special architectural or historic interest, unless listed building consent has been first obtained from the district planning authority. There also exists a procedure by which a local planning authority can serve a building preservation order in respect of a building threatened with demolition which it may wish should be listed. This provides a breathing space of six months. Compensation is, however, payable if in due course the building is not listed.

Applications for listed building consent must be advertised and expressly brought to the notice of certain amenity groups and public bodies. Against a refusal of listed building consent appeal lies to the Secretary of State.

The position of owners of listed buildings is safeguarded to some extent by provisions of the legislation. Compensation may be payable in respect of refusal to grant listed building consent, or the modification or revocation of a consent previously granted. If consent is refused and the owner is unable therefore to make reasonably beneficial use of the building he may serve a listed building purchase notice on the local authority. On the other hand, owners who fail to take appropriate care of listed building may find themselves served with a "repairs notice" requiring specified works to be done to ensure proper preservation of the building. If such steps are not taken in accordance with the notice served there exists a power for the Secretary of State to authorise the local authority to compulsorily purchase the building, subject to payment of compensation at site value only. A palliative exists in that a local authority may, under the Local Authorities (Historic Buildings) Act 1962, make grants towards the preservation and maintenance by private owners of historic buildings. Owners may also seek assist-

ance from the National Heritage Memorial Fund, administered by English Heritage under the National Heritage Act
1983.

Conservation Areas

A local authority power with a similar objective to that of
control over individual listed buildings is the power to
declare an area a "conservation area"[1]. This is valuable
where a group or cluster of buildings warrant protection on
architectural or historic grounds even though individually
none may merit listing as a historic building. Around 5000
conservation areas have been created. The effect of creating
a conservation area is to subject applications for planning
permission to greater public scrutiny. There must be local
advertisement of applications, so providing members of the
public and amenity groups with ample opportunity to make
known their views. Also, in conservation areas, whatever
may be the position elsewhere, the **demolition** of buildings
comes clearly within local authority control.[2] Although it is
fair to regard conservation areas as primarily a matter of
urban planning control, the powers may be valuable also
in rural areas, protecting, for example, buildings clustered
around a village green or in some cases an entire village.

Trees

Provisions of the legislation also provide special protection
for individual trees, groups of trees and woodlands by the
Tree Preservation Order procedure. This will be considered
more fully below in Chapter 4.

Open Sites

Akin to the positive requirement that owners of historic
buildings maintain them in good repair is the, admittedly
much more limited, requirement that owners of open sites
should not allow the condition of such sites to deteriorate
so as to be detrimental to the amenity of the locality. District

---

[1] The power dates from the Civic Amenities Act 1967.
[2] See above, p 29.

planning authorities have power to issue notices requiring such waste land to be tidied up[1].

RUS IN URBE

In 1902 Ebenezer Howard wrote his famous and influential book *Garden Cities of Tomorrow*, in which he proposed the construction of new towns to relieve the stresses of overcrowded urban life. His objective was an urban environment in which every householder would be able to glimpse at least green fields, while still enjoying the advantages of city life. This notion of *Rus in Urbe* was soon realised in some measure by the development, by private enterprise, of Welwyn Garden City and Letchworth before the first World War.

After World War II the "new town" idea was adopted energetically by the central government. Under the New Towns Act 1946 and its successors some twenty-six new towns have been built in Britain in order to help relieve congestion in overcrowded cities, and to ease housing shortages that had been made acute by the devastations of enemy action. Few of these towns may resemble Howard's ideal garden cities but they have certainly gone some way to the achievement of his principal objectives. Howard's ideas can be seen also, influencing recent pressures for a "greening" of the city which may improve the look of town centres generally in the future.

No further new towns are at present planned under the machinery of the New Towns Acts, but currently private enterprise is pressing for planning permission to develop considerable areas of open countryside in the South-East of England.

The *Rus in Urbe* concept may also be seen behind the idea of the "green belt". This is really nothing more than an area of land encircling a large city or urbanised area which is designated as intended to be kept free from substantial development, thus restricting the creeping enlargement

---

[1] T.C.P.A. 1990, s. 215. Note also, Public Health Act 1961, s. 34.

of the urban area. The concept was given statutory effect in the case of London by the Metropolitan Green Belt Act 1938 (pre-dating the general comprehensive controls of the TCPA 1947), but elsewhere the observance and continued existence of a green-belt depends entirely on the administration by the local planning authority of the ordinary controls over development under the planning Acts. The total area of land designated as green-belt is increasing: it doubled in area between 1979 and 1989. Nevertheless, in recent years green-belts have been under increasing threat; there were indications from central government in the early 1980s that land in a green-belt could perhaps be released for housing development where suitable building land was in acutely short supply. However, a strong green-belt policy has more recently been reasserted. For example, PPG6 states categorically that major out-of-town shopping developments have no place in the green-belt nor, generally, in the open countryside.

One of the latest developments in planning law, and one which may almost be called a barnacle on the 1947 scheme, is the introduction of Enterprise Zones and Simplified Planning Zones. The Enterprise Zones date from 1980, and in such areas industrial and commercial enterprises are able to establish themselves and develop their businesses free from most planning permission requirements. Very generous exemptions for local and national taxes also apply. In Simplified Planning Zones, under legislation dating from 1986, the planning but not the fiscal advantages apply. The aim of these zones is the revitalisation of economically depressed areas. The absence of planning controls has led to concern about the likely poor aesthetic quality of inner city redevelopment in these areas. "Old eye-sores being replaced by new ones". The problem is mainly of concern to those seeking to improve city environments and is therefore rather beyond the scope of this book. One safeguard may, however, be noted. This is that such zones cannot be made in relation to any land forming part of a National Park, Area of Outstanding Natural Beauty, or a Conservation Area.

CONCLUSION

This chapter has attempted to provide a bare outline of the modern legislation on planning control. The legislation's drastic restrictions on the rights of owners to enjoy and use their land as they please has assured both the complexity of the subject and also that much litigation would result. The old maxim *sic utere tuo ut alienam non laedas* ("so use your own property in any manner that does not harm the rights of another") now fails to convey the very great constraints imposed by the community as a whole on the actions of owners of land. Even the Englishman's castle may be invaded by the officers of the local planning authority armed with an enforcement notice.

APPENDIX TO CHAPTER 2

APPEALS AND INQUIRIES

Procedure

In many of the situations discussed in various parts of this book there is a statutory right to appeal against a decision taken, or order made, by some organ of the executive (very commonly a local authority) to a Minister of the Crown, usually the Secretary of State for the Environment. The commonest example of such a right is the right of appeal against a refusal of planning permission, or against the terms of an enforcement notice; but such rights of appeal "to the Minister" are a common feature of British public administration and apply also, to take examples relevant to later chapters, to the service of notices in relation to Sites of Special Scientific Interest[1] and orders diverting or closing public footpaths[2]. Similar procedures involving public inquiries also apply in situations where legislation requires ministerial confirmation of an act or order of a local author-

---

[1] Wildlife and Countryside Act 1981, s. 29, as amended by Wildlife and Countryside (Amendment) Act 1985. See further, Chapter 4, below.

[2] Highways Act 1980, ss. 118, 119 and Schedule 6. See further, Chapter 3, below.

ity or other body: for example, a compulsory purchase order.

In matters of detail the procedure regulating such appeals will vary from one context to another; but the basic pattern is reasonably uniform, and can be outlined in general terms.

On receipt of the notice, order, or decision against which it is desired to appeal, notice of the appeal must be lodged with the Secretary of State within a specified period of time. The Secretary of State will then refer the case to a "person appointed by him" (commonly called an "inspector", though this term does not appear in the legislation). The inspector will arrange for a local inquiry to be convened, unless, in the case of the less important planning appeals (of which there are a large number), it is decided, with the appellant's agreement, to determine the case on the papers by "written representations".

Where there is to be a local inquiry, advance notice must be given of the time and place at which it is to be held. Inquiries will normally be in the locality of the site in question and are often held at the town hall.

Prior to the hearing the appellant will often be invited to state the grounds of his appeal, and the administrative body against whose action or decision the appeal is being brought may be required to disclose matters upon which it proposes to rely at the hearing. The idea is that advance disclosure aids preparation for the hearing, and assists the orderly presentation of fact and argument at that hearing.

The hearing itself will normally take place in public. The appellant will open his case and call his witnesses in support. He may be represented by a solicitor or barrister, or he may choose to argue his own case. Both he and his witnesses will be subject to cross-examination by the opposing local authority or other body. Then the public authority will be entitled to make their own submissions and call their own witnesses, subject of course to cross-examination on the part of the appellant. Both the appellant and the public authority are entitled, immediately after any of their witnesses have been cross-examined, to re-examine the witnesses to clear up any ambiguities or difficulties revealed in the cross-examination; but not at that stage to try to introduce any fresh evidence. Matters of procedure will be under the control of the inspector, who will normally not insist on any high degree of formality. However, he will be anxious to ensure that all evidence is relevant to the subject-matter of the inquiry. The inspector must, however, ensure that he gives the appellant a fair opportunity of calling any evidence he may genuinely require. Failure to afford an appellant a proper opportunity to present his case may give rise to a successful court challenge on grounds of breach of "natural justice"[1]. Other points of note are that witnesses are not required to give evidence on oath, and civil servants, when called, are not expected to give evidence to **justify**, as distinct from explaining, a government policy.

At the end of the proceedings the appellant will normally, either himself or through his advocate, make a final speech. Following this, the inspector will commonly arrange to visit the site, which he will do in the presence of all the parties. At such a visit fresh argument will not be allowed, but the parties may be permitted to point out salient features which have been referred to during the oral hearing.

After the close of the inquiry the inspector will either give his determination on behalf of the Secretary of State, or he will prepare a report with recommendations to enable the Secretary of State to make the final decision. In either case the decision will be notified by letter to the appellant. Decision letters include a summary of the evidence heard, the inspector's findings of fact, and his conclusions, leading to his determination of recommendation. The appellant will then normally have a right of appeal to the High Court exercisable within six weeks from the date of the decision letter. On such an appeal the appellant is confined to allegations that there has been some error of procedure or that the decision or order is not within the powers of the Act in question. In other words, while the "merits" of a decision

---

[1] *Nicholson v Secretary of State* (1977) 76 LGR 693.

may dominate argument at the initial stages and also before the minister, argument before the courts is confined to questions of compliance with legal rules and procedures. From the High Court a further right of appeal lies to the Court of Appeal and eventually to the House of Lords.

The procedure outlined above will be followed even in relation to the most major issues, such as controversial development within a National Park, or the proposed construction of a new oil terminal or nuclear power station. However, in such cases, where many persons and much evidence will be heard, it is now customary for the inspector to convene a pre-inquiry hearing at which all the parties likely to be involved at the "inquiry proper" endeavour to settle the order in which the various issues are to be discussed and the order of the speeches of those taking part.

Funding of Objectors?

A matter of some current concern in connection with inquiries is that of the funding of objectors. The issue is whether those who object at inquiries should be entitled to assistance from central government funds towards their legal costs and other expenses? Such objectors might be, for example, a local group of residents objecting to the proposed route for a village or town bypass; or, perhaps, an amenity society such as the Council for the Protection of Rural England, objecting to a public body's proposals for development within a National Park or Area of Outstanding Natural Beauty. In cases like these there is a danger that the "contest" at a public inquiry may seem a rather unequal fight; the objectors, with such funds as they can scrape together, taking on the local planning or highway authority, a public corporation or a large public company (*eg* some of multinational mining and quarrying companies). If the inspector is to be sure of being fully informed on all relevant issues, perhaps it is necessary that public funds be available to assist objectors. The principal difficulty with any such proposal is in determining the criteria by which such financial assistance should be awarded. Clearly all objectors cannot be given an entitlement to whatever sums they feel they need. Objectors, for example, who object simply to protect the value of their properties may seem less deserving than those who wish to object on landscape or other environmental grounds. Likewise, some amenity groups may seem to possess resources which may make them less strong contenders for public funding: compare the "group of local residents", referred to above, with the National Trust. These issues are clearly difficult ones, quite apart from the further problems of seeking such funding at a time of severe restraint in public expenditure.

CHAPTER 3

ACCESS TO THE COUNTRYSIDE

In this chapter our primary concern will be to describe the law relating to footpaths and other public rights of way, together with orders which may be made affording, to the public, rights of access to open country. These various laws give to members of the public certain rights, by virtue of which they may explore and enjoy the countryside; and the exercise of these rights is not dependent or conditional upon the consent or approval of the owner or occupier of the land in question.[1]

Such access "as of right" in accordance with the principles of law to be considered does not, of course, constitute the only means by which the public may visit and make recreational use of the countryside. In addition should be stressed the very considerable extent to which the public are permitted, by the consent of the owners of the land, to visit prime scenic locations, though sometimes only on payment of entrance fees. One thinks here of the extensive land-holdings of the National Trust,[2] the Forestry Commission[3] the water companies, the proliferation of the Country Parks,[4] and also the more commercially orientated enterprises of owners of financially burdensome landed estates. In such ways there has been opened up a multitude of opportunities for the moderately enterprising town dweller to enjoy, with the owner's agreement (indeed often exhortation), many facets of the countryside.

---

[1] For the "Country Code", which should of course be complied with in the exercise of these rights, see below p. 255.
[2] See below at p. 151.
[3] See below at p. 143.
[4] See below at p. 118.

PUBLIC RIGHTS OF WAY

Introduction

The existence in England and Wales of a dense labyrinth of footpaths, bridleways, tracks and roads which are open to general public use as of right is invaluable in terms of the recreational amenity of the countryside. **Public** rights of way need to be distinguished from **private** rights of way (called easements). The former benefit the public as a whole: the latter simply allow a particular property owner rights over his neighbour's land. It has been estimated that public footpaths and bridleways alone total some 140,000 miles (of which the bridleways amount to some 28,000 miles); an average of roughly two miles for every square mile of land, though this average belies substantial regional differences — thus Hereford and Worcester has a footpath and bridleway density over four times that of Lincolnshire. Though most of the countryside is not in law open for the public to roam at will[1], the use of such public rights of way, shown on maps and often sign-posted on the ground itself, does in fact afford access to, or to the vicinity of, most points of beauty or interest. The main areas of general inaccessibility comprise land used by the Ministry of Defence for military exercises and weapons testing, the problem being exacerbated by the fact that modern weaponry apparently requires ever-larger expanses of land for testing and personnel training. In this connection fiercest controversy has centred upon the continued use of particularly attractive landscape in Wiltshire and Dorset and the Northumbria National Park for these purposes. Critics have argued that the Ministry of Defence has failed to take proper account of the recreational needs of the more densely-populated counties of the south of England in deciding which areas of open landscape it needs to retain for such purposes; and that such land, although properly requisitioned at a time of emergency, should by now have been returned to agricultural use and general public enjoyment. However, here as elsewhere,

---

[1] *A.G v Antrobus* [1905] 2 Ch 188. See, however, below at p. 90 for possibility of access agreements and orders in relation to "open country". Note also the rights over commons described below at pp. 168–170.

"simple solutions" prove problematic and conservation arguments may run counter to the promotion of public enjoyment. These areas, it is said, are not easily restorable to ordinary use owing to the numbers of unexploded shells littered about. Moreover, ironically, they consitute valuable nature reserves. For example, the denial to the public of enjoyment of some of the hills and coastline of Dorset has very effectively preserved the flora of the chalk downs of the Purbeck Hills behind Lulworth Cove from the despoliation which would otherwise have occurred.

The bulk of the network of public rights of way has existed for generations, in many cases for centuries; and came into being for reasons quite different from that which constitutes their main present value, that of accommodating the leisure needs of visitors to the countryside. Many paths still existing today were worn originally by people walking to and from their work, going to market (droveways) or to church (churchways), or simply travelling from village to village, or from town to town. This historical aspect to public rights of way can add a dimension to the pleasure obtained by the modern user. Whether or not the correct answer be known[1] it may at least be of interest to consider, when walking a path, whether its origin was Neolithic feet, the military might of the Romans, the medieval pilgrimages to Glastonbury, Canterbury or Bury St. Edmunds, the miners and packhorses trudging to and from the lead and tin mines, the geometrical creations of the parliamentary enclosure surveyors of the late eighteenth and early nineteenth centuries, or a public path creation order made only last year by the local county or district council!

Although the law of public rights of way originated as part of the common law, it has been much modified by statutes over the last century. This has, perhaps inevitably, resulted in considerable complexity in the law. The statutory developments have, however, gone some way to bringing the law into line with modern needs; securing a reasonably fair balance between the respective rights and interests of

---

[1] Note G. K. Chesterton's speculation: "Before the Roman came to Rye or out to Severn strode, The rolling English drunkard made the rolling English road".

farmers and other landowners, on the one hand, and the general public on the other.

Public Rights

To Pass and Repass

Public rights of way recognised by the modern law are, broadly, of three kinds: carriageways, bridleways and footpaths. These may be referred to compendiously as "highways". What rights do members of the public have in respect of such rights of way? The basic principle is that the law confers on members of the public generally the right to "pass and repass" along rights of way "on their lawful occasions". In so doing they do not commit trespass against the owner of the land over which they pass. In addition to such journeying, members of the public may also do things which may be regarded as "reasonably incidental" to passage; stock illustrations being to pause in order to rest or in order to admire a view. But persons using a right of way must not use it for purposes other than those described above; and if they do so they become trespassers on the land in question. Thus, in 1893, a court held that a man who went onto a public right of way, crossing a grouse-moor belonging to the Duke of Rutland, not for the purpose of passage but in order to interfere with the grouse-shooting of the Duke and his friends, was liable to the use of reasonable force to remove him as a trespasser[1]. Likewise, in 1900, a sporting journalist was held to have been trespassing when he walked up and down a right of way over Newmarket Heath, not to get from one place to another but simply in order to note the form of racehorses as they were being exercised[2].

It is evident, therefore, that those who wander off the route of a right of way, or who use a right of way for an improper purpose, thereby become trespassers. What, however, is the consequence of this? Trespass is, generally speaking, a civil wrong but not a criminal offence. The aim

---

[1] *Harrison v Duke of Rutland* [1893] 1 QB 142.

[2] *Hickman v Maisey* [1900] 1 QB 752. See also *R v Pratt* (1855) 4 El & Bl 860; *Randell v Tarrant* [1955] 1 All ER 600.

of any court proceedings will be to **compensate** the land-owner rather than to **punish** the trespasser; and proceedings will be in the civil courts (county court or High Court) rather than the criminal courts (the Magistrates' Courts or the Crown Court). Quite apart from taking court proceedings to obtain damages, the law gives the landowner the right to use reasonable force to "eject" the trespasser; and also, if repetition is expected, to seek an injunction (a court order forbidding or requiring a particular course of action) against the wrongdoer. If **more** than reasonable force is used to remove a trespasser the person so ejecting the trespasser will himself commit both a civil wrong and a criminal offence. Ejectors, accordingly, should act with restraint! Where damages are sought against a trespasser these are assessed so as to compensate for any damage done by trespasser: if no substantial damage was done in trespassing the damages will be nominal (*ie* a token amount). If an injunction has been obtained any person to whom it is addressed who fails to comply with its terms is guilty of contempt of court, the penalty for which can be a fine or a term of imprisonment or both. However, in the usual situation, where no injunction has previously been obtained against the trespasser, the trespasser will not be liable to criminal penalties unless his actions whilst trespassing involve the commission of some criminal offence. Such would be the case if he has committed acts of criminal damage; for example, by deliberately or recklessly breaking down a fence. Except in circumstances such as these the warning commonly seen that "Trespassers will be Prosecuted" may be considered to have been correctly described as a "wooden lie".

To these general statements about trespass to land not, of itself, giving rise to criminal liability certain exceptions exist. Thus, in respect of some ownerships or uses of land bye-laws may have been made rendering trespass a criminal offence. This will commonly be the case in relation to land owned by the Ministry of Defence and by British Rail. Similarly, as we shall see, bye-laws have sometimes been made to exclude the public from nature reserves where their presence, either throughout or just at particular times of the year, might be harmful to flora or fauna. Another instance where legislation has imposed criminal sanctions for trespass is in connection with "squatting" in residential houses (Criminal Law Act 1977); and criminal sanctions in relation to squatters were extended by the Public Order Act 1986 to deal with the then much publicised problem of "hippy" convoys parking their caravans, and settling, on agricultural land. The 1986 Act provides that a police officer who reasonably believes that two or more persons entered land as trespassers, intend to reside there for any period, and have been asked to leave, may make a direction under the Act that those persons leave the land provided two further conditions are satisfied. These conditions are that the trespassers must either—

(*i*) have caused damage to property on the land, or have used threatening, abusive or insulting words or behaviour towards the occupier or his family or an employee; or

(*ii*) have brought, between them, twelve or more vehicles onto the land.

In other words these provisions do not deal with entirely peaceable trespasses not involving a substantial number of vehicles. Such, less "troublesome" trespasses must be dealt with by the civil procedures outlined above.

Where a direction has been made, as described, under the 1986 Act, it becomes a criminal offence for a person knowing that the direction has been made, and that it applies to him, to fail to leave the land as soon as is reasonably practicable; or, having left, to return to the land as a trespasser within a period of three months. A uniformed constable who reasonably suspects a person to be committing either of these offences may arrest that person without need for a magistrate's warrant.

Kinds of traffic

Having considered the purposes for which the public may use public rights of way we come now to the forms of "traffic" which may use such ways: and here lies the difference between the three kinds of highway—footpaths, bridleways and carriageways. The public have the right to use a footpath on foot only, though it has been held[1] that this does not prevent passage with the "usual accompaniment" of a walker. It was, therefore, held to be permissible to push a perambulator along a footpath, and the rule would also clearly cover accompaniment by a dog.

In the case of bridleways, the public may pass on foot or on horseback or may lead a horse on foot. In addition to horses the rights extend to use with ponies, asses or mules. Also, some bridleways may be driftways and here the rights extend to the driving of cattle. Since 1968, the riding of pedal cycles has been allowed on bridleways provided that cyclists give precedence to pedestrians and persons on horseback[2]. This right may, however, be restricted by orders or bye-laws made by a local authority; and since the highway authorities maintenance obligations only relate to suitability for use on foot or by horse, the surface may not be such as to be conducive to easy cycling.   The use made of bridleways, for cycling has increased very considerably in the last few years with the advent, and great popularity of all-terrain mountain bikes. Over a million such bikes were sold in 1989. In some areas the activities of such cyclists have given rise to concern. The concern has focused both on the inconvenience which may be caused to other users of bridleways, and also on damage which may be caused to the surface of the path and to the landscape in general. For example, the attractions of the slopes of Box Hill in Surrey for stunt-riding are resulting in damage to the faces of the hill's chalk slopes. A Code of Conduct on Mountain Bike riding has recently been produced by the Countryside Commission. This stresses that riding other than on carriageways and bridleways will usually require the consent of the landowner.

---

[1] *R v Mathias* (1861) 2 F & F 570.
[2] Countryside Act 1968 s. 30.

Carriageways afford the most extensive rights of use: they may be used on foot, on or leading a horse, or by any kind of vehicle.

These various rules relate to the form of traffic for which the right of way was dedicated or was created. Although use other than by the appropriate means may amount to a trespass, such use will not necessarily involve the commission of a criminal offence. However, an offence **will** be committed in any case where a motor vehicle is driven along a footpath or bridleway[1]. Moreover, where appropriate bye-laws or orders have been made by district[2] or county councils[3] in respect of particular footpaths, it may be an offence to cycle or ride a horse on those paths[4]. In relation to cycling the Cycle Tracks Act 1984 should also be noted. This authorises county councils to designate particular footpaths as "cycle tracks", thus giving rights to cyclists which would otherwise not exist.

Dogs

Some further mention should be made of the matter of dogs and public rights of way. Although there is no general obligation to keep a dog on a lead on a right of way, orders may be made by county councils imposing such an obligation in respect of specified ways[5]. Moreover, under the Dogs (Protection of Livestock) Act 1953, a criminal offence is committed by the owner or person in charge of any dog which, on any agricultural land, "worries livestock"[6]. When the dog is in the charge of a person other than the owner, the owner is nevertheless liable to prosecution in addition to the person in charge unless he can prove that he reasonably believed the person in charge to be a fit and proper person

---

[1] Road Traffic Act 1972 s. 36. The section prohibits such driving "without lawful authority". Such authority may appear in statute (*e.g.* the Chronically Sick and Disabled Persons Act 1970 s. 20) or may arise by consent of the owner of land.

[2] Local Government Act 1972 s. 235. (bye-laws).

[3] Road Traffic Regulation Act 1967 ss. 1 and 12, as modified by the Wildlife and Countryside Act 1981 s. 60 (traffic regulation orders).

[4] It is also an offence generally to cycle or ride a horse on a **footway:** Highways Act 1835.

[5] Road Traffic Act 1972 s. 31.

[6] 1953 Act s. 1(1).

to be in charge. The expression "worries livestock" is defined in wide terms; it includes not only attacking and chasing cattle, sheep, goats, swine, horses or poultry, but in the case of sheep there is extra protection by virtue of the provision, added by the Wildlife and Countryside Act 1981, that worrying includes "being at large (that is to say not on a lead or otherwise under close control) in a field or enclosure in which there are sheep." The reference to "field or enclosure" would seem to exclude the operation of this provision to open upland. The 1953 Act does not apply to police dogs, guide dogs, trained sheep dogs, working gun dogs, or more contentiously perhaps, packs of hounds. In addition to the 1953 Act a self-help remedy is afforded to a farmer whose livestock are being chased or attacked by a dog: he may shoot the dog without any obligation to compensate its owner[1].

As regards civil liability to pay compensation for harm done by a dog, the position may be summarised as follows. Under the Animals Act 1971, the keeper of a dog is generally liable in damages only where the dangerous characteristics of the particular animal were already known to him when the incident in question occurred. In other words, as the saying goes, "each dog is allowed its first bite". If such characteristics are known to the keeper (or his employee or his family), the keeper is liable even though he may, in fact, have taken reasonable steps to try to keep the dog under control. There is, however, one situation where a stricter rule than this operates. Where a dog does damage by killing or injuring livestock (including poultry) the keeper of the dog is liable to pay for the damage even though the dog has no known prior history of such behaviour, and even though the keeper may have taken reasonable trouble to try to keep the dog under control.

Creation of Public Rights of Way

Public rights of way may in law come into existence in either of two ways: by the original common law method of "dedication and acceptance", or by the operation of statu-

---

[1] Animals Act 1971 s. 9.

tory powers. We shall consider each of these methods in turn.

Common Law

Dedication and acceptance involves the dedication by the owner of the land, to the public generally, of certain rights over that land and acceptance of those rights by the public. Dedication to a section of the public only (*eg* to local residents) is not sufficient to create a public right of way[1]. In some cases it may be possible to point to positive acts of dedication by the owner of the land, but more usually dedication is presumed from long user. The common law rules about dedication have, in practical terms, been superseded by statutory provisions providing for dedication to be presumed if certain conditions are fulfilled. The modern law is to be found in the Highways Act 1980[2]. This states that "when a way has been actually enjoyed by the public as of right and without interruption for a full period of 20 years, the way is to be deemed to have been dedicated as a highway unless there is sufficient evidence that there was no intention during that period to dedicate it." An important point to note about this section is that it does not provide that **any** twenty year period of uninterrupted user as of right gives rise to the presumption. The twenty year period during which such user must be shown is the one calculated back from the date at which the right of the public to use the way is called into question. This is quite a significant limitation. A case in 1953 illustrates the operation of the principles[3]. Members of the public had used a path across a piece of land between 1914 and 1940. Between 1940 and 1947 the land had been requisitioned and public use of the path discontinued. In 1948 the owner locked a gate and posted notices fobidding public use of the path. It was held by the court that no statutory presumption of dedication arose, because the twenty year period during which uninterrupted user had to be shown was the period dating back from 1948 (when the right of the public to use the way was

---

[1] See *Poole v Huskinson* (1843) 11 M & W 827.
[2] H.A. 1980 s. 30.
[3] *De Rothschild v Buckinghamshire C.C.* (1957) 55 L.G.R. 595.

brought into question) and that public use had not been continuous during that period because of the requisitioning between 1940 and 1948. The period of over twenty years of use prior to 1940 was not of relevance because although the requisitioning in 1940 led to the use stopping, there was no "calling into question" of the right to use the path at this time. It should be noted, however, that this rule that public user must take place without interruption over the twenty years prior to challenge relates only to the **creation** of rights of way. Once created a right of way remains such even if not used for any length of time. Hence the maxim: "Once a highway, always a highway."

For the statutory presumption of dedication to operate the user must not only have spanned twenty years without interruption by the owner, but also the user must have been "as of right". Thus, if a way has been enjoyed by express permission rather than by claim of right; or if use has been made of a route secretly, the users not believing themselves to have a right of way; or if use has been "open" but the users believing themselves trespassers, the condition is not satisfied[1].

Owners of land over which members of the public are asserting, in fact non-existent, rights of way must therefore take some care that by their inaction they do not unintentionally allow such rights to become established. It is, however, possible for an owner to prevent this by only a small amount of effort. In the first place he may show that he is not acquiescing in the establishment of a new right of way by interrupting periodically the public's use. Interruption requires something physical, such as blocking the way or personal challenge. It is not sufficient simply to tell users that they have no right of way[2]. A common practice of owners is to close routes used across their property for one day each year, though one day each twenty years would actually suffice. Often Christmas Day or Good Friday are dates chosen, though these dates have no legal significance

---

[1] *Hue v Whiteley* [1929] 1 Ch 440; *Jones v Bates* [1958] 2 All ER 237.
[2] *Per* Hilbery J. in *Merstham Manor Ltd. v Coulsdon and Purly UDC* [1937] 2 KB 77.

in this connection. Another way in which an owner may prevent a right of way becoming established is, even where he allows uninterrupted user to establish the statutory presumption of dedication, to do certain things which the statute provides will rebut (*i.e.* counter) that presumption. Thus, it is provided that where a notice has been erected and maintained by a landowner, and the notice is visible to users of the "way" and is in terms inconsistent with an intention to dedicate a right of way, the notice shall suffice to rebut the presumption of dedication[1]. It is also provided that in the event of such a notice being torn down or defaced the owner may, rather than re-erecting and continuing to maintain it, instead inform the local county council that no right of way is dedicated, and to the same effect[2]. Another course of action is for the owner of land periodically to submit maps and statements to the county council, together with sworn declarations stating that the rights of way shown are the only ones dedicated. This also will rebut the statutory presumption of dedication[3].

Statutory powers

Quite apart from this traditional method of establishment of public rights of way by actual or presumed dedication and acceptance, there are various procedures for creation of such ways by the exercise by public bodies of statutory powers. Historically, an important example of this were the powers contained in the numerous Inclosure Acts, which authorised commissioners to enclose open land and to create public rights of way in order to allow villagers access to the new enclosed fields. In recent times, the more important provisions have been those conferring on county and district councils powers to create footpaths and bridleways, either compulsorily or by agreement with landowners[4]. Such agreements with landowners may also be made by parish (or, in Wales, community) councils[5]. However, in such cases no

---

[1] Highways Act 1980 s. 31(3).
[2] H.A. 1980 s. 31(5).
[3] H.A. 1980 s. 31(6).
[4] H.A. 1980 ss. 25–29.
[5] H.A. 1980 s. 30.

payments may be made to the landowners, as is permitted by district and county councils; nor are parish or community councils under the duty that applies to districts and counties[1] to carry out such work as is necessary to bring such paths into a fit condition for use by the public.

The power to make a compulsory "public path creation order" exists where a county or district council considers there to be a need for such a path in their area and that it is expedient for the path to be created having regard to:

(a) the extent to which the path would add to the convenience or enjoyment of a substantial section of the public, or to the convenience of persons resident in the area, and

(b) the effect which the creation of the path would have on the rights of persons interested in the land (account being taken of their rights to compensation)[2].

Procedure is governed by Schedule 6 to the Highways Act 1980. If the order is unopposed it is confirmed by the local authority itself. If opposed, the order is submitted to the Secretary of State who will appoint an inspector to hold a local inquiry[3] or, at least, afford objectors an opportunity of being heard. The Secretary of State will, in the light of the inspector's report and recommendations, decide whether or not to confirm the order (with or without modification). In fact, this power to create public footpaths and bridleways is not commonly used. In particular its use simply to create a new path has been rare except in relation to long-distance routes[4]. The powers are, however, sometimes used alongside diversion and extinguishment orders[5] to secure local rationalisation of paths.

---

[1] H.A. 1980 s. 27.
[2] H.A. 1980 s. 26(1). Compensation is governed by s. 28.
[3] For this procedure, see above, pp. 55–59.
[4] See below, p. 87.
[5] See below, p. 85.

Definitive Maps

Procedure

Although a footpath or bridleway, once created by any of the methods described above, does not in law cease to be such simply because it is not used or becomes obstructed or overgrown or is simply forgotten, there was clearly a danger that, as use of paths became less a benefit to local people and more a rural amenity for town residents, the number of usable footpaths might diminish, and doubts set in as to the rights of the public to use particular paths. The best safeguard, recommended by the Hobhouse Committee in its Report on Footpaths and Access to the Countryside and put into legislative effect in 1949[1], was to impose a duty on local authorities to survey their areas and to produce definitive maps and written statements of all footpaths and bridleways. The procedures whereby these maps and statements have been prepared have been complex. Before a **definitive** map may come into existence there has had to have been produced earlier **draft** and **provisional** maps; each of these being open to public inspection. Any representations or objections from members of the public about the inclusion or omission of ways on the **draft** maps have had to be taken into account, following a local inquiry, in producing the **provisional** map, with a right of appeal to the Secretary of State against the local authority's decision. Objections by landowners to ways shown on the **provisional** map have been determined by appeal to the Crown Court. The provisional map has then been followed by the **definitive** map.

Under the 1949 Act the duty to prepare definitive maps was imposed on county councils only. This ensured coverage of most of the countryside and all county councils had completed their definitive maps by mid-1982. The urban areas of the larger cities, having former county borough status, and the inner London area were, however, not subject to surveying obligations under the original legislation; and although legislation has now extended obligations to the cities generally, the inner London area remains exempt.

---

[1] National Parks and Access to the Countryside Act 1949.

The procedures, outlined above, for making the maps and statements have also been streamlined to some extent by provisions of the Wildlife and Countryside Act 1981.

Legal effect

What then, is the legal significance of the definitive map? The legislation provides[1] that the map and statement are conclusive evidence as to the existence, at the date to which the map applies, of any public rights of way shown and described. It is thus conclusive that a public right of way of the particular nature shown exists (*eg* footpath or bridleway) and that the way is of the width described, and in the position described, in the written statement. It is important to note, however, that the absence of an indication of a public right of way is not conclusive evidence that no public right of way exists; nor does the fact that a way is shown as a footpath or a bridleway rule out the existence of more extensive public rights to use the way, for example to use a "footpath" on horse or to use either by vehicle[2]. Definitive maps and statements thus certainly "enshrine" those rights which they show, but in so doing they do not preclude persons from establishing the existence of omitted rights of way by the traditional methods of proof of actual or presumed dedication and acceptance.

A word of caution is, however, here necessary. These apparently "enshrined" rights are more precarious than might perhaps have been expected under the legislation. As we shall shortly see, if a right of way has been mistakenly entered on the map (or included as bridleway instead of as only a footpath) the map is liable to modification procedures. In other words the map as it stands at any point in time is definitive—it does not, however, follow that the map cannot be corrected[3].

It is obviously of importance that the information con-

---

[1] Wildlife and Countryside Act 1981 s. 56.

[2] W.C.A. 1981 s. 56(1); *Andover Corporation v. Mundy* [1955] JPL 518.

[3] *R v Secretary of State for the Environment, ex p. Simms* [1990] 3 All ER 490, overruling the decision in *Rubinstein v Secretary of State for the Environment* [1988] JPEL 485.

tained in definitive maps and statements should be readily available to members of the public. For this reason county councils are required to ensure that a copy of relevant parts of the map and statements is available for public inspection, free of charge and at any reasonable time, in each district and, where practicable, in each parish[1]. The information on the definitive maps has also been incorporated onto modern Ordnance Survey maps. Footpaths and bridleways are marked in green on the, appropriately named, green covered "Pathfinder" Maps (Second Series). At a scale of 1:25,000 these maps show both rights of way and the existence and shape of fields, making them the most suitable for walking in the countryside. The Second Series should soon cover the whole of England and Wales. Rights of way are also shown on modern, purple-covered "Landranger" maps. The scale of these is 1:50,000; a scale which permits the walker to locate and use well-defined paths, but may make accurate path-finding difficult where the route is overgrown, ploughed over, or simply not walked often enough to be self-evident[2].

Modification

The making of definitive maps and statements has taken a good deal of time and effort on the part of county councils. Once made, proper arrangements for keeping the information up to date are necessary if the documents are to retain their value. The plan of the 1949 Act was for the survey authorities to undertake, periodically, comprehensive re-surveys of their areas. The Wildlife and Countryside Act 1981 has altered this scheme to one under which county councils are under a duty to keep their definitive maps and statements under **continuous review,** and to make modification orders as and when necessary[3]. Modifications to the map and statement may be necessary for a variety of reasons. For example, to include paths previously omitted; or to exclude paths previously included erroneously; to cor-

---

[1] W.C.A. 1981 s. 57(5).
[2] 1:25,000 is the metric equivalent of the former 2¼ inches to the mile maps; 1:50,000 the equivalent of the "inch to the mile" maps (1:63,460).
[3] Wildlife and Countryside Act 1981 s. 53(2)(b).

rect misrouting and misdescriptions of ways; to reflect orders or agreements creating new paths; or orders "stopping up", diverting, widening or extending existing paths. In relation to certain of these reasons for modification[1] any member of the public may apply to the county council for a modification order. The member of the public must comply with the procedure laid down in the legislation, and also with regulations issued by the Department of the Environment[2]. These require, for example, that all owners and occupiers of the land affected be notified. The county council is required to investigate and consider any such application and then notify the applicant of its decision. Against a refusal to make a modification order the applicant may appeal to the Secretary of State. If the Secretary of State considers that a modification order should be made he can give instructions to this effect to the county council.

Where modification of a definitive map is sought, it is necessary for the applicant to prove error by cogent evidence. Given that matters in dispute may well relate to events prior to inclusion in a map some decades ago, local authorities have been encouraged to give ample publicity in the community to applications for modification. By this means it is hoped that when decisions are taken they are taken on the basis of as full and complete information and evidence as can be obtained.

In cases where the council is minded on its own initiative to make a modification order, it is required[3], first, to consult with the appropriate district and parish councils and then to publish its intended order. Objectors may then lodge representations within six weeks, whereupon the matter must be referred to the Secretary of State who, following a local inquiry or private hearing before an inspector, will decide whether or not to confirm the order. Such an order

---

[1] W.C.A. 1981 s. 53(5). But not when the modification is simply to record the effect of some other legal procedure such as stopping up or diverting a path. In such cases rights of objection will have been afforded at that earlier stage.

[2] W.C.A. 1981 Sched. 14: Wildlife and Countryside (Definitive Maps and Statements) Regulations 1983 (S.1 1983/21).

[3] Again, except in cases where the modification is simply to reflect the effect of some other legal procedure in the course of which objections will have been heard.

may also be challenged in the High Court though on strictly limited grounds only, and within a period of six weeks from confirmation[1].

Obstruction of Rights of Way

Nuisance

Members of the public using a footpath or bridleway have to accept obstructions which were there when a right of way came into being, such as trees or stiles and gates; but otherwise the obstruction of a right of way, such as putting a barbed wire fence across a footpath, constitutes what is called a public **nuisance.** If such a nuisance exists any member of the public wishing to exercise his right of passage is entitled to remove the obstruction, in legal parlance to "abate" the nuisance. Furthermore, criminal proceedings may be taken against any landowner or other person causing such an obstruction[2]. In this context "obstruction" has been held to include the erection of gates across a bridleway; even though the gates were readily openable, being attached in the centre by a loose piece of twine[3].

The law of nuisance applies not only to the physical obstruction of public rights of way, it also covers other actions which, without physically barring the way, may prevent public use of the highway. So, for example, a landowner who fires guns across a right of way or hits golf balls in such an area, or who keeps fierce animals in a field crossed by a right of way will be committing a nuisance if by doing so he puts the reasonable user of the highway in fear of injury. In this context one particular instance of such interference with the public's rights has been made a specific criminal offence. Thus, it is an offence for a farmer to keep at large a bull, exceeding ten months in age, in any field or enclosure crossed by a public right of way. An exception exists, however, where the bull is kept along with cows and heifers so long as the bull does not belong to one of the

---

[1] Wildlife and Countryside Act 1981 Sched. 15. For more details of this standard administrative appeal procedure, see above, pp. 55–59.

[2] Highways Act 1980 s. 137.

[3] *Durham C.C. v Scott*, (The *Times* May 28, 1990).

following seven specified breeds[1]: Ayrshire, British Friesian, British Holstein, Dairy Shorthorn, Guernsey, Jersey and Kerry. Presumably ramblers should enquire of any bulls they meet their age and breed! The theory behind the legislation is that foreign breeds of beef bulls are less aggressive than domestic breeds of dairy bulls. Not all, however, are convinced of this and the matter remains contentious. Even where no **criminal** offence is committed a farmer may be **civilly** liable in damages if a bull with known dangerous propensities injures a person using a right of way.

Ploughing

The ploughing of fields over which exist public rights of way is a matter which has given rise to a good deal of controversy; particularly so in view of the fact that an increasing proportion of paths which formerly skirted around small fields now bisect new large fields as farmers have removed hedges to enhance agricultural efficiency[2].

The extent of this problem was revealed in a survey commissioned by the Countryside Commission which was completed in 1989. A major finding of the survey, carried out by over a thousand volunteers, was that although most of the footpath and bridleway network in England and Wales was in fact in reasonable shape, its amenity value was marred by the incidence of obstacles. The survey found that obstructions to users, such as fences, overgrowth of vegetation (*e.g.* crops in fields), flooding and muddiness of bridleways, and in particular the ploughing of paths, meant that people intending a two mile walk stood a two in three chance of not being able to complete their route. Those intending a five mile route had only one chance in ten of getting through!

Concern at the problem caused by the ploughing of footpaths led in 1990 to important new legislation. The Rights of Way Act 1990 has amended and developed earlier legislation, and the present rules about ploughing may be summarised as follows.

---

[1] Wildlife and Countryside Act 1981 s. 59.
[2] These would often be appropriate cases for diversion orders: see below, p. 85.

To begin with, it is clear that if a right of way was originally dedicated subject to the right to plough, the public cannot complain and must re-tramp the way afresh after each ploughing. Where dedication has been presumed by twenty years user as of right and without interruption, the reservation of a right to plough will depend on the practice during that critical period[1]. In cases where, however, no reservation of a right to plough exists the act of ploughing will constitute a criminal offence[2]. In this connection the 1990 Act has extended the criminal law so that it is now an offence not only to plough a path without legal authority but also to "disturb the surface" of a path or bridleway so as to "render it inconvenient for the exercise of the public right of way". Proceedings in respect of these offences may be brought only by highway or other specified local authorities. Individuals or amenity groups cannot bring private prosecutions.

To these offences an exception, however, exists, designed to meet genuine agricultural needs. Where a footpath or bridleway crosses agricultural land, or land which is being brought into agricultural use, then if the farmer wishes, in accordance with the rules of good husbandry, to plough or otherwise disturb (*eg* by harvesting activities) the surface of the land, and it is not reasonably convenient in so doing to avoid disturbing the surface of the right of way he may do so provided certain conditions are complied with. The right to plough does not apply to paths around the edges of fields, only to those crossing fields; and where a path is lawfully ploughed the farmer is under a duty to make good the surface of the path, so as to make it reasonably convenient for the exercise of public rights, not later than two weeks from the time ploughing began in cases where ploughing is for sowing; where ploughing is not for sowing, reinstatement must be within 24 hours. In either case extensions may be granted by the highway authority up to a period of not more than 28 days. This is intended to take account of difficulties

---

[1] *Mercer v Woodgate* (1869) LR5 QB26.
[2] Highways Act 1980 s. 134(5A): subsection (5A) added by the Wildlife and Countryside Act 1981.

presented by adverse weather conditions. Failure to make good the surface constitutes a criminal offence[1] alongside that of unlawful ploughing. Again, criminal proceedings in respect of these offences may only be brought by local authorities (counties, districts, parishes, communities), thus ruling out private prosecutions being brought by groups such as the Ramblers' Association[2]. County councils, as highway authorities, are under a duty to enforce these rules about ploughing and restoration[3] but there has been a measure of criticism of their zeal in this regard. In addition to the power, and duty, to prosecute, the county council may in a case where there has been disturbance of the surface of a path so as to make it inconvenient to use, or unlawful ploughing, or a failure to restore the surface, give fourteen days' notice to the farmer of its intention to enter onto the land itself to reinstate the path. If the farmer still fails to do the work himself within that period the council may carry out the reinstatement and recover its reasonable expenses from the farmer[4].

Another problem dealt with in the 1990 Act has been the growing of crops in fields so as to encroach, obscure, and make impassable, rights of way. The Act makes it an offence for an occupier of agricultural land to allow any crop, other than grass, to encroach so as to render any footpath or bridleway inconvenient for the exercise of the public right of way. Breaches of this provision can, unlike the earlier provisions, be prosecuted by any individual or organisation, and the Act places an express enforcement duty on highway authorities. There is here also a power, on having given notice, for the local authority to take action directly by cutting a way through the crop and then recovering its costs from the landowner.

---

[1] H.A. 1980 s. 134(4).
[2] H.A. 1980 s. 134(6).
[3] H.A. 1980 s. 134(6).
[4] H.A. 1980 s. 134(8)(9).

Maintenance

Duties of Highway Authorities

Highway authorities (county councils) are by law under a duty to maintain all highways[1], including footpaths, in such a condition as is reasonable in view of the nature and volume of traffic that may be expected to use the way[2]. This duty is, accordingly, relatively light in the case of paths across fields or open countryside. However, even in respect of such paths it is the duty of the highway authority to prevent or remove obstructions, be they natural or artificial, and to preserve the right of way. These duties arise from the common law and have been bolstered by statute[3]; they cover both the taking of physical action to prevent and remove obstructions, and also the taking of legal proceedings, such as the prosecution of offenders[4] or the seeking of injunctions or declarations.

In addition to the duty imposed on county councils, as highway authorities, to maintain highways the legislation has conferred discretionary powers on district, parish and community councils to undertake maintenance of footpaths and bridleways if they so wish[5]. Where districts exercise such powers they have a right to have their expenses reimbursed by the county council. Where parishes so act their expenses may be reimbursed at the discretion of the county council (or a district council which is exercising maintenance

---

[1] H.A. 1980 s. 41. Strictly speaking this duty relates only to "highways maintainable at public expense"; highway authorities having powers, rather than a duty, of maintenance of privately maintainable ways. See *e.g.* s. 57. The distinction between highways maintainable at public expense and other highways is a complex one, beyond the scope of this book. See further, H.A. 1980 ss. 37 and 38.

[2] In *R v High Halden (Inhabitants)* (1859) 1F & F 678 it was held that the duty was to maintain the highway so as to be reasonably passable at all seasons of the year. The duty includes the maintenance of footbridges.

[3] *Bagshaw v Buxton Local Board of Health* (1875) 1 Ch D 220; Highways Act 1980 s. 130 (statutory **duty** on highway authorities to assert and protect the rights of the public to the use and enjoyment of any highway; **powers** given to district councils to do the same).

[4] *e.g.* under Highways Act 1980 s. 137 (wilful obstruction) or s. 134(5), (5A), (unlawful ploughing). Note also the offence under the National Parks and Access to the Countryside Act 1949 of erecting a sign or notice containing false or misleading information likely to deter public use of a right of way.

[5] H.A. 1980 ss. 42, 43 and 50.

powers). In addition, district councils have power to assert and protect public rights in respect of any public right of way in their area[1], and parish and community councils have power to make representations to county councils about rights of way which have been stopped up or obstructed[2]. If these representations prove to be well-founded the county council comes under a duty to take proper proceedings. The making of such representations can be a very useful form of local activity by parish and community councils. It is a worthwhile practice to include in such representations a request that the county council should inform the parish council of the action it intends to take, and to report on progress being made in the matter.

Powers of Individuals

So far we have confined our attention to the duties and powers of local authorities in relation to the protection of rights of way. However, such authorities have many other responsibilities and calls upon their funds, and so cannot be relied upon always to survey fully the state of paths and to act with vigour where need arises. The Countryside Commission estimated that in 1986/7 some £14m was spent on rights of way maintenance (about £100 per mile). It recommended that this figure be increased by fifty per cent. It also calculated that judged by reference to footpath usage this still provided an amenity much more cheaply per use (10p) than did provision of swimming pools or country parks. These might be five or ten times as expensive to provide per individual user.

What action may be taken by private individuals in relation to rights of way which are obstructed or are in poor repair? As long ago as 1630[3], it was declared by the courts that any of the King's subjects passing along a highway and finding an obstruction might take steps to unblock the path by removing the obstruction. A word of caution is necessary, however, in relation to this self-help remedy. An obstruction

---

[1] H.A. 1980 s. 130(2).
[2] H.A. 1980 s. 130(6).
[3] *James v Hayward* (1630) Cro Car 184.

may only be removed if it is preventing use of the path; if it can be walked around whilst remaining on the right of way, such clearance of the way is not authorised. Moreover, in a case in 1932[1], Maugham J stressed that the common law permitted only the taking of the minimum action necessary to make the way passable. Thus, for example, when a locked gate is found across a path it would be lawful to remove the lock; it would be to exceed self-help powers to remove the gate itself. Individuals who exceed their common law powers may be sued for damages for trespass, and may face prosecution for criminal damage[2].

Apart from this self-help remedy there is also a useful procedure under the Highways Act[3] by which an individual may enforce the duty of the highway authority to maintain the highway. The procedure involves serving a notice on the highway authority. If, then the highway authority fails to reply, or replies denying that the way is a highway, or denies that it is a publicly maintainable highway, the individual can take proceedings in the Crown Court for an order that the way be put into proper repair. The court will grant the order if it finds that the way is indeed a highway maintainable at public expense and is out of repair. If the highway authority admits its obligation to maintain the way in question, any dispute about the extent of maintenance required by law will be determined in the Magistrates' Court.

There is, however, an important limitation to this procedure. It can only be used to enforce the duty of the authority to maintain and repair highways; it does not extend to enforcement of the duty to keep ways free from obstruction. Thus in a case in 1975[4], it was held that the procedure was not apt to enforce the duty to remove a wire fence, or effluent from a cess-pit which was obstructing public use of paths; it was appropriate, however, in relation to paths which have vegetation growing from their surfaces

---

[1] *Seaton v Slama* (1932) 31 LGR 41.
[2] Criminal Damage Act 1971.
[3] Highways Act 1980 s. 56.
[4] *Hereford and Worcester C.C. v Newman* [1975] 1 WLR 901.

making them impassable. In the latter instance the vegetation growth meant that the surface of the right of way was in disrepair. In this connection a distinction must also be drawn between growth of shrubs or trees **beside** a right of way and growth from the surface of the way itself. The former may obstruct passage along a way; but only the latter involves disrepair requiring maintenance, and so enforceable by the procedure described above. An alternative exists in that proceedings may be taken in the High Court to enforce any duty imposed by the law on a public body. However, such proceedings are much more expensive than the procedure described above.

Gates and Stiles

The maintenance of gates and stiles which lawfully exist across footpaths or bridleways is a matter of some importance. The basic rule[1] is that they are required to be maintained in a safe and usable condition by the owner of the land[2]. However, the owner can recover a quarter of his costs in so doing from the highway authority, and the authority may pay more than this if it wishes. In default of maintenance by the owner of the land the highway authority (or in some cases the district council) may, having given fourteen days' notice, undertake the work itself and charge some or all of its costs to the owner, as it thinks fit. The rule, referred to above, about recovery of expenses from the highway authority applies only in the absence of agreement to the contrary. Thus, where a highway authority has granted permission[3] for the erection of a stile or gate which would otherwise have constituted an unlawful obstruction, that grant of permission will also make clear on whom the cost of maintenance shall fall.

Waymarking

Since 1968 there has been an obligation on highway authorities to erect and maintain direction posts at all points where a

---

[1] Since the Countryside Act 1968.
[2] Highways Act 1980 s. 146.
[3] H.A. 1980 s. 147.

public footpath or bridleway leaves a metalled road, except where the agreement of the parish council is obtained to the effect that signposting in particular places is not necessary[1]. They are also empowered, though not obliged, to erect such waymarks generally as they consider necessary. Such waymarking may, with the consent of the highway authority, be undertaken by parish or community councils. In this connection the Countryside Commission has issued advice about waymarking, suggesting the use of a special sign, yellow for footpaths and blue for bridleways. Further, since the Wildlife and Countryside Act 1981, local authorities (counties and districts) have been authorised to appoint wardens to "advise and assist the public in connection with the use of" footpaths, bridleways etc. in their areas[2].

The Countryside Commission has recently drawn attention to the unsatisfactory state of waymarking of paths. Its survey in 1989, referred to earlier, disclosed real difficulty in determining where many paths intersected with roads, and the Commission has advised the need for some 280,000 more signs to be put in place.

Diversion and Stopping Up

According to the traditional common law, "once a highway, always a highway"; in other words a public right of way once established exists forever, and is not forfeited owing to any lack of public use[3]. At common law the only way in which a right of way might be lost was by physical extinction. Thus when a right of way is washed away by erosion of the sea or a river the way is lost: there is no common law right in such circumstances to deviate along adjoining land[4].

The position at common law is, however, modified in some respects by certain legislative provisions. There are numerous Acts of Parliament which provide for the "stopping up" (*ie* extinguishment) or the diversion of public rights of way.

---

[1] Countryside Act 1968 s. 27.
[2] Wildlife and Countryside Act 1981 s. 62.
[3] See *e.g. Turner v Ringwood Highway Board* (1870) LR 9 Eq 418.
[4] *R v Bamber* (1843) 5 QB 279.

The earliest of these statutory provisions was in the Highway Act 1835; now replaced by the Highways Act 1980 section 116. Under this provision the highway authority, perhaps on the request of a landowner, may apply to a magistrates' court for an order that the way be stopped up as being unnecessary, or that the way should be diverted to a new route on the ground that the new route is either nearer or more commodious to the public. The "new" route in such a case will be inspected by the magistrates before approval, and the consent of the local district and parish councils must have been obtained before any such order is made. In other words, such councils can **veto** the closure or diversion under this procedure. In order to assist the magistrates in reaching a fully informed decision it is provided that any objector to the stopping up or diversion may appear before the court and has a right to be heard[1].

In practice, however, this is a rather elaborate and expensive procedure. To appear as an "objector" before a Magistrates' Court is a more awesome experience than to appear before a local public inquiry. A Department of the Environment Circular (1/83) has therefore recommended that this procedure be used only in cases involving closure or diversion of **roads**. In relation to **footpaths** and **bridleways**, the procedures laid down in sections 118 and 119 of the 1980 Act are to be preferred. This procedure consists of the making by the local county or district council of a "public path extinguishment order" or a "public path diversion order". Notice of the making of such orders must be placed in the local press; and a copy of the notice and a copy of the orders must be served on parish or community councils. The grounds upon which such orders may be made are substantially similar to those outlined above in connection with section 116. If objections are lodged to any such order, the Secretary of State will, before deciding whether or not to confirm the order (with or without modification) appoint an inspector who will hold a local public inquiry, afford objectors a private hearing, or order that the matter be

---

[1] H.A. 1980 s. 116(7).

considered on the basis of written representations[1]. Where a parish or community council has objected a full public inquiry is usually held.

In addition to these **general** powers of stopping up and diversion, there are also powers conferred by other Acts of Parliament which are important in particular contexts. Thus, under the Town and Country Planning Act 1971[2] powers are given to local planning authorities to make extinguishment and diversion orders in order to enable development, for which planning permission has been granted, to be carried out. The procedure is similar to that outlined above in relation to orders made under sections 118 and 119 of the Highways Act 1980. It should be noted, however, that the power is not exercisable **after** development has been carried out in order to deal with inconvenient public rights of way[3]. Other examples of statutes authorising the stopping up or diversion of public rights of way include the Acquisition of Land Act 1981[4], the Open Cast Coal Act 1958[5], the Land Powers Defence Act 1958[6], and the Civil Aviation Act 1981. In each of these, and many other, cases the standard administrative procedure of "order subject to ministerial confirmation", with the possibility of a local public inquiry, must be followed.

Long Distance Routes: National Trails

Over the last quarter of a century there have been established a number of long distance routes (in 1989 renamed "national trails"), consisting of a series of linked rights of way. Where necessary the gaps between pre-existing rights of way have been bridged by the making of dedication agreements with landowners, or in cases where such agree-

---

[1] H.A. 1980 Schedule 6. See further on this standard administrative procedure, above, pp. 55–59.

[2] H.A. 1980 ss. 209, 210, 214, 215.

[3] See *Ashby v Secretary of State for the Environment* [1980] 1 All ER 508.

[4] Orders in respect of land acquired compulsorily by public authorities, and also land acquired by agreement which could have been acquired compulsorily in default of agreement: 1981 Act s. 32.

[5] Orders to **suspend** public rights of way in order to allow open cast mining: 1958 Act s. 15.

[6] Orders in respect of land used for various defence purposes: 1958 Act s. 8.

ment has not been forthcoming by the making of public path creation orders.

Legal provision for such routes to be established dates from the National Parks and Access to the Countryside Act 1949[1]. The Countryside Commission (formerly the National Parks Commission) initiates proposals for consideration and approval by the Secretary of State. The proposals show any need for new paths to be created and the need, if any, for the provision of ferries, accommodation, meals and refreshments along the route: they also estimate capital outlay necessary and annual maintenance and running costs.

Once proposals are approved by the Secretary of State the onus shifts from the Countryside Commission to the county councils through which the route passes. It is they who negotiate agreements with landowners and make any necessary orders, though these initial expenses are defrayed entirely by the Countryside Commission. Once established, three-quarters of the maintenance cost of the routes is borne by the Commission. Long distance routes are shown as such on the appropriate definitive maps, and are also clearly waymarked "on the ground" by distinctive symbols.

The earliest of the routes to be established was the Pennine Way. Opened in 1965, this route follows the spine of northern England for around 250 miles, from Edale in Derbyshire to Kirk Yetholm in the Scottish border country, passing on its way through three National Parks. The painstaking work necessary to secure complete linkage of rights of way is demonstrated by the fact that the ministerial approval for the Pennine Way was granted as far back as 1951. Since the Pennine Way there have been opened a further thirteen long distance routes. A number are coastal paths (*e.g.* Pembrokeshire; Somerset and North Devon, North Cornwall, South Cornwall, South Devon, Dorset coast — approximately 500 miles of almost continuous coastal walking); others have historical links (*e.g.* Offa's Dyke path) or follow prominent landscape features (*e.g.* South Downs Way, North Downs Way, Ridgeway). Some parts of the

---

[1] Ss. 51–55.

routes are bridleways; and the South Downs Way is such for the whole of its course.

These routes have certainly achieved popularity with walkers, both those walking entire lengths and those walking shorter stretches. A principal attraction is the clear waymarking. However, such popularity has brought problems. Some stretches of the routes are becoming seriously worn. It has been estimated that 120,000 pairs of boots tramp up Ingleborough each year; and a quarter of a million people walk each year in the general area of the Pen-y-Ghent, Whernside and Ingleborough. This makes walking difficult (sometimes a matter of walking at the bottom of viewless troughs) and, as walkers steer beside the worst worn tracks, the width of paths grows, causing some hillsides to resemble sites of motor-cycle scrambles.

The solutions appear to be twofold. First, to incorporate, at least at the busiest spots, certain lessons that have been learnt about the technique of path maintenance; and secondly, to create more such paths and to publicise well-marked walks along other "unofficial" long distance routes. As regards official long distance routes the work is nearly complete on the Thames Path: a path along the river from its source to the Houses of Parliament, and on to the Thames Barrier. Feasibility studies have also been conducted into a trail in the Hadrian's Wall area, into a Cotswold Way and a Glyndwr Way in central Wales. There have also been extensions to some existing paths. For example, extending the South Downs Way westward. The Countryside Commission has also proposed a Pennine Bridleway, following the spine of the pennines and taking a similar but not identical route to the Pennine Way. The bridleway's route would be designed to avoid areas of vulnerable upland peat. Another significant feature of this proposal is the development of a network of linking routes to join the nearby conurbations to the main trail. As with other recent proposals for new trails the Countryside Commission has emphasised the need for commercial sponsorship in order to meet the costs involved in their creation.

In addition to these official routes a number of unofficial long routes are quite well-known, some being the result of local authority initiative; others the publications and writings of rambling organisations, national and local, and freelance writers. Examples include the Viking Way in Lincolnshire, and the Robin Hood Way in Nottinghamshire. A number of such recreational paths have been grant-aided by the Countryside Commission. Many are more suitable for just a few hours walking than are the long-distance trails, often being designed to allow circular routing.

In addition to the valuable work done by the Countryside Commission mention should be made of a recent proposal by British Waterways to establish a new 140 mile long distance path along the Grand Union Canal between London and Birmingham. It will be vehicle free, will only involve walkers having to cross four roads, and as many as twenty eight railway stations lie within the waterway's corridor. Implementation of the plan is eased by the fact that the entire path already exists, and that 85% of it is adequately surfaced. It will be less demanding physically than some of the other trails. The route will be designed to permit cyclists access where, but only where, towpath width makes safe use by cyclists and walkers possible.

ACCESS ORDERS AND AGREEMENTS

As was stressed at the start of this chapter, the network of public footpaths and bridleways is of considerable value to the general public in exploring and enjoying our, largely privately-owned, countryside. In areas of intense cultivation, or of enclosed livestock farming, the various rules described above would seem to strike a fair balance between the needs and interests of members of the public and of landowners. However, in areas of more open landscape the rules are, perhaps, more restrictive as to public rights than is desirable if the public are to be able to make the best possible use of the countryside for recreational purposes. One particular deficiency with the rules discussed so far is that public rights of way must be along defined routes joining distinct locations. There can be no public right to wander at will even upon open land. This was made clear in a case in 1905 in which it was held that the public could not have acquired a right to wander at will around Stonehenge[1].

There are, of course, many places where the public are allowed to roam at will with the manifest consent of the landowner. Of particular significance here are the large land-holdings of the National Trust[2] and also the numerous Country Parks[3]. In other areas consent of the owners may be less overt but public access generally seems to be allowed. Nevertheless, the absence of any legal right to walk according to one's will, or even to walk at all, over large tracts of open countryside—moors, heaths and uplands generally—became, in the 1930s, a matter of considerable controversy. The main conflict was between the residents of the industrial cities of the Manchester and Sheffield areas seeking solace from the Depression by walking in the Peak District hills, and the owners of those hills who wanted to fence the public out in order to preserve their value as grouse-moors. Similarly, at this time, the water companies were unwilling to allow public access to land they owned which constituted water catchment areas, fearing pollution to water supplies. Disputes between these factions culminated in the 1930s in pitched battles between walkers and gamekeepers, protests involving many thousands of people, and, most celebratedly, the mass trespass on Kinder Scout in 1932. A consequence of these actions was the Access to Mountains Act 1939; though this Act was soon replaced and extended by the provisions of the National Parks and Access to the Countryside Act 1949. This Act provides for the securement of rights of access to areas of "open country": an expression which is widely defined as land consisting "wholly or predominantly of mountain, moor, heath, down, cliff or foreshore (including any bank, barrier, dune, beach, flat or other land adjacent to the foreshore)" and also any wood-

---

[1] *A.G. v Antrobus* [1905] 2 Ch. 188. See, further, below Chapter 5 on rights of access to common land.
[2] See, further, below, p. 151.
[3] See, further, below, p. 118.

D

lands rivers and canals in the countryside[1]. In relation to such areas, rights of access may arise either by agreement between the county council and the landowner (such agreements binding successors in title to the land), or by a compulsory order made by the county council[2]. Such access agreements and orders must be shown on a special map maintained by the county council. Where, by agreement or order, rights of access exist they may be enjoyed by the public subject to such conditions as may be set out in the agreement or order. Such conditions may, for example, exclude public access to certain areas; such as around farm buildings.

The 1949 Act obliges county planning authorities to survey their areas and assess the "access requirements" of the area. They must then take appropriate action to secure rights of access for "open-air recreation" in such "open country". Despite the strong terms of the legislation it must be said that access orders have very rarely been made in practice, and even access agreements are not very common. Some critics have pointed to landowner domination of county councils for this lack of action. The only area where much progress has been made is in the Peak District where the National Park Authority has negotiated agreements over quite extensive areas of moorland, permitting walking and climbing but not extending to activities such as horse-riding or motor-cycling. Over 60% of such "access" land in England and Wales lies within the Peak District.

RIVERS, CANALS AND THE FORESHORE

The public have rights of navigation over tidal rivers, and non-tidal rivers may be navigated where a public right of way of such nature has come into existence by long use[3]. Such rights of navigation must, however, be exercised in accordance with any bye-laws which may have been made

---

[1] National Parks and Access to the Countryside Act 1949 s. 59(2) and Countryside Act 1968 s. 16.
[2] N.P.A.C.A. 1949 s. 16.
[3] See further, below p. 204 on fishing rights.

by the British Waterways Board, or the National Rivers Authority, or other statutory body.

Canals are artificial streams which were created by private individuals (such as the Duke of Bridgewater) or companies, in either case under the authority of Acts of Parliament. Most were constructed in the period between 1761 (opening of the Duke of Bridgewater's canal) and the middle of the nineteenth century, when the railways and later the roads replaced the canals as the principal arteries of commercial traffic. The canals are mostly now owned by the British Waterways Board, which is responsible for their maintenance, and for the control of cruising and the commercial use of the canals. No member of the public has any rights of navigation over canals, but the BWB customarily allows such use in accordance with its bye-laws, and it may and does make charges for permitting such use. The recreational use of canals is, of course, becoming ever more popular.

These inland waterways extend to about 2000 miles, though many decades of neglect has meant much silting up, disrepair of lock-gates, and growth of vegetation in the canals. Both rivers and canals are of great importance in terms of the habitats they provide for wildlife and plants, though the still-water habitat of canals is quite different from that of a flowing river. Also of value are the "feeder" reservoirs which were built at intervals beside many canals and from which the water level in the canals is topped up. A concern of environmentalists in recent years has been that work done to rivers to make them less prone to flooding has made many river banks less congenial than before to small river-side animals, the vegetation being much reduced and soft mud being replaced by stone or concrete. River engineers are, however, within limits imposed by budgets, becoming more sensitive to these matters in the planning and implementation of their river engineering projects.

Canals have towpaths, and these are in some cases, though usually are not, public rights of way[1]. Nevertheless the BWB commonly permits walkers, and also cyclists, to

---

[1] But access orders may be made, as described, above, p. 90.

use these paths. The towpaths are very often in a better state of repair than the canals themselves and are of very considerable recreational value, being well defined routes which are safe to walkers and cyclists from the dangers of motorised traffic.

The foreshore, the area of our coast between high and low water marks, is the property of the Crown[1] except where it has been sold or leased by the Crown to some other person or body, such as a lord of a manor or, more typically in modern times, to a local authority. No general rights of access exist, but as every seaside holiday-maker will be aware access is customarily permitted. Where the foreshore is owned or leased by the local authority its use may be restricted by bye-laws, or other limitations imposed by the local authority as owner. In any case, at places where much public use is made of the foreshore (*e.g.* at seaside resorts) the land immediately above high water mark is usually publicly owned. Although no legal right to wander at will exists in relation to the foreshore, it is possible in law for a public right of way to have come into existence in the ways discussed earlier in this chapter. However, given the nature of the foreshore and the requirement that a right of way must follow a defined route it is rare for such rights to exist.

There is a general public right of navigation over the sea, and this includes the foreshore at high tide. No owner of land adjoining the coast is, however, obliged to allow public access to the foreshore or sea by crossing his land unless a public right of way across the land exists. He may fence his land **from** the foreshore, but without the consent of the Secretary of State may not extend fences **across** the foreshore as this may interfere with the public's rights of navigation[2].

ACCIDENTS IN THE COUNTRYSIDE

Accidents do unfortunately occur to even the most careful adults and children making recreational use of the country-

---

[1] See further, below, p. 153 on the Crown Estates.
[2] Coastal Protection Act 1949 s. 34.

side. They may be caused by the condition of the surface of a footpath, by the collapse of branches of trees, by attacks from bulls or other animals, or in numerous other ways. In what circumstances may a person who suffers injury be able to sue for damages the owner or occupier of the land in question; or in the case of injuries caused by footpaths being in a dangerous condition, sue the local highway authority having responsibilities for their maintenance? A full discussion of this area of the law is beyond the scope of this book, but it may be appropriate to outline some of the general principles applicable and the factors which may be relevant to liability.

The starting point is that occupiers of land are expected to take reasonable care as regards the safety of persons whom they may reasonably expect to come onto their land. The obligation is to take reasonable care, and this is a matter to be determined in the light of the particular circumstances of each case. In making this assessment certain factors may be of special significance. Thus, where unsupervised young children are reasonably expected to come onto a person's land his obligations as regards their safety may be greater than where adults only are expected. In particular this may be the case where there are on the land potentially dangerous things which may be allurements to children, such as ponds or tree branches which may make tempting swings. Adults may be expected, to a degree, to look after their own safety, but if the presence of unsupervised children is foreseeable the occupier of the land may be under a duty to check the condition of the water's edge or examine whether the branches are sound or rotten. In this connection a second factor may be relevant to liability. In deciding whether or not reasonable care has been taken in respect of those likely to be present the courts take into account whether the injured visitor was an invited guest or was a trespasser. Understandably, the steps which should be taken to secure the safety of guests are of a higher order than those which the law requires in respect of foreseeable trespassers. In other words, returning to our earlier example, if an occupier of land invites children onto his land he will be expected to take greater care as to their safety than if the children are unwelcome trespassers. Nevertheless some obligation exists even in respect of trespassers. If land is in a condition which may present danger to trespassers this may require reasonable steps to be taken to fence the land adequately to keep those trespassers out, or at least may oblige the occupier to give clear warning of the perils.

Until quite recently an occupier could exclude liability towards those who suffered injuries by the posting of prominent notices to that effect on the land itself, or by the insertion of appropriately worded clauses in any contract of admission to the property. Such notices or clauses are now, in relation to "business occupiers", governed by the terms of the Unfair Contract Terms Act 1977, which makes them ineffective to exclude liability in so far as they relate to death or bodily injury. They may, however, still be effective in relation to other kinds of harm. For example, the exclusion of liability in respect of torn or damaged clothing. Here the effectiveness of the exclusion notice or clause will depend on the court's view as to its reasonableness.

Following the enactment of these provisions some concern was expressed at doubts created as to the continued ability to exclude liability for death or personal injury in connection with the dangerous state of premises where a landowner (who might very likely make business use of his land, such as by farming it) allowed persons onto his land for recreational or educational purposes. Accordingly, the Occupiers' Liability Act 1984 now makes clear that any such liability will not be a business liability unless granting such persons such access falls within the business engaged in by the occupier. In other words a farmer in business in that capacity can still allow educational or recreational access to his land subject to exclusion of liability so long as he does not make such activity a part of his business use of the land.

Recovery of damages may also be affected by the extent to which the injured person's own carelessness may have contributed to the accident. Such "contributory negligence" will lessen the amount of damages awarded against a defendant occupier by a proportion equivalent to the degree to which the plaintiff's own carelessness contributed to his accident.

Lastly we may note the possibility of the local highway authority being liable in damages in respect of accidents occurring as a result of the condition of a public footpath. The surface of such paths belongs to the highway authority and liability depends on the authority having had a reasonable opportunity of being aware of the dangerous condition of the path, and of their having failed to take reasonable steps to remedy its condition within a reasonable period of time[1].

---

[1] See *eg Hayden v Kent CC* [1978] 2 All ER 97.

CHAPTER 4

PROTECTION OF SPECIAL AREAS

INTRODUCTION

In this chapter we shall consider the law and practice of amenity and nature conservation with reference to a number of particular kinds of location. Some such areas may warrant special legal provision simply because of their visual beauty; others for reasons of habitat protection. And very often both motives may coincide. The areas we shall consider are diverse in their characteristics, from craggy mountain ranges to lowland wetlands, and areas as large as Dartmoor to ones as small as a village duck pond. Any list of types of land which are valuable in terms of scenic amenity, or habitat for flora or fauna, will be a long one: open mountains, moorlands, heaths, downlands, woodlands, marshes and wetlands, meadows, lakes, rivers and estuaries, coastal dunes and cliffs, and villages and buildings. The law must provide for effective conservation of each of these different environments and features if we are to continue to enjoy a rich and varied landscape, flora and fauna.

A variety of legal methods have been devised to attempt to achieve this protection. Thus, we shall examine the protection which may be afforded to an area as a consequence of designation as a National Park, an Area of Outstanding Natural Beauty (AONB), a Conservation Area, a Site of Special Scientific Interest (SSSI) or an Environmentally Sensitive Area (ESA). We shall also consider the powers which exist to establish Country Parks, Nature Reserves and Marine Nature Reserves. Following that we shall consider legal provisions which relate to the public enjoyment of, and conservation of, other areas quite independently of any special designation or establishment under statutory powers.

This will involve, principally, a discussion of laws relating to trees and woodlands; and the chapter will end with some reference to the activities of two major "private" landowners, each of whom generally manage their lands with a keen appreciation of the needs of conservation. We refer here to the National Trust and the Crown Estates.

Before considering each of these matters, certain points of general significance may be made. We shall see that, very commonly, conservation is sought without going so far as taking the land in question into public ownership. The land is left in private hands but limitations or controls may operate as to what the owner may do on or with that land. An increasingly common legislative device to try to secure some regulation of a landowner's activities is that of the management agreement entered into, voluntarily, by the landowner and an appropriate public body (*e.g.* the Countryside Commission, Nature Conservancy Council, National Park Authority, or local authority). Such agreements may provide financial incentives to the landowner to use his land in ways which are least detrimental and most beneficial to the environment. The aim in the move towards management agreements is to avoid too much of a "Thou Shalt Not" image of conservation, and so far as possible to secure ends by voluntary means and by arriving at an agreed programme of land management. This last aspect is particularly important. Conservation of the countryside is by no means a matter simply of leaving it alone; it is not just a question of outlawing a long list of environmentally detrimental practices. The landscape we wish to preserve, together with its plants and wildlife, is very largely an artificial one. It is the product of man's activities over the last few thousand years. To maintain the countryside as we wish it to remain what is required is the continuation of a wide variety of agricultural practices, otherwise the mixed landscape may degenerate to primaeval forest, managed woodlands become mere wildernesses, and so forth. Effective conservation therefore is as much about the encouragement of practices which maintain cherished features as it is about forbidding or deterring more obviously harmful activities. It is in this respect that management agreements and the "voluntary principle" of conservation are to be commended compared with excessive reliance on prohibition alone.

We may now consider in turn each area or category of specially protected land. In relation to each we shall draw attention to deficiencies in the law's provisions or in the practical operation of principles or procedures. Some of these criticisms are substantial ones; nevertheless, it may be noted at the outset that collectively the laws we shall consider do provide at least some degree of special protection for a quite substantial proportion of the countryside of England and Wales.

NATIONAL PARKS

There are in England and Wales ten areas which have been designated as National Parks. From north to south these are the Northumberland National Park, the Lake District, the North York Moors, the Yorkshire Dales, The Peak District, Snowdonia, the Pembrokeshire Coast, the Brecon Beacons, Exmoor and Dartmoor. The legal process of creation of National Park status for an area is that of "designation" as such by the Countryside Commission (formerly called the National Parks Commission: 1949–1968) followed by "confirmation" by the Secretary of State. The governing legislation, the National Parks and Access to the Countryside Act 1949, authorises such designation and confirmation in relation to "extensive tracts of country" which in the opinion of the Commission are worthy of protection by reason of their natural beauty and the opportunities they afford to the public for open air recreation.

An important point to stress at the outset is that our National Parks differ from similarly designated areas abroad, such as Yellowstone or Yosemite in the United States, in that legal ownership of the land is unaffected by designation. Certainly a proportion of the land in the National Parks is owned by public bodies, such as the Forestry Commission, or by the National Trust, which, for example, owns about a quarter of the Lake District, but, equally, much is in purely private ownership. The creation of an area as a National Park may limit things which an owner may do on or with his land by way of stricter application of especially extensive planning controls;[1] it does not, however, deprive him of his ownership of the land. Our National Parks are areas which are farmed and "lived in" by some 300,000 people; and the consequent need for there to be employment to support the inhabitants of the small towns and villages gives rise, as we shall see, to certain problems. In no way are our Parks intended to be uninhabited areas of landscape unmarked by man's activities, as is the pattern in the U.S.A.

Origins and Development

Notwithstanding the retention of private ownership, the kinds of areas which have been designated as National Parks are areas in respect of which members of the public have long assumed, though wrongly, some general right of access and common enjoyment. One does not forget the fact of private ownership of the "suburban semi" or even of intensively cultivated farmland, but one may tend to do so in relation to extensive areas of open upland, mountain and moorland. This was adverted to by the poet Wordsworth in his *Guide to the Lakes*, in which he commented that the Lakes are:

> "a sort of national property, in which every man has a right and interest who has an eye to perceive and a heart to enjoy."[2]

But Wordsworth was a better poet than a lawyer, and in due course the absence of public rights of access to, and enjoyment of, such areas became a matter of much contention. Until the start of this century the number of visitors from the cities to these open areas was small. It was in the 1920s that conflict began to become apparent between landowners seeking to protect their grouse moors from dis-

---

[1] See below, p. 109.
[2] Quoted in *Fifty years of National Parks:* a valuable booklet, published by the Council for National Parks, tracing the history of the work of its predecessor, the Standing Committee on National Parks.

turbance, and ramblers from the cities seeking solace from the grimness of the urban depression. The absence of public rights of way over vast tracts of open land, and hence its unavailability for public recreation, led to the mass trespass by several thousand on Kinder Scout in 1932, the establishment, by federation of local groups of the Ramblers' Association in 1935, and also to a widespread feeling that the law should recognise areas such as these, though privately owned, as a part of the nation's heritage. As such they should, it was increasingly felt, be made subject to a legal regime which would allow public enjoyment, whilst, at the same time, providing necessary safeguards against despoliation.

Although there had been unsuccessful attempts by private members to introduce legislation in 1884 and 1908, it was pressure from groups such as the Council for the Protection of Rural England, and also from influential individuals, which led to a government inquiry which recommended the creation of National Parks.[1] This Report, coinciding with economic crisis and change of Government, did not give rise to any immediate action and so, in 1936, there came together a number of individuals and amenity and access groups to form a Standing Committee on National Parks. The Standing Committee campaigned for parliamentary action, but, again, the period immediately prior to and during the second World War was not a time for such legislation. Nevertheless, the campaign was assisted by the images of rural England presented by the press to the public as the England which was being fought for; moreover some members of the SCNP served in influential positions in the civil service during the war years. Even before hostilities were over the idea of National Parks was accepted by government in principle,[2] and Reports after the war furnished detailed proposals and schemes. Most notably, the Dower Report followed closely the principal ideas of the SCNP.[3] The essential idea behind the designation of National Parks was stated to involve selection of extensive

---

[1] The Addison Report (1931).

[2] Report of the Scott Committee on Land Utilisation in Rural Areas in 1942 (Cmd 6378), and White Paper on Control of Land Use, in 1944 (Cmd 6537).

[3] Cmd 6628 (1945). John Dower had been a founding member of SCNP.

areas of, relatively wild, beautiful countryside and there to **preserve** the characteristic landscape beauty, to **protect** wildlife, buildings and places of architectural and historic interest, and to **provide** access and facilities for open-air public enjoyment of the areas. It was assumed that established farming use would continue; at this time the idea of farming being conducted in such a way as to be of concern to conservationists had not yet dawned. Following the General Election of 1945 a committee under Sir Arthur Hobhouse[1] toured the various areas suggested by Dower for National Park status. This committee narrowed down to ten Dower's original list of twelve areas—the present ten, plus the South Downs and the Norfolk Broads. Eventual legislation came in the National Parks and Access to the Countryside Act 1949. The ten National Parks were all established in the period 1951–57, starting with designation of the Peak Park and culminating with that of the Brecon Beacons. Together the National Parks comprise 13,618 square kilometres; approximately 9% of the land area of England and Wales.[2]

The Norfolk Broads

The failure to have designated the Norfolk Broads as a National Park was, however, a matter of continuing controversy. The Broads are shallow lakes which were created as recently as medieval times by the flooding of peat workings—very much a man-made area of "natural" beauty. The forty or so Broads are connected by waterways and constitute a valuable recreational area of some 50,000 acres of open water and nearly 100 miles of navigable channels. They are also of immense importance as habitat for birds and wetland plants. In 1949 the National Parks Commission, and in 1976 its successor the Countryside Commission, attempted to secure National Park status for the area. The desire for the Broads to be a National Park was for two principal motivating reasons. A wish that there should be

---

[1] Cmd 7121 (1947).

[2] The National Parks Review Panel has in 1991 reported to the Countryside Commission recommending National Park status for the New Forest (and for the consideration to such status for the S. Downs, N Pennines, and Cumbria Mountains).

a National Park so favourably sited to serve the densely-populated south-east of England, as the Peak Park and the Lake District serve the industrial north of England; and, perhaps more importantly, to give to a single Park Authority wide powers to promote and to protect the area.

The chief problems facing the plants, birds and animals of this area are familar ones: pollution of waterways as the numbers and proportion of motor vessels compared with sailing boats has increased; erosion of banks as more, and more turbulent, craft use the broads; the drainage of wetlands to convert land from pasture to arable; and fertiliser runoff from agricultural land. The need for a single authority to plan and regulate the "amenity" and "conservation" future of this area increasingly became acknowledged.

Some degree of co-ordination of action on the part of the numerous district and county councils was achieved by their establishment in 1978 of a joint planning committee, thus permitting a more strategic approach to planning across the Broads region. This did not, however, suffice fully to tackle the areas needs, in particular in relation to issues of navigation and water pollution. The various local authorities, in due course promoted a private bill in Parliament to establish a Broads Authority with wider and greater powers than those of the joint committee. This bill foundered in the autumn of 1985, but prompted a Government bill which in due course became the Norfolk and Suffolk Broads Act 1988. This established, as of April 1989, a new, Broads Authority. The legislation has created for the Broads a legal framework very much akin to that which we shall describe for National Parks. It was, however, felt by government to be appropriate to establish a special regime for the Broads rather than simply to confer National Park status because of the particular features of the area; a region of rivers, lakes and wetland rather different from the other Parks. The Broads Authority consists of members appointed by each of the constituent district and county councils, members appointed by the Countryside Commission and the Nature Conservancy Council, members appointed by the Great Yarmouth Port and Haven Commissioners and the

National Rivers Authority, and by the Secretary of State. In addition to becoming the sole district planning authority for the Broads area, its more general functions are to manage the Broads for the purpose of conserving and enhancing natural beauty, promoting public enjoyment, and protecting the interests of navigation. In discharging these functions the Authority is required, amongst other things, to have regard to the needs of agriculture and forestry and the economic and social interests of those who live and work in the area. As we have noted in connection with the National Parks, the aim is that the Broads shall be managed and protected as thriving and "working" areas of landscape. The intention is not that these areas be set aside as protected museum pieces.

The new Broads Authority is required as one of its first tasks to prepare a "Broads Plan" in which it must set out its policies for the achievement of its various statutory objectives. The plan is to be published, initially in draft, and this is to be followed by a consultative process. In addition, the Authority is under a duty to prepare a map showing the areas within the Broads whose natural beauty it considers it to be particularly important to conserve. Both this map and the Plan are then to be kept under review, and modified as and when appropriate.

In order to assist its protection of the Broads area the Authority has power under the 1988 Act to make orders in respect of particular areas of grazing marsh, fen marsh, reed bed or broad-leaved woodland; and in respect of any of these specified areas to specify certain operations which appear to the Authority likely to affect the area's character or appearances. Where this power is exercised an obligation arises on persons generally not to undertake any such operations on the land in question without having first given written notice to the Authority and then –

—having received the **written consent** of the Authority; or
—having **waited for three months** following the giving of written notice, and still not have received a decision from the Authority giving or refusing consent; or

—having **waited for twelve months** from the giving of written notice, in cases where the Authority has refused consent.

Anyone acting in breach of these provisions commits a criminal offence. It will be noticed that these provisions, in themselves, do not authorise the permanent prohibition of any activity. Rather, they provide for the designation of particular activities, in specifically defined areas, and provide that those activities shall be delayed for a three or twelve months period during which time discussions can take place with the owner of the land. Such discussions may lead to a modification to the planned operation being agreed, or to a voluntary or statutory management agreement being entered into, to the satisfaction of the Authority. Where discussions are less fruitful, time should remain during which the Authority, along with other interested bodies (the NCC will have been informed) can consider taking action under other legislation; such as, for example, seeking the compulsory purchase of the land and its creation as a nature reserve.

As regards navigation, the Act requires the Authority to establish a special Navigation Committee, consisting not only of members of the Authority itself but also of members with navigation interests who are not also members of the Authority. The functions of the Authority in connection with navigation are very broadly stated as being to maintain the navigation area to such standard as it thinks fit, and also to improve and develop the area for navigation as it thinks fit.

In connection with the various functions described above the Authority has wide bye-law making powers, and also has powers to do anything necessary or expedient for the purpose of carrying out its general functions.

The establishment of this new Authority has done much to create an eleventh National Park. Considered alongside the enhanced water pollution activity of the National Rivers Authority, the prospects for the Broads, as very significant areas of habitat and recreational value, seem better assured than hitherto.

National Park Administration: Local or National Interests?

Returning to our discussion of the establishment of the National Parks, there was created at national level a National Parks Commission. This was, however, a rather different creature from that envisaged by the various reports mentioned above. These had recommended a powerful central body which would exercise **executive** functions in the management of National Parks. This it would do through local committees consisting of an equal number of members appointed by the National Parks Commission and by the local authorities in whose areas a Park was situated. The expenses of these committees in developing the amenities of the National Parks for the benefit of the population of the country generally would be borne by the central exchequer. In fact, the 1949 Act introduced significantly different arrangements. A National Parks Commission was established, but as an "advisory" rather than an "executive" body, and management functions were bestowed on the local authorities in the Park areas rather than on the committees proposed. In a way this was logical enough. Given the very extensive town and country planning responsibilities which local authorities had only recently been accorded under the Town and Country Planning Act 1947, it seemed to the Government only natural to assume confidence in local authorities to administer the National Parks. There were, however, worries from the start about this scheme. Essentially, the fears were that local authorities would be likely to be unduly influenced by local considerations, rather than viewing the Parks as national resources; and that they would be less willing to spend the sums of money necessary to realise the full amenity potential of the Parks, central funds bearing much but not all such expenditure. These early concerns seem not to have been unfounded. Expenditure on the National Parks was, particularly in the early years, significantly less than the various Reports had recommended; and local authorities have on many occasions found themselves in a dilemma, torn between their "local" concerns for the industrial and economic well-being of their areas and their broader "national" concerns for the protec-

tion of the unspoilt beauty of the Parks as recreational areas
for the benefit, mostly, of "outsiders".

Boards and Committees

The detailed administrative arrangements under the 1949
Act were altered slightly at the time of the local government
reorganisation of 1974. The present position is as follows.
In the Peak Park the planning and management functions
are in the hands of a **joint board** (the Peak Park Joint
Planning Board); and in the Lake District the former joint
board became, on local government reorganisation, the
Lake District Special Planning Board. In contrast, the
remaining eight National Parks have National Park **Committees**, or, where the National Park straddles county boundaries, **Joint Committees**. The distinction between the boards
in the Peak and Lake Districts and the local authority committees found elsewhere is of some significance. A board
may "precept" for its expenses on the several district councils within a National Park. In other words it has power to
ensure that it receives the funds it desires for its activities.
The position of a committee is rather different. It submits
claims in respect of its proposed expenditure to the finance
committee of the local authority or authorities of which it
is a committee or joint committee. The finance committee
will then consider the proposed budget in the light of other
calls on local authority funds and of expenditure constraints
generally. It may well, therefore, choose not to allow the
claim in full. Given these differing arrangements as to finance it is not surprising that it is in relation to the Peak
Park and the Lake District National Park that the activities
of the Park Authorities have been most marked.[1]

At one time a second distinction between the boards and
the committees was of importance. Whereas the **boards** had
always contained a proportion of members nominated by
the Secretary of State in addition to local authority nomi-
nees, the **committees** consisted almost entirely of local coun-
cillors. This difference in composition resulted in the boards

---

[1] The Review Panel (above p.103) has recommended that *all* Parks should be
run by independent boards as in the Lake District and the Peak Park.

taking a rather more "national" view of their functions than the committees. Since 1968, however, the position has been that in respect of both the boards and the committees the membership consists of at least a third appointed by the Secretary of State, following consultation with the Countryside Commission.[1]

Apart from planning and the National Park management powers, other local government functions are in the Parks undertaken by the ordinary county, district and parish councils.

We may turn now to the legal consequences which follow from designation of an area as a National Park and the establishment of a board or committee. The effects are, broadly, two-fold. There are certain differences to note as regards the operation of planning controls; and the park authority, be it a board or committee, may exercise certain statutory powers to promote the amenity of the Park. We shall consider each of these matters in turn.

Planning

In the two National Parks which have planning boards these boards exercise the planning functions normally exercised by county and district councils. In other words development plan matters, the control of minerals, and also the day-to-day operation of development control (through planning permission and enforcement decisions) are functions of a single body with responsibilities covering the whole area of the Park. In the other National Parks these various planning functions are exercised by the special planning committees appointed by the county council or councils. In all the Parks the boards or committees have management as well as planning responsibilities; and in all the Parks the ordinary planning role of the district councils is much-reduced, though they do retain certain functions in relation to tree preservation and replacement, and waste land.[2]

As regards the **substance** of planning control the main

---

[1] Countryside Act 1968 Schedule 4, subsequently replaced by Local Government Act 1972 Schedule 17. Note also, Wildlife and Countryside Act 1981 s. 46.

[2] See, generally, Local Government Act 1972 s. 182.

special provisions in relation to National Parks arise from the fact that special Development Order provisions apply to these areas,[1] thereby reducing the categories of development which are exempt from the requirement of obtaining planning permission. In addition, in the Peak Park, the Lake District and Snowdonia the ambit of ordinary planning control was **more** extensive by virtue of the Town and Country Planning (Landscape Areas Special Development) Order 1950.[2] This extended planning controls in those Parks, to the design and external appearance of agricultural and forestry buildings. The 1950 Order did not apply, however, to the *siting* of such buildings. However, in 1986 these controls were extended to all the National Parks, and were amended to cover siting. More recently, the Environment White Paper of autumn 1990 has promised that these controls will be extended throughout the whole of England and Wales, and no longer be confined only to the most scenic areas.

As well as these special legal rules the actual, day-to-day, exercise of planning controls is marked by a policy of development constraint in these areas, as described earlier in Chapter 2.[3]

Management

The management of the National Parks is the responsibility of the park authorities; that is, the planning boards and committees. The Local Government Act 1972 imposed on the authorities an obligation to prepare, and to review every five years, a "management plan" setting out their policies for the management of the Park and the exercise of their functions in relation to the area. Plans are produced in consultation with both the Countryside Commission and the district councils within the Parks.

More recently the Wildlife and Countryside Act 1981 has required the preparation, by the county planning authority within each National Park, of maps showing areas of mountain, moor, heath, woodland, down, cliff and foreshore

---

[1] For the General Development Order, see above, p. 28.
[2] S.1 1950/729.
[3] See, above, p. 46.

whose natural beauty it is thought particularly important to preserve. Such maps are required to be prepared in accordance with guidelines as to criteria for assessing "importance" issued by the Countryside Commission, and are to be reviewed every five years.[1]

The National Park authorities have a number of specific legal powers, in addition to those possessed by local authorities generally and discussed elsewhere in this book, which they may exercise in order to achieve the aims and objectives of the Parks. They may, for example, provide accommodation, refreshments, camping sites and car parks. However, since such activities may be costly and the authorities have not been over-generously funded, progress in such matters has been rather slow. An important power dating from the 1949 Act and which has been extensively used is the power to appoint Wardens,[2] who give advice to users of the Parks which is often of importance in terms of safety, and they keep a wary eye open for infringements of the law or the country code or other threats to the ecology of the Park. The Park authorities have not, perhaps, been able to play the part envisaged by the advisory committees of the 1940s in exploiting to the full the recreational potential of the Parks. Nevertheless, in addition to specific legal powers the National Park authorities also pursue their general objectives by means of consultation with public bodies and landowners, giving advice on matters upon which they have developed special expertise, and giving publicity and disseminating information to the public about the Parks.

Appraisal

With what degree of success have the Park authorities achieved their basic objectives of preserving the unspoilt natural beauty, and of promoting public enjoyment, of the designated areas? In terms of planning control over relatively minor private development in National Parks the record has been reasonably impressive. More difficulty has

---

[1] 1981 Act s. 34, as amended by the Wildlife and Countryside (Amendment) Act 1985, s. 3.

[2] The Wildlife and Countryside Act 1981 has now conferred powers to appoint wardens on local authorities generally.

been experienced in preventing intrusions by public sector bodies, and in relation to the more major development proposals of private industry. For example the Central Electricity Generating Board succeeded in building a nuclear power station in the Snowdonia Park; oil refineries and an oil terminal have been constructed on Milford Haven on the boundary of the Pembrokeshire Coast Park; military use has been made of areas owned by the Ministry of Defence within the Dartmoor and Northumbria Parks; and, especially in the Peak District, large-scale quarrying of hillsides has been permitted. In some cases central government has been itself responsible for controversial development in National Parks: the route chosen by the Department of Transport for the Okehampton by-pass provides an example of this. On the other hand, numerous proposals which would have had adverse effects on the landscape have not been allowed; and some of those which have been allowed have been subjected to strict conditions as regards siting and landscaping. The Llyn Celyn reservoir in Snowdonia, the development within closely defined limits of Milford Haven, and the underground pumping of water from Ullswater and Windermere are examples of this. For the future, it is likely that demand for limestone from quarries within the Parks will increase, as large quantities of this material are required to operate flue-gas-desulphurisation at electricity generating stations. Action to alleviate the problem of "acid rain" may therefore itself have deleterious effects on landscape.

A problem which planning controls have been unable to counter has been the effect on the natural beauty of the National Parks resulting from changes of agricultural use and from forestry.[1] Particular concern has been focused on the loss of heather moorland on Exmoor and on the North York Moors as a result of ploughing for more intensive agriculture or for afforestation. In this connection a provision of the Wildlife and Countryside Act 1981 should be noted. Under section 42 the Secretary of State may designate particular moorland or heath areas within any National

---

[1] The exemption of such matters from planning controls was explained in chapter 2, p. 32.

Park for special protection. Following such designation it becomes an offence to plough or otherwise convert to agricultural use such land if the land has not been agricultural land within the previous twenty years. It is also an offence to carry on on such land any other agricultural or forestry operation specified in the ministerial order and which is likely to affect the character and appearance of the area. No offence is committed, however, in either case if the consent of the county council has been obtained; or if after three months notice has been given the request has neither been granted nor refused; or if the action takes place over twelve months after giving notice even if consent has been refused. The idea of the scheme is thus not to forbid such actions, but to subject them to a period of delay during which discussions and negotiations may take place between the local authority, bodies such as the Nature Conservancy Council and the Countryside Commission, and the landowner. The landowner may be persuaded to enter into a statutory management agreement, binding on the landowner and also his successors in title,[1] or it may be appropriate in some cases to protect a valuable area by making it a Site of Special Scientific Interest[2] or a Nature Reserve. In the latter case powers of compulsory purchase are available, if necessary.[3]

Any assessment of the success or otherwise of the National Parks must stress a fundamental difficulty which has faced those responsible for them. The statutory task has been that of promoting two aims which may on occasions conflict: the preservation of amenity and the promotion of public enjoyment. To promote one regardless of the other is relatively easy: to regard each as an essential and equal objective poses problems. Public enjoyment on a large scale necessitates road-building or at least road-widening, car parks, caravan and camping sites, hotels, cafés and restaurants. These may be planned so as to minimise scenic

---

[1] For example, with the local authority under s. 39 of the 1981 Act.

[2] This will enable the NCC to offer a management agreement: Countryside Act 1968 s. 15.

[3] National Parks and Access to the Countryside Act 1949, s. 17. Nature Reserves and SSSIs are further considered later in this chapter.

harm but not to eliminate such harm entirely. Moreover, the presence of visitors in large numbers may put at risk certain habitats for plants and wildlife. The suggestion has therefore been made that the legislation be amended so as to impose a primary obligation to preserve unspoilt beauty and a subsidiary obligation to promote public enjoyment.[1] However, any such change would be to alter fundamentally the concept of the National Parks as originally conceived.

AREAS OF OUTSTANDING NATURAL BEAUTY

In considering the events which led to the establishment of the National Parks reference was made to the influential Dower and Hobhouse Reports. These proposed also that alongside the National Parks, which would be positively managed to secure the aims of landscape protection and public enjoyment, there should be designated other areas of particular landscape beauty. These other areas would generally be smaller in size than the National Parks, and would not be under the superintendence of any special managing authority in the way envisaged for the Parks; but the fact of such designation would constitute clear official recognition of the importance of preserving the attractiveness of the areas.

Procedure

The National Parks and Access to the Countryside Act 1949 implemented these basic recommendations. It gave to the National Parks Commission, now the Countryside Commission, power to designate areas as Areas of Outstanding Natural Beauty,[2] and, to date, some thirty-eight areas have been afforded this status. Together these areas represent around 20,000 square kilometres: about thirteen per cent of the land area of England and Wales. Designation takes place after consultation with local authorities, advertisement

---

[1] See, for example, the Report of the National Park Policies Review Committee (Sandford Report) 1974. Also, National Parks Review Panel Report (1991): add wildlife conservation as statutory duty; and make clear that public enjoyment means quiet enjoyment.

[2] NPACA 1949 s. 87

in the *London Gazette* (an HMSO publication containing official notices) and in local newspapers, and consideration of any representations, in favour or against, made by interested persons. Individual landowners are not, however, directly notified. Designation orders made by the Countryside Commission do not come into effect unless and until confirmed by the Secretary of State. Where representations have been made against any such designation the Secretary of State may choose to convene a local public inquiry, before arriving at his decision. A recent example of this occurred in 1985 in respect of the Countryside Commission's proposed designation of a large area of land in the northern Pennines near Hadrian's Wall as an AONB. The proposal was, in due course, confirmed.

Size

There is nothing in the legislation imposing any upper or lower limit to the size of an area which may be designated as an AONB, and indeed they do vary enormously in size — the Scilly Isles being only 16 square kilometres compared with the 1738 square kilometres of the North Wessex Downs. However, it may be said that they are mostly smaller than the National Parks, but larger than the Country Parks which we shall consider shortly. Some criticism has been levelled at the substantial size of certain of the designated areas. If large areas are designated there is a risk that those wishing to act to the detriment of landscape may argue that not all of a very substantial area should merit equal and full protection. The Cotswolds, the North Wessex Downs, and the North Pennines AONBs, covering areas of 1507, 1738, and 1998 square kilometres respectively, are each larger than most of the National Parks.[1] The problem, of course, is that if a large area is indeed an area of outstanding natural beauty it deserves protection as a whole; and to divide it up into "pockets" of especially outstanding beauty may be damaging to the other areas of only outstanding beauty!

---

[1] Pembrokeshire Coast Park (583 sq km), Exmoor (686 sq km), Dartmoor (945 sq km), Northumberland (1031 sq km), Brecon Beacons (1344 sq km), Peak District (1404 sq km), North York Moors (1432 sq km).

Unlike the National Parks, which were all created between 1951 and 1957, designation of AONBs has continued steadily throughout the period since the confirmation of the first such area, the Gower peninsula, in 1956. Early designations included the Quantock Hills, the Lleyn peninsula and the Northumberland Coast; recent additions to the list of AONBs have included the High Weald, Cranbourne Chase and the West Wiltshire Downs, the Clwydian Hills in Wales, the North Pennines, and the Howardian Hills. It may also be noted that most of the stretches of coastline which the Countryside Commission has declared to be "heritage coasts" (not a statutory designation) fall within AONBs.

Legal Consequences

What are the legal consequences of confirmation of a designated area as an AONB? In terms of direct legal protection the answer is "surprisingly little". The 1949 Act confers general powers on local authorities to preserve and enhance the natural beauty of such areas;[1] but central government grant in aid of such matters is less generous than in connection with the National Parks, and accordingly local authorities have not been active in this respect. The 1949 Act also authorises local authorities to appoint wardens for AONBs[2] in order to enforce local authority byelaws and to advise and assist the public. Finally, the 1949 Act requires that the Countryside Commission be consulted in relation to development plan[3] proposals affecting an AONB. However, there is no such obligation to consult the Commission about actual development proposals; though **if** consulted, the Commission is willing to give its advice.

The intention behind the AONB provisions of the 1949 Act was that designation would signal to local planning authorities the importance of applying strict development control policies to the area in order to preserve its natural beauty. In this connection a difference of emphasis between

---

[1] N.P.A.C.A. 1949 s. 11.
[2] 1949 Act s. 92 (applicable to National Parks also).
[3] As to which see, above, p. 38.

National Parks and AONBs is discernible. In considering the National Parks it was noted that both the protection of landscape and the promotion of recreational use are statutory objectives. As regards AONBs the emphasis has been on protection rather than recreation; thus, for example, central government grant aid towards local authority expenditure treats more favourably projects to enhance landscape than those for recreational purposes. This may avoid certain of the special dilemmas referred to in connection with the National Parks, but the more general problems associated with rural planning control[1] certainly remain. Indeed they become problems writ large because of the particular scenic attractions of such areas. The general policy of development constraint in rural areas should apply with particular strictness in AONBs, the onus on the developer being in such places greater than elsewhere. In addition to this the special Development Order provisions referred to in connection with National Parks also apply to AONBs, thus bringing certain, normally excluded, development within the ambit of development control.

Appraisal

With what degree of success has this development constraint policy protected AONBs? A fair conclusion might be to say that although such a policy is necessary it is not, by itself, sufficient. As stressed before, agriculture and forestry are activities which are carried on largely beyond the ambit of planning controls and each can have a very significant impact on the landscape. Much of the beauty of AONBs is not a "natural beauty" at all: it is a landscape fashioned by traditional forms and practices of agriculture and forestry, and the nature of the landscape changes if those practices alter. In AONBs, perhaps more than elsewhere, sufficient public money needs to be made available to finance management agreements with landowners, designed to secure continuation of scenically attractive agriculture and provide compensation for lost profits in not pursuing other forms.

---

[1] See, above, p. 46.

COUNTRY PARKS

Although the National Parks are of very great importance as areas for leisure and recreation, it was apparent from the outset that they would not be sufficient alone to meet the needs of the increasingly mobile urban populations. The National Parks are at some distance from the most densely populated south-east of England, and only the Peak Park is close to large city areas. In addition, therefore, to the National Parks there was a need to assist the day, or half-day, tripper to gain an experience of the countryside closer to his town home. With this intention the Countryside Act 1968 conferred on county and district councils powers to establish and manage Country Parks.

Local Authority Powers

Country Parks may be established on land which the local authority owns; or it may purchase land, either by agreement or compulsorily, for this purpose. The Act also provides for a Country Park to be established on privately owned land by agreement with the owner.[1] Having established a Country Park the local authority must allow access free of charge, for purposes of recreation and exercise, to all members of the public whether or not locally resident.

Within a Country Park the local authority may provide car parks, toilets, refreshment facilities and such other amenities as they think appropriate. Examples of such amenities, sometimes provided, include adventure playgrounds for children, nature trails, camping and caravanning sites, and facilities for fishing, boating and water sports on any lake or pond within the Park.[2] Although entry to a Country Park must be free of charge, reasonable charges may be made for car parking and the use of any of the amenities provided.

The Countryside Commission has power to recommend in relation to particular Parks whether the expenditure of the local authority should qualify for 75% central exchequer

---

[1] Countryside Act 1968 s. 7.

[2] These latter matters are specifically authorised by section 8 of the 1968 Act.

grants. Since the obtaining of such financial assistance is of obvious importance to local authorities, this power of recommendation has given the Countryside Commission power to exert some influence over the location and nature of such Parks.

Appraisal

The Country Park idea has proved to be a considerable success. A large number have been established; the majority in the first ten years following the 1968 Act when around 150 were created. By 1988 a total of 220 had been established. They have afforded an experience of the countryside to many city residents; an experience which in some areas of intensified agriculture is not always easy for the uninitiated to gain without assistance. Conversion of much pasture to arable cultivation and the common, albeit unlawful, practice of growing crops over footpaths, or even of ploughing them up, have led to the ironic situation that the "growth in demand for outdoor recreation has been paralleled by a great decline in the suitability of much of the countryside for these purposes".[1] The Country Parks have therefore been especially valuable in the regions with least open country and most arable land. At the same time the Country Parks have had some beneficial effects in relieving, to a degree, pressures of congestion at other traditional beauty spots and day-trip locations. And in so far as Country Parks often embrace precious habitats for flora and fauna, the Parks are commonly managed with a view to conservation as well as simply to provide leisure and recreation. Approximately a quarter of Country Parks contain SSSIs.[2]

Local authorities have shown a good deal of flair in their presentation of country parks. It is common to provide a wardens service and information kiosks to meet the visitors' enquiries about the area; and, often, well written information pamphlets are provided. When the site has historical associations (such as one at Bosworth in Leicestershire) or historic buildings these matters can, if appropriately

---

[1] Bryn Green, *Countryside Conservation* p. 185.
[2] See below, p. 127.

explained, enhance considerably the interest of visitors. A good example of this is in the Sherwood Forest Country Park, where the displays at the Visitors' Centre help to explain and bring to life the traditions of Robin Hood and Maid Marian. In this particular connection, the value of Country Parks in the gentle education of young, and less young, people may be of significance. Well-marked nature trails, for example, may help stimulate an interest in, and an understanding of environmental matters; and the greater the proportion of the community with first-hand experience of the countryside the stronger the conservationist lobby is likely to become.

On a smaller scale, but in some ways similar to Country Parks, we may mention also the power given to local authorities by the Countryside Act 1968 to establish picnic sites, and also camping sites for holiday and recreational purposes.[1] By 1988, some 264 picnic sites had been created under this power.

CONSERVATION AREAS

These areas have already been considered in the chapter on planning. Although more commonly to be found in urban areas, there are numerous villages which are, or contain, conservation areas. The protection afforded to these areas lies in the additional publicity attaching to planning permission applications, the application of special Development Order provisions to such areas (excluding some of the usual exemptions from the need for planning permission), and protection afforded to trees against being felled or otherwise destroyed without local authority consent.[2] Furthermore, many local authorities have followed advice from the Department of the Environment and have established special advisory Committees for the conservation areas in their districts. These consist of members of the authority and also co-opted members from local amenity societies and other interested bodies.

---

[1] 1968 Act s. 10. Note, also, the Highways Act 1980, s. 112 (picnic sites and public conveniences for users of main trunk road).

[2] See above, p. 52; and below, p. 149.

NATURE RESERVES

The designations considered so far have had as their principal aims, variously, the protection of scenic landscape beauty and the promotion of public recreational use of the countryside. We turn now to designations designed principally to preserve the habitats of our flora and fauna, in order to maintain the very rich diversity of plant, animal and bird life which exists in our countryside. Areas designated for this reason may in some cases be of little scenic attraction and restrictions on public access may sometimes be essential to successful habitat protection. However, where such areas are of scenic beauty and of recreational value public access is usually permitted in so far as the land is in public ownership and the overriding protection objectives are not endangered. We shall consider in turn each of the following: National and Local Nature Reserves, Marine Nature Reserves, Sites of Special Scientific Interest, and Environmentally Sensitive Areas.

National and Local Reserves

The power to establish nature reserves was given by the NPACA 1949. This provides that the Nature Conservancy Council or any local authority may establish such a reserve;[1] and defines nature reserves as land managed so as to provide opportunities, under suitable conditions and control, for study and research into the flora and fauna or geological or physiographical features of an area, or simply for the purpose of preserving and protecting the flora or fauna or such features.[2] In the light of this definition it can be appreciated why nature reserves have sometimes been called "outdoor" or "living" laboratories.

The establishment of a nature reserve may be by taking ownership of the land in question, either by agreement or by the exercise of powers of compulsory purchase; or may be by leaving the land in private ownership, and entering into agreement with the private landowner concerning the

---

[1] 1949 Act ss. 17 and 21.
[2] 1949 Act s. 15.

management of the land. There is also in the 1949 Act a power to acquire land compulsorily for management as a nature reserve in circumstances where there has been breach of such an agreement previously entered into. Where agreements have been entered into these may provide for payments to be made to landowners in respect of the costs of works undertaken and also to provide compensation in respect of restrictions imposed on the owner by the terms of the agreement. Reserves which the NCC considers to be of national importance may be designated by that body as National Nature Reserves, and it is in respect of such areas of "national importance" that the NCC may itself establish reserves or enter into agreements with landowners. The powers of local authorities to establish, or enter into agreements for, nature reserves are exerciseable wherever it appears to the authority to be expedient in the interests of the locality. Such reserves are usually called Local Nature Reserves although if the NCC considers such a reserve to be of national importance it may designate it a National Nature Reserve. Such designation gives the NCC certain powers in respect of the reserve. Although, as shown above, the powers of local authorities may be couched in wider terms than those of the NCC, local authorities have perhaps understandably not regarded nature reserves as a first call on their resources. Accordingly there are over 230 National Nature Reserves, extending to over 1,650 square kilometres, compared with some 176 Local Nature Reserves, covering a very much smaller area. Of the National Nature Reserves only a small proportion are on land actually owned by the NCC. Most have been established by nature reserve agreements with the landowners, or by leasing land from the landowner.

Byelaws

Following the establishment of a nature reserve by the NCC or a local authority there should be published in the locality a formal declaration of the existence of the reserve. This will then enable the NCC or the local authority, as the case may be, to make bye-laws in relation to the reserve.[1] Such bye-laws may cover a variety of matters necessary for the protection of the reserve, such as prohibiting or restricting access by members of the public and prohibiting actions likely to disturb or endanger any living creatures. The bye-laws may not, however, interfere with the rights of entry and access of the owners and occupiers of the land. Restrictions on the activities of owners or occupiers may, however, be contained in the nature reserve agreements, backed up by powers of compulsory purchase in the event of breach.

Non-Statutory Reserves

The discussion so far has concentrated on nature reserves established and managed under statutory powers. In addition mention must be made of the numerous non-statutory reserves under the control of private bodies. Thus, for example, the Royal Society for the Protection of Birds has in the last two to three decades increased its landholdings from about a dozen bird sanctuaries to over a hundred reserves extending to over 125,000 acres. These reserves are predominantly of value for bird protection, over ninety per cent of British breeding birds having nested on RSPB reserves. Moreover the reserves support high proportions of British populations of a number of species, such as black-tailed godwits, bitterns, and red-necked phalaropes. RSPB reserves are also of importance in terms of animal and plant habitat. For example, populations of red deer, red squirrels and otters thrive at certain reserves. The reserves include a wide variety of kinds of territory—woodland, moorland, estuaries and other wetlands. The reserves are not restricted to RSPB members, but many are closed at certain times of year to avoid disturbance of the birds. Other private reserves exist on land purchased by County Trusts for Nature Conservation. There are over forty such Trusts and they now operate under the umbrella of the Royal Society for Nature Conservation. The County Trusts have established over 1,300 reserves extending to more than 110,000 acres. Over half of these reserves are, or include, SSSIs.

---

[1] 1949 Act s. 20.

Another example of a private body establishing nature reserves is the Woodland Trust. This body, established in 1972, has acquired and now manages over 400 woods of a wide variety of ages, sizes and types. Over 70 of these are ancient woodlands of especial ecological importance. The Trust spends over £2m each year on new woodland acquisition and management. Like the RSNC it sees itself as having an important role in stepping in and buying areas at risk of harm.

The activities of these and other bodies are of considerable importance. It must be remembered, however, that purchases by such private bodies can be by agreement only, since these bodies have no powers of compulsory purchase. Moreover, once the land has been acquired the powers of these bodies are simply those of the ordinary landowner. They have no power to make and enforce bye-laws regulating access to, or conduct within the reserves.

In recent years some attention has been drawn to what might be called *de facto* reserves. These are areas which, without being specially designated or managed as reserves, nevertheless exist as relatively congenial and safe habitats for birds, animals and plants. A good example is motorway verges.[1] These areas, which are out of bounds to the public and the grass of which is not regularly cut, provide sanctuaries for much wildlife. The bee orchid, for instance, grows beside the M20 in North Kent. The verges of other roads can also provide valuable habitats but considerable harm has in the past been done in this connection by county councils in their cutting and spraying practices. In many areas, however, the councils are now attempting to preserve verges as linear nature reserves by avoiding chemical herbicides and taking care about the time of year and the heights at which they cut. Road-safety is, of course, of prime importance and overgrown verges can hamper visibility. However, it seems that along most roadsides a reasonable balance may be struck between the demands of the motorist

---

[1] Other examples include country churchyards, the less well tended areas of golf courses, and the areas beside railway lines.

and the maintenance of congenial habitats, provided a little thought is given to the matter.

MARINE NATURE RESERVES

A further category of statutory nature reserve has been provided for by the Wildlife and Countryside Act 1981.[1] These are Marine Nature Reserves. Such reserves may be established on land covered continuously or intermittently by tidal waters, or over parts of the sea adjacent to Great Britain and within territorial waters. The procedure for the establishment of such a reserve is for the NCC to make application to the Secretary of State for an area to be so designated and for the Secretary of State to confirm designation. The 1981 Act lays down an elaborate procedure for publication by the Secretary of State of draft orders and for consultation with appropriate bodies, such as local authorities. A local inquiry must be held if there is opposition to a proposal. Marine Nature Reserves are to be managed in all instances by the NCC; and the aims for the reserves will be comparable to those in respect of reserves on land—to preserve and protect marine flora and fauna and geological and physiographical features of special interest, and to enable studies to be undertaken within the reserve.

Bye-Laws

The 1981 Act provides for the NCC to make bye-laws, with the consent of the Secretary of State, for the protection of any marine nature reserve.[2] The proposed bye-laws must be published as part of the Secretary of State's draft designation order, so that consultation and objection can relate not just to the desirability of a reserve at the particular location but also can extend to the proposed regime for management of the reserve. Such bye-laws may provide, amongst other things, for the prohibition or restriction of entry to persons or vessels; may prohibit the killing, taking, destruction, mol-

---

[1] 1981 Act s. 36 and Schedule 12.
[2] 1981 Act s. 37. See, for example, the Wildlife and Countryside (Byelaws for Marine Nature Reserves) 1986 (S.1. 1986 No. 143).

estation or disturbance of animals[1] or plants in the reserve; may prohibit the doing of anything which will interfere with the sea bed; and may prohibit the deposit of rubbish. These wide bye-law-making powers are, however, subject to some significant limitations. The Act provides that the bye-laws shall not prohibit or restrict the exercise of any right of passage by a vessel other than a pleasure boat, and prohibition of rights of passage of pleasure boats must not be total but must be related to particular parts of the reserve at particular times of year.[2] Furthermore, it is provided that nothing in the bye-laws shall make unlawful the discharge of any substance from a vessel;[3] and nor shall the bye-laws interfere with the statutory functions of such bodies as local authorities, the NRA, or any other persons.[4] Bye-laws may also be made by local fisheries committees constituted under the Sea Fisheries Regulation Act 1966. These must also be published with the draft designation order so that local fishermen may know how their activities are to be restricted.

Appraisal

The marine environment may, at least until quite recently, have been regarded as a "cinderella" area as regards conservation. Much harm has been done by such practices and activities as the discharge of sewage into the sea (a practice which distorts the natural marine environment), scallop fishing which is damaging to the seabed and its life, bait-digging which can starve wading birds of lugworms (as well as producing eyesores on the landscape), and dredging operations.

Progress in the designation of Marine Nature Reserves has been rather slow. The NCC intended the Scilly Isles to be the first such reserve, but this plan foundered upon fierce opposition by local fishermen. The first actual designation came in 1986 and was of Lundy, a small island off the coast of Devon. Situated amongst the warm currents of the Gulf

---

[1] This expression would in this context include fish and birds.
[2] 1981 Act s. 37(3).
[3] See, however, below p. 247, on dumping at sea.
[4] 1981 Act s. 36(6).

Stream this area contains an abundance of coral, including the sunset star coral. Following Lundy, the NCC secured the designation in 1990 of Skomer and Bardsey islands off the Welsh coast where large populations of seabirds, such as Manx Sheerwaters, razorbills and Kittiwakes depend on clear sea waters for food. Other areas which the NCC would like designated, and in respect of which consultation is taking place include the Menai Straits where deep tidal rapids support specialist survivors in turbulent waters, and Loch Sween in Scotland where there are colonies of massive sponges.

The NCC's programme centres not only on securing the prohibition or restriction of harmful activities in these especially valuable areas, but also on furthering public knowledge of, and interest in, the marine environment. To this end it is hoped that information centres may be established in these areas and glass-bottomed boats be made available to show the non-diving public the riches which lie below the surface of the sea.

SITES OF SPECIAL SCIENTIFIC INTEREST

Original Scheme

This designation dates, along with the National Parks, AONBs, and Nature Reserves, back to the important NPACA 1949, though the law is now principally to be found in the Wildlife and Countryside Act 1981. The procedure is that where the NCC is of opinion that any area of land outside a nature reserve is of special interest by reason of its flora or fauna, or its geological or physiographical features, the NCC should notify the fact to the local planning authority. The local planning authority is then under a duty, when considering an application for planning permission for development in such an area, to consult with the NCC prior to coming to a decision.[1] Moreover, a circular issued by the Department of the Environment has exhorted such consultation also in relation to proposed development outside, but in the vicinity of, an SSSI which might adversely affect that

---

[1] General Development Order 1988

site (*e.g.* by altering drainage, or by noise).[1] The planning authority is not obliged to follow the advice of the NCC. However, it usually will do so; and where it proposes to grant permission contrary to such advice, this may be a suitable case for the Secretary of State to exercise his power to "call in" the planning application for determination himself[2] following the holding of a local inquiry.

Deficiencies

The identification of sites of special scientific interest, and the assessment of the likely consequences for those sites of development proposals, has been a demanding and important part of the work of the NCC. By 1990 the Council had designated as SSSIs over 5,300 of Great Britain's most important wildlife and geological areas, together amounting to some 16,270 square kilometres or 7% of total land area. Most of these sites are in private ownership.

The system of planning restraint was certainly of some value, but was found inadequate by itself to protect the designated areas. The 1949 Act was passed at a time when the actions of farmers and foresters were not foreseen as being a threat to the environment; and since most of their activities are, as we noted in chapter two,[3] outside the scope of planning controls, the system of notification of sites to the local planning authority was in this context of little value. Another deficiency of the original arrangement was that the activities of the nationalised industries were outside the scope of ordinary planning control.

Present Law

A number of important changes were therefore made by the Wildlife and Countryside Act of 1981 to seek to secure a greater degree of protection for sites. The NCC is now obliged not simply to notify local authorities of sites, but must also notify the Secretary of State and also the owners and occupiers of the land in question. The notification to

---

[1] DOE Circular 108/77.
[2] See, above, p. 43.
[3] See, above, p. 32.

the owners and occupiers must specify the flora or fauna or geological or physiographical features which make the site one of special interest, and it must also specify any operations which appear to the Council to be likely to damage that flora or fauna or those features. This notification requirement applies not only to "new" sites, but also to pre–1981 Act sites if the enhanced protection afforded by the 1981 Act is to apply to them.

As originally enacted the 1981 Act included a provision giving owners and occupiers a right to make representations and objections, and obliged the NCC to consider any such representations and objections duly made. The scheme was, however, defective in that the notices to owners and occupiers inviting comment had to be issued prior to the notification, and hence the commencement, of a site as an SSSI. Since not less than three months opportunity to comment had to be given, the result was to give owners and occupiers at least three months advance warning during which they could act in relation to the site as they pleased before the constraints introduced by the 1981 Act for SSSIs would come into operation. In other words, the procedure constituted official notice that if owners wished to plough or drain land, or do other prejudicial acts, they should do so immediately!

This problem has now been met by the Wildlife and Countryside (Amendment) Act 1985.[1] This has amended the 1981 Act so that the statutory requirement to hear the views of owners and occupiers now arises upon, rather than prior to, notification of a site as an SSSI. Again, at least three months' opportunity to comment must be given; and within nine months of the original notification of the site, and having considered representations, the NCC must either confirm or withdraw the notification. If the NCC fails to do either of those things within the nine months period the consequence is that the original notification ceases to have effect.

What is the consequence of the notification of a site as

---

[1] 1985 Act s. 2.

an SSSI? The 1981 Act provides that the owner or occupier shall not carry out, or cause or permit to be carried out, on land notified as an SSSI any operations specified in that notification unless certain conditions are complied with. These conditions are that written notice of the proposed operations shall have been given to the NCC and that **either** their written consent has been obtained, **or** that the operations carried out are in accordance with a management agreement previously drawn up with the NCC,[1] **or** that four months have elapsed since written notice was given to the NCC[2] For such operations to be carried out, without reasonable excuse, except in accordance with one of these three conditions constitutes a criminal offence. The Act specifically provides that it shall be a reasonable excuse if the operations in question are ones for which planning permission has been obtained. Since the NCC should have been consulted prior to the grant of such planning permission this provision is readily explicable. It is also a reasonable excuse if the operation was an "emergency operation", particulars of which were notified to the NCC as soon as practicable.

The "Voluntary Principle"

It can be seen from the account given above that the emphasis of the 1981 Act is on voluntary restraint on the part of owners and occupiers rather than on clear statutory prohibition. The principle has been that sites will be safe provided that owners and occupiers are made aware, by the notification procedures, of the scientific importance of their land, know what kinds of actions are likely to be harmful to a site, and are offered reasonable sums under management agreements in compensation for voluntarily accepting that they should not act so as to damage the site. Whether or not this voluntary approach would prove adequate was much contested during the passage of the 1981 legislation, and has remained a controversial matter. In particular, the policy of "buying off" owners and occupiers by offering generous compensatory sums, under management agreements, has

[1] Under N.P.A.C.A. 1949 s. 16 or the Countryside Act 1968 s. 15.

[2] The 1981 Act originally specified **three** months. This was extended to four months by the Wildlife and Countryside (Amendment) Act 1985 s. 2(6).

been contentious. Although it might be likely to be a successful policy, provided adequate sums are made available to support such agreements, the principles behind the policy have been doubted. Contrasts have been drawn with the position of persons seeking to do things with, or on, their land which would be profitable, but for which planning permission is necessary. For example, building and operating a factory. If such permission is refused by the local planning authority, this will prevent the owner from making this more profitable use of his land. Nevertheless there is no question of any compensation being given to him, notwithstanding that his freedom of action has been curtailed in the interests of the general public good. Why, it is asked, should those who wish to destroy or damage SSSIs be in a more favoured position?

Another criticism has been that the system may be open to abuse. A compensatory grant may be sought by a person who has never had any genuine intention to do things which would be harmful to a site, but who knows that such sums may be offered him if he pretends that he intends to do those things and then agrees not to do so!

Resources of the NCC

Quite apart from these matters, the success of the SSSI system depends very much on the NCC having adequate manpower to identify and monitor sites, and having sufficient funds to offer attractive agreements to owners and occupiers. The NCC has faced difficulties in each of these respects. The tasks of notifying owners and occupiers of around 4000 pre–1981 designated sites of the activities likely to be prejudicial to those sites, of dealing within four months with notifications of intent to do damaging acts,[1] and generally of monitoring SSSIs, have imposed considerable burdens on the Council. In 1988 the NCC concluded 435 management agreements and nine nature reserve agreements in respect of SSSIs. It was also in the process of negotiations in relation to some 1100 other agreements. Payments for

---

[1] The period of four months is, in fact, extendable by agreement: 1981 Act s. 28(6A) and (6B).

the 435 new agreements would amount to £4.8 million, on top of some £3.1 million payable annually under earlier agreements.

Appraisal

Designation of a site as an SSSI does not, of itself, guarantee the site's protection from harmful activities. Statistics published annually by the NCC show the extent of damage done to such sites. The figures distinguish between sites damaged, either entirely or in part, to such extent that they have permanently lost their special scientific interest and will be denotified as SSSIs; sites which have suffered long-term damage; and sites which have suffered short-term damage. Cases of short-term damage are, as might be expected, the most numerous, amounting to some 160 in 1988. Quite commonly in these instances discussion with the landowner in question results in some alteration to agricultural practice which will, in due course, lead to reversal of the damage. A common example would be to achieve a change in the timing, or intensity, of grazing. Management agreements will compensate for any lost productivity. Instances of long-term damage are numerically fewer, but have given the NCC cause for considerable concern. A feature which is worthy of note in respect of such damage is that during the 1980s the amount of lasting damage done by agricultural activities progressively declined, the chief culprit becoming, instead, works carried out by public bodies with the sanction of either planning permission or a Private Act of Parliament. This reminds us that SSSI designation does not make a site inviolable. It simply constitutes official and public acknowledgment of the special importance of the site. However, this importance may have, in due course, to be weighed with other issues, of finance and practicability of alternatives, when development proposals are being considered. Such balancing decisions will always be difficult and controversial. The environment White Paper of 1990 explains: "even where nature conservation interests have been fully considered there will be times when these have to be overridden by more pressing legitimate interests, for example, the North Devon link road and the Dersingham By-pass, where the benefits of the roads outweighed the loss of small areas of SSSI. In other cases such as that at Lodmoor, Dorset, the conservation argument outweighed the economic benefits and permission was refused". At the time of writing fierce debate exists about the proposed M3 extension, south of Winchester. The approved plan is to cut a wide and deep path for the dual-carriageway through Twyford Down, notwithstanding damage caused to several SSSIs and archaeological sites, rather than to build a tunnel through the hillside: the latter option having been costed at some additional £91 million.

"Super-SSSI's": Nature Conservation Orders

A slightly higher degree of protection may be afforded to particular sites by their designation not simply as SSSIs under section 28, but as "super-SSSIs" under section 29 of the 1981 Act. Designation of such sites is by the Secretary of State, following consultation with the NCC, and is by means of what is called a Nature Conservation Order. By 1989, some eighteen such super-SSSIs had been designated. The power may be exercised in respect of:

(i) land which because of its flora or fauna or geological or physiographical features is of "special interest" and for the purpose of securing the survival in Great Britain of any kind of animal or plant, or of complying with international obligations; or

(ii) land which because of its flora or fauna or geological or physiographical features is of "national importance", and for the purpose of conserving any of its flora or fauna or such features.

The protection afforded to super-SSSIs is in many respects the same as for ordinary SSSIs. The differences lie in the following matters. The level of fines which may be imposed in respect of offences committed in relation to super-SSSIs is higher than in respect of ordinary SSSIs.[1] Moreover, the requirement not to take action until at least three months

---

[1] Compare sections 28(7) and 29(8) of the 1981 Act.

notice has been given to the NCC is strengthened by a provision that if the NCC offer to enter into a management agreement or offer to purchase the land the three months period becomes thereby extended. This is to give the NCC a longer period during which discussions and negotiations between the NCC and owners and occupiers may take place. The three months period becomes instead one of twelve months in a case where no such agreement is reached, or three months from the rejection or withdrawal of an offer to enter into such an agreement if this period exceeds twelve months.[1] Furthermore, if the NCC chooses to exercise its powers of compulsory acquisition no action may be taken by the owner or occupier which may damage the super-SSSI even though it may take longer than the three months period for these procedures to be implemented. In this situation the action may lawfully only take place if the compulsory purchase order is withdrawn or the Secretary of State decides not to confirm the order.

These various provisions give to the NCC a more generous period of time during which to negotiate voluntary agreements with owners, or in the last resort to purchase the land compulsorily, than is the case with ordinary SSSIs. The compulsory purchase powers exerciseable are those which the NCC possesses to acquire land to establish nature reserves. However, as with ordinary SSSIs the value of the rules depends, ultimately, on the availability to the NCC of adequate man-power and funds.[2] Finally, one further protective feature applicable to super-SSSIs, though not to ordinary SSSIs, may be mentioned. The 1981 Act provides that upon conviction for having destroyed or damaged a super-SSSI contrary to the terms of the Act, the court may, in addition to the power to impose a fine, make an order requiring the defendant to carry out, within a period specified in the order, such operations for the purpose of restoring the land to its former condition as it specifies in the order. Failure on the part of the defendant to comply with

---

[1] 1981 Act s. 29(6)(b).
[2] Note, also, in this connection the compensation provisions of the 1981 Act s. 30.

such a restoration order constitutes a further offence. Moreover, where restoration has not been undertaken as ordered, the NCC is empowered to enter onto the land to carry out those operations and may then recover its expenses reasonably incurred from the person in default.[1] It is, perhaps, a weakness of the legislation that these provisions apply only to super-SSSIs and not to SSSIs generally.

ENVIRONMENTALLY SENSITIVE AREAS

This is the most recently invented category of specially protected area. Its origin lies with the United Kingdom's membership of the European Community. Community funding is available to assist with the protection of areas where wildlife and landscape are of special importance and are particularly vulnerable to changes in agricultural practice[2]. The matter is governed in United Kingdom legislation by the Agriculture Act 1986.

Designation of Areas

This Act provides that the MAFF may by order designate an area as an Environmentally Sensitive Area (ESA) if, following consultation with the Secretary of State for the Environment, the Countryside Commission and the Nature Conservancy Council, it appears that it is particularly desirable to:

—conserve and enhance the natural beauty of the area; or
—conserve the flora or fauna or geological or physiographical features of the area; or
—protect buildings or other objects of archaeological, architectural or historical interest in the area.

The MAFF must also consider that the maintenance or adoption of particular agricultural methods is likely to facilitate such conservation, enhancement or protection; and must also obtain Treasury consent.

---

[1] 1981 Act s. 31.
[2] Under E.C. Regulation 797/85 Art. 19.

Agreements

Having designated an area as an ESA the MAFF may then make agreements with owners and occupiers of land in that area by which such persons agree, in consideration of "incentive" payments to be made by the Minister, to manage their land in accordance with the provisions of the agreement. In other words, agreements will provide for cash payments to farmers who agree not to engage in environmentally detrimental practices or who agree to revert to more environmentally beneficial forms of agriculture. The order which designates an area as an ESA may specify provisions which must be incorporated into all such agreements within that area. These provisions may, for example, relate to the particular requirements as to agricultural practices, methods, operations, or the installation or use of equipment, the period or minimum duration during which such agreements must last, the consequences of breach of an agreement's requirements, and the rates or maximum rates of payments to be made. It may be seen that much flexibility is left as to the particular terms of agreements as between different ESAs, but that within an ESA the intention of the Act is for agreements to be fairly standard form as between different landowners and the ministry.

Unless an agreement provides to the contrary the terms are binding on successors in title to the person who originally made the agreement. When agreements have been made the MAFF is required to keep under review the effect on the area of performance of the obligations under the agreement, and to publish from time to time such information about those effects as it considers appropriate.

The Areas

Early in 1986 the Countryside Commission and the NCC made recommendations to the MAFF as to appropriate areas for such designation, and also presented their views about "management guidelines" and grant levels. From an original list of 46 areas for consideration the two bodies settled on 14 areas of England and Wales which they proposed should be designated as ESAs. These areas were of considerable variety, showing the numerous different ways in which modern farming techniques and practices may be harmful to landscapes and habitats. In August 1986, the MAFF designated five of the areas recommended, and schemes in respect of these areas came into operation early in 1987. The original five areas designated were:

The Norfolk Broads—where an earlier experimental scheme in respect of the Halversgate Marshes had already been operating, offering farmers £50 an acre to continue traditional grazing practices rather than draining and ploughing their land for arable cultivation.

Pennine Dales—where protection of the traditional stone-walled hay meadows has been needed against more intensive methods of livestock farming involving draining and reseeding pastures and cutting the grass for silage.

Somerset Levels—where the grazing marshes have been threatened by the prospect of continued drainage and ploughing for arable.

Southern Downs (Eastern half)—where already very much of the chalk grazing downland has been ploughed for arable cultivation.

West Penwith (Cornwall)—where management guidelines will need to take account of the need to protect the prehistoric archaeological interest of this area from being harmed by the "improvement" of the dairy farmland.

Since 1987 the process of designation has continued. By 1990 a total of nineteen areas had been established in Great Britain as a whole. In England and Wales there were added to the original list: Breckland, North Peak, Shropshire Borders, Suffolk River Valleys, South Downs (West), and the Test Valley. Total land area designated amounted to 7960 square kilometres (or 3.5% of total agricultural land).

The scheme appears to be popular both with farmers and with conservationists. Some 4700 farmers had, by 1990, joined the scheme. This represents a very satisfactory take-up rate. The only area where there appears to have been reluctance to join the scheme has been the Test valley. On joining the scheme a farmer enters into a five year agreement under which he will receive an annual payment at the rate per hectare prescribed for the area, in return for following the prescribed farming practices which have been set down for that area. The practices may have positive and negative aspects. For example, the farmer may have to refrain from draining his land and agree to fertiliser restrictions; he may also have to maintain hedges, barns and ponds.

ARCHAEOLOGICAL AREAS

Protection of areas of archaeological importance is provided for by the Ancient Monuments and Archaeological Areas Act 1979. This Act authorises the designation, as an area of archaeological importance, of any areas which appear to the Secretary of State, or to a county or district council, to merit the protection of the Act.[1]

Such designation orders have been made in respect of five towns (Canterbury, Chester, Exeter, Hereford and York) but not in respect of any archaeologically rich areas of countryside.

Once an area has been so designated it becomes an offence for any person, including the owner of the land, to carry out certain kinds of operations on the land unless he has served a notice relating to those operations on the appropriate authority at least six weeks previously.[2] The appropriate authority is normally the district council, although if it is a local authority itself which proposes to perform the operations the operations notice is served on the Secretary of State. The kinds of operations to which the notice requirements apply are ones which disturb the ground, flooding operations and tipping operations.

---

[1] 1979 Act s. 33.
[2] 1979 Act s. 35(1).

These provisions are designed to give advance warning of potentially damaging operations. What steps may be taken on receipt of such information? The Act provides for the appointment of persons competent to undertake archaeological investigations as "investigating authorities".[1] When an operations notice has been served the investigating authority acquires the right to enter onto the land in question, at any reasonable time, to inspect the site in order to record any matters of archaeological or historical interest, to determine whether any excavations would be desirable, or to observe the operations being carried out so as to be able to examine and record any items of historical or archaeological interest discovered during those operations.[2] When the investigating authority considers that excavation is desirable it may acquire power to do so provided that it serves an excavation notice on the "developer" within four weeks of the service of the operations notice. The period allowed for excavation is, generally, six months starting from the date of service of the operations notice. During this period of excavation the operations described in the operations notice must not be carried out.

In addition to this protection afforded to areas of archaeological importance, the 1979 Act also provides for the protection of particular "ancient monuments" by means of a process of "scheduling". Monuments protected in this way take a wide variety of forms, ranging in age from the constructions of Britain's very earliest inhabitants to the military defences erected during World War II. Some are easily recognisable (*e.g.* the stone ruins of medieval castles), others exist only as earthworks or appear to the untrained eye as merely an unevenness across a ploughed field. These latter kinds of feature are particularly vulnerable to damage by modern agricultural practices and equipment. The 1979 Act, consolidating and strengthening the terms of earlier legislation, provides that any such scheduled monument shall not be demolished, destroyed, damaged, removed, repaired, altered, added to, flooded or covered up without

---

[1] 1979 Act s. 34.
[2] 1979 Act s. 38(1).

first the Secretary of State for the Environment having granted consent. Breach of this obligation constitutes a criminal offence. In certain circumstances an entitlement to compensation may follow a refusal of such consent. In addition, payments may be sought from English Heritage (formerly the Historic Buildings and Monuments Commission) in return for entering into management agreements. Such agreements are usually for a five year period and will compensate the landowner for agreeing to take action to protect the site (*e.g.* by the erection of fencing) or for agreeing to cultivate the area in particular ways (usually avoiding deep ploughing) which help protect the site.

The Government is currently reviewing the operation of the 1979 Act. It is expected that amongst proposals for amendment will be a new offence of removing objects from a scheduled site.

Finally, it may be noted that none of the provisions of the 1979 Act confer on the public any rights of access to monuments or sites.

LIMESTONE PAVEMENTS

The Wildlife and Countryside Act 1981 makes special provision, in section 34, for the protection of limestone pavements. These are defined as "areas of limestone which lie wholly or partly exposed on the surface of the ground and have been fissured by natural erosion". In relation to such locations the Act provides that where the NCC or the Countryside Commission consider that any land comprising a limestone pavement is of special interest by reason of its flora, fauna or geological or physiographical features it shall be under a duty to notify that fact to the local county planning authority. The planning authority will then be in a position to take this into account in considering applications for planning permission for mineral extraction.

The section then proceeds to authorise the Secretary of State or the county planning authority to make limestone pavement orders. Such orders may be made when it appears that the character or appearance of a limestone pavement would be likely to be adversely affected by the removal of the limestone or by its disturbance in any way. The effect of such an order is to make it a criminal offence for any person to remove or disturb limestone on a limestone pavement to which such an order applies, unless there is a reasonable excuse for such action. It is, further, expressly provided that it shall constitute a reasonable excuse if the actions were authorised by a grant of planning permission. This covers mineral extraction which has been approved under planning controls; however, since agricultural actions affecting such areas are subject to deemed permission rather than granted permission, it seems that the general agricultural exemption from planning control does not take agricultural damage beyond the scope of this protection. Accordingly, removal of limestone by a landowner to use as lime for fertiliser will be an offence where a pavement order has been made.

This relatively new protection is intended to give special recognition to the importance of limestone pavements as habitats for many kinds of wild plants.

TREES AND WOODLANDS

Introduction

The areas so far considered in this chapter have received protection by a process of designation, thus bringing into operation certain legal safeguards and conferring powers and duties on public authorities with respect to those areas. We turn now to consider the protection afforded to certain kinds of land quite apart from any special designation. We begin with trees and woodlands, and will then consider the activities of the National Trust, Crown Estates Commissioners, and certain other landowners, each of whom own much land of prime importance in terms both of recreation and the protection of habitats, and manage their lands with conservation in mind.

The importance of trees and woodlands to the conservation of our countryside can hardly be over-stated. Quite apart from the visual attractions of individual trees and areas of woodland in the landscape, trees are vital for the maintenance of a diverse natural world. Trees help purify the atmosphere, they prevent soil erosion and the leeching of soil nutrients, and provide habitats for birds, small mammals and a wide variety of flora.

It is a matter of considerable concern that the world's trees are under serious threat.[1] Dangers arising from clearance of tropical rain forest to provide what, because of climate and soil changes, may only be short-term cultivatable land are beyond the scope of this book. However, even confining ourselves to this country the extent of deforestation has been so great that Britain has less trees per acre than almost any country in Europe, having only about 10% forest and woodland cover. Furthermore, there has been disquiet in recent years about the nature of the tree cover to be found in Britain. Commercial considerations have resulted in a very high proportion of plantings this century being coniferous, and the extent of traditional, ancient, broadleaved, deciduous woodland has declined to total now only about 700,000 acres. The disadvantages of coniferous woodlands are two-fold. First, they provide much less in the way of wild-life and plant habitat than do many forms of broadleaved woodland; and, secondly, there has been a tendency for coniferous plantations to be blanket-planted across a landscape in geometric pattern bearing little or no relation to the natural contours of hill and dale, and so spoiling the visual beauty of the countryside.

The loss in Britain of much of its woodland demonstrates very clearly the impact of man on his environment. Over most of Britain, except for the highest mountain regions and waterlogged lowland areas, woodland is the natural vegetation; sometimes referred to as the "climax" vegetation, the vegetation that would exist in particular physical conditions (soil, climate etc) independent of human activity. And Britain was, of course, once very much a wooded country. The form of tree cover varied somewhat according

---

[1] See, below, p. 225 on the problems for forests caused by "acid rain".

to region; with oak, ash, beech, elm, lime and poplar being the main trees of the deciduous broadleaved woodlands of England and Wales, and coniferous forest predominating in the Scottish Highlands.

Forest clearance began surprisingly early. Until relatively recently this was thought to have begun in a significant way only in post-conquest medieval times. However, recent researches have demonstrated the very marked effects of man in the Neolithic and, more particularly, the Bronze Ages (*i.e.* from about 3,000 BC). Clearance began on the lighter soils of the limestone and sandstone uplands, leaving large forests on the heavy clay lowlands; and this process continued through the Roman, Saxon and medieval periods right through to modern times. The reasons for felling trees have varied with time and place. Originally clearance was mainly to provide grazing land and cultivatable land in the initial ages of agriculture; at later times the need for timber for shipbuilding and for house construction was of importance, as well as the burning of charcoal for iron ore smelting and generally the use of timber as fuel. From relatively early times concern has existed at the depletion of the forests. In Elizabethan times, for example much planting of oaks took place in order that timber for shipbuilding should be in ready supply.

In this section we shall be principally concerned with the activities of the Forestry Commission, and with the powers of local planning authorities in relation to trees and woodlands.

Forestry Commission

Some reference was made earlier, in chapter 1, to the Forestry Commission. Established in 1919, its aim was to secure a degree of public control over timber resources. It was not, however, a matter of nationalising the forests. The Forestry Commission has sought to achieve its aims in two ways: by, on the one hand, acquiring existing woodlands and other land upon which it has created new plantations; and, also, by securing the permanent dedication of privately owned woodlands to forestry and then to support the private owners by grants and other technical and scientific assistance. In other words it both manages its own forests, and supervises the private sector. Privately owned woodlands remain of immense importance. About half the timber felled annually is from such woodlands, and this includes most of the hardwood timber. With the recent privatisation policy of government being applied to publicly owned forests the importance of privately owned woodlands is likely to increase.

Statutory Objectives

From the inception of the Forestry Commission in 1919 through to, and including, the Forestry Act 1967 the statutory aims of the Commission were stated primarily in terms of the control and management of timber production on a commercial basis, without significant reference to the importance of forests for recreation, as places of scenic beauty or as rich habitats for wildlife and plants. Thus, the original aims were to develop and ensure the best use of the country's timber resources and to promote efficiency in the timber industry, to undertake research relevant to the needs of forestry, to combat forest and tree pests and diseases, to advise and assist in training in forestry and to administer controls and schemes for assisting private woodland owners. The aims also included those of advancement of knowledge and understanding of forestry and trees in the countryside, and to ensure the use of forest management systems and practices which safeguard the environment; but these appeared to be subsidiary objectives only. For many years concern was expressed at the failure of the Commission to allow, or to make adequate provision for, public access to their forests; an apparent lack of concern for the visual amenity of their plantations;[1] and failure to undertake forestry in ways which promote rich habitats, for example by ensuring the continuance of broadleaved woodland and by "selection felling" rather than the ecologically more catastrophic practice of blanket felling. A good deal has, however, now changed. Increasing demands for countryside

---

[1] "Troops of soldiers marching up the hillsides".

recreation which became apparent during the 1950s and 1960s resulted in the Commission taking measures to accommodate these needs. The Commission embarked on a programme of creating forest walks, establishing visitors centres, caravan and camping sites, and letting forest cabins and disused cottages for holidays. As such, valuable steps have been taken in making available the recreational potential of Forestry Commission land to the public. But what about visual amenity? Here again the Commission has improved its planting techniques. Recent plantings, under the guidance of landscape architects, have been more sensitive in relation to topography, and have consisted of mixtures of species so as to produce variation of foilage colour and growth forms, as well as the use of screens of deciduous broadleaves such as beech and oak. The incorporation of reasonably wide forest drives within new plantations has the two-fold benefit of facilitating public access to forest interiors and also of acting as a fire-break; increased incidence of forest fires being an unfortunate, but apparently inevitable, consequence of public enjoyment of these areas.

Most recently the Wildlife and Countryside (Amendment) Act 1985 has now made quite clear the environmental as well as the commercial and recreational obligations of the Commission. Section 4 of the 1985 Act[1] modifies the general duties of the Commission so that in discharging their functions under the Forestry Acts the Commission shall, so far as is consistent with the proper discharge of those functions, endeavour to achieve a reasonable balance between (*a*) the development of afforestation, the management of forests and the production and supply of timber and (*b*) the conservation and enhancement of natural beauty and the conservation of flora, fauna, and geological or physiographical features of special interest.

A matter which aroused a good deal of controversy during the 1980s was the way that government grant and tax relief policies seemed inimical to nature conservation. Policies encouraged afforestation of the wrong kinds and in the

---

[1] Amending the Forestry Act 1967.

wrong places. The argument over proposals to drain and plant forest over the Flow country in Caithness reached such a pitch that, as a result, the policies were considerably modified so as to seek to promote, rather than frustrate, conservation objectives. Thus, in 1985, a new broadleaved woodland grant scheme was announced, and within three years the proportion of broadleaves in new private planting had increased from 9% to 17%. In 1988, the Forestry Commission replaced this with a new Woodland Grant Scheme, also offering higher rates of grant for broadleaf plantings. A significant feature of this Woodland Grant Scheme is that it has been designed to secure planting which positively enhances both the visual and the recreational potential of the countryside. Applicants for grants are required to specify their intentions in respect of such matters as landscape planning, wildlife conservation, and the protection of water courses. Also in 1988, commercial woodlands were removed entirely from the scope of income and corporation tax reliefs. Thenceforth governmental support was to be by way of specific grant schemes incorporating environmental considerations, rather than by tax advantage. Another scheme which should be mentioned in this context is the Farm Woodland Scheme, an experimental scheme linked to the general policy of set-aside of agricultural land and the "extensification" of agriculture.

In these ways it is hoped to encourage planting at the rate of some 45,000 hectares a year. In addition, support is being given by government for the development of new Community Forests on the degraded urban fringes of Tyne and Wear, South Staffordshire and East London (with several other proposals also being considered); and for the development of a new national forest in the East Midlands. This latter project will involve, over a 40 year period, the creation of a forest of some 40,000 hectares (150 square miles). It is the aim of the Government to achieve this by means of substantial private and voluntary sector investment.

Controls over the Private Sector

So far as management of the Forestry Commission's own forests is concerned the outlook appears to be reasonably promising, with policies showing more sensitivity to the interests of conservation and amenity than has always been the case hitherto. What protection, however, does the law afford to trees and woodlands in **private** ownership? Also, what controls exist over undesirable private-sector afforestation: undesirable either in terms of site, such as the ploughing of moorland for tree planting, or in terms of species?

Tree Preservation Orders

The first matter to be remembered is that the ordinary planning controls over the development of land do not apply to forestry. Thus, trees and woodlands may be planted or cut down without the need for planning permission. However, this statement needs qualification in certain respects. To begin with, local authorities may protect trees by making Tree Preservation Orders. Such Orders may be made at any time by the district planning authority in respect of a single tree, a group of trees or an area of woodland where this action may help to conserve the amenity of the area. Regulations have been made prescribing the form the Order should take; it must, for example, include a map showing the position of the tree or trees to which it applies.[1] Orders are made first in draft form and do not come into effect unless and until confirmed by the district planning authority. In situations where there is a likelihood of threat to a tree or trees between the draft stage and confirmation, the draft may be made so as to come provisionally into effect on the date specified in the draft (usually the date it was made). In such a case the provisional order will cease to have effect unless confirmed within 6 months. Orders made must be available for public inspection, and copies must be sent to owners and occupiers of the land in question.[2] Within 28 days objection may be made to a T.P.O. and any such

---

[1] Schedule to the Town and Country Planning (Tree Preservation Order) Regulations 1969.

[2] 1969 Regulations, s. 5.

objections must be considered by the district planning authority in deciding whether or not to confirm its order. Once a T.P.O. is in force it becomes an offence for any person to cut down, top, lop, uproot, wilfully damage or wilfully destroy any tree covered by the order without the consent of the district planning authority. An exemption exists, however, in respect of trees which are dying or dead or have become dangerous, or where such action is necessary to prevent or to abate a nuisance;[1] moreover, the provisions do not apply to action by certain public authorities. It is no defence to a criminal prosecution to plead ignorance of the fact of the T.P.O., or belief that consent has been obtained: the offence is one of "strict liability".[2] In addition, where any tree or trees are removed, uprooted or destroyed in breach of a T.P.O. the owner is under a duty to plant a replacement or replacements of appropriate size and species. The T.P.O. will then apply to the replacement tree or trees. Applications for consents in relation to trees subject to T.P.O.s are made to district planning authorities. Consent, if given, may be either conditional or unconditional; a common condition to a consent requires the replacement of a tree by one or more new plantings in the vicinity. Against refusal of consent, or against conditions imposed, there is a right of appeal to the Secretary of State. In certain cases compensation is payable to any person suffering loss through refusal, or only conditional grant, of consent.[3]

The environment White Paper of autumn 1990 has promised a streamlining of administrative procedures associated with T.P.O.s, and also an extension of the scope of such orders so that they may be used to protect not just trees and woodlands but also hedgerows. The disappearance of hedgerows in post war years has been a matter of very considerable concern in terms both of habitat loss and landscape appearance. Some hedgerows are of very ancient origin, perhaps marking county or parish boundaries, and may deserve protection for that reason also. A recent report

---

[1] T.C.P.A. 1990 s. 198(6).
[2] *Maidstone B.C. v Mortimer* [1981] JPL 112.
[3] T.C.P.A. 1990 s. 203.

of the Countryside Commission, describing changes to the landscape of post war Britain has suggested that the rate of loss of hedgerows has been greater in the years since 1980 than in the earlier period, notwithstanding increased awareness of the importance of habitat retention. The extension of the T.P.O. procedure to hedgerows has, therefore, been long advocated and now seems likely soon to occur. The White Paper proposes also that farmers should be entitled to grants to help them manage the hedgerows properly. These changes will be in addition to other changes in recent years to farm grant and subsidy schemes, which have been designed to give financial encouragement to the retention, and even the new planting, of hedgerows.

Conservation Areas

Allied to the T.P.O. protection of trees is the protection afforded to trees in a Conservation Area.[1] The legislation provides that all trees, except the smallest (under 3″ d.b.h. — diameter at breast height *i.e.* 4′ 6″), in such an area shall be protected to the following degree. Action such as forbidden by a T.P.O. may not, on pain of criminal penalty, take place unless written warning has been given to the district planning authority, and either consent is given or 6 weeks elapses without a T.P.O. being made.[2] A further exception relates to the felling, lopping or uprooting of trees less than 4″ d.b.h. where this has been done to promote the growth of other trees.

Other Planning Controls

A further way in which planning authorities may have influence on trees is through their grants of planning permission. Such grants may be made subject to conditions requiring that existing trees be retained in the new development, or that trees be replaced, or that "additional" trees be planted. The T.C.P.A. 1990, s. 197 imposes a clear duty on planning authorities to consider these matters, and the need for T.P.O.s, when granting planning permission. In these ways

---

[1] See further, above, p. 120.
[2] T.C.P.A. 1990 s. 210.

planning authorities can play some part in the maintenance of trees and woodlands, and also may minimise scenic damage, for example, where industrial building is permitted in rural areas, by insisting on adequate tree screening.

The Countryside Commission, in 1987, reviewed its policies in respect of forestry in the countryside. As regards local authority planning, it has recommended that development plans, produced by local authorities to guide planning permission decisions, should include forestry as an item in its own right. In other words, each county should survey its area and formulate a strategic forestry policy, indicating where afforestation would be acceptable and the type of planting appropriate. In addition to this, the Commission recommends that planning controls over the development of land should be extended so as to apply to afforestation covering an area of five hectares or more. Such planting would therefore require the grant of planning permission. In certain particularly sensitive landscape areas such controls should apply in respect of afforestation proposals of .25 hectares or more. Furthermore, in all areas it should be obligatory, before planting an area larger than .25 hectares, to prepare a plan of operations prior to commencement. This plan would have to be approved by the Forestry Commission. Failure to comply with these obligations would render the "developer" liable to enforcement action, and would render him ineligible for grant aid.

Felling Licences

The felling of privately owned trees and woodlands is controlled not only by local planning authorities, in the ways mentioned above, but also by the need to obtain a Forestry Commission felling licence in certain cases. The Forestry Act 1967 prohibits the felling of any tree without licence[1] except in the case of trees of not more than 8 centimetres d.b.h., fruit trees or trees in an orchard, garden, churchyard or public open space. The requirement of obtaining a licence also does not apply to trees to be felled under an approved plan of operation under a Forestry Commission Woodland

---

[1] 1967 Act s. 9(2).

Grant Scheme.[1] Nor does it apply to trees which are dead, dangerous, causing a nuisance, or badly effected by Dutch Elm disease. There is also a general permission to fell trees to obtain relatively small amounts of timber for primarily non-commercial purposes.[2] In determining whether to grant a felling licence the Forestry Commission takes into account interests of amenity, landscape and nature conservation. Somewhat complex arrangements exists for liaison in decision-making in cases where a T.P.O. exists in respect of a tree or trees for which a felling licence is sought.

The Forestry Act 1986 has strengthened these legal provisions by empowering the Forestry Commission to require replanting by a person convicted of having unlawfully felled trees. Against such a "restocking notice" an appeal lies to the minister. Notices will require not only replanting but also maintenance of the trees in accordance with the rules and practices of good forestry for a period not exceeding ten years.

THE NATIONAL TRUST

The National Trust[3] is a voluntary body, founded in 1895, with the principal object of acting as a corporation for the holding of land of natural beauty and sites and houses of historic interest for the nation's continued use and enjoyment. In the early years its acquisitions were mostly areas of high landscape value. Since the second world war it has concentrated its attention equally on the preservation of buildings of historical or architectural interest. The Trust is now the owner of some 625,000 acres of land, about half of which consists of tenanted farms and to which the public are not afforded free access in the same way as to the Trust's open country landholdings. However, the Trust works in close co-operation with its tenants to improve public access,

---

[1] 1967 Act s. 14.

[2] 1967 Act s. 9(3).

[3] The full name is the National Trust for Places of Historic Interest or Natural Beauty. Membership has increased rapidly in the post-war period. There were 35,000 members in 1935, 100,000 in 1961, the one million mark was reached in 1981, and the two million mark in 1991.

and any restrictions on access to its open land are usually justified in terms of protection of young plantations and the need to keep the public away from certain nature reserves, especially during the breeding season. The Trust is currently reviewing the scope for the designation of **new** rights of way across its properties. The Trust encourages its tenant farmers to be conservation-minded in their agricultural practices but does not always have legal powers to enforce its will. Approximately one-eighth of the total coastline of England, Wales and N. Ireland is owned by the Trust, in many cases along with the immediate hinterland. Much of this coastline was purchased out of funds raised from the Enterprise Neptune Campaign dating from 1965 and relaunched in 1985. In addition to this the Trust owns over 200 historic buildings, all or most of 22 villages, and more splendid gardens than any other single owner in the world. In addition to land and buildings owned by the National Trust it also holds the benefit of restrictive covenants over a further 75,000 acres. Here the land remains in "private" ownership subject to restrictions, which the Trust can enforce, on the owner's and his successors' use of the land. In this way an owner of land may preserve its future amenity without parting with its ownership.

Inalienability

Under the National Trust Act 1907, land held in freehold by the National Trust may be declared by the Trust to be "inalienable", which means that the Trust thereafter cannot sell or otherwise dispose of the land except under the authority of an Act of Parliament specifically passed to authorise that transaction. This statutory inalienability is obviously of significance in encouraging benefactors to give property to the Trust during their lifetimes or to leave their property to the Trust on their deaths.

Trust property, although inalienable, is not immune from compulsory acquisition by a government department, local authority or other public body having such powers. However, certain safeguards do exist in that rather more elaborate procedures apply than in cases where the compulsory purchase is of other land. Following the making of a compulsory purchase order in the ordinary way and the standard local public inquiry into objections, by a Department of the Environment inspector, the inspector's report is considered by the Secretary of State. Instead, however, of a decision by the Secretary of State to confirm being final, the matter must in the case of National Trust property be placed before a special committee of members drawn from both Houses of Parliament. The committee will itself hear evidence and argument and will submit a resolution either in favour of or opposing the order for the consideration and approval of Parliament. This procedure makes apparent the special degree of protection afforded to National Trust land. It does not, of course, prevent compulsory acquisition in a case where this is, in all the circumstances, nevertheless considered appropriate.

THE CROWN ESTATES

Crown Estate land is administered by a body called the Crown Estate Commissioners under the terms of the Crown Estate Act 1961. The lands in question are the property of the Crown; as distinct from the private estates of the reigning monarch, and from land owned by government departments and agencies and administered by the Property Services Agency. Originally, profits from the Crown Estate went to the reigning monarch. However, since the time of George III, sovereigns have surrendered such profits to the central exchequer in return for Civil List payments. Crown Estate land comprises a diverse range of types, city centre properties and agricultural land, forests and foreshore. Although the Commissioners are expected to manage this portfolio of properties so as to make profits for the Exchequer, this goal is not their only concern. The Commissioners are conscious of the need for policies which balance commercial considerations against the protection and enhancement of the countryside and the conservation of the Estate's older buildings. The idea is that those responsible for the Sovereign's estate should try to set high standards, for others to follow, in both rural and urban estate management. Similar considerations apply as to the management of the estates of the Duchy of Cornwall, amounting to around 130,000 acres. The personal interest in conservation of the present incumbent of the Dukedom, H.R.H Prince Charles, ensures that an attempt is made to "marry" profit-orientated and environmentally sound estate management practices. The Crown Estate Commissioners manage around 170,000 acres of agricultural land in England and Wales, about 67,000 acres of common land in Wales,[1] about half the foreshore around the coast and tidal waters of the United Kingdom,[2] the Windsor Estate, as well as having mineral and sporting rights which are of considerable value. The Commissioners encourage tree and hedgerow planting, and often only allow a tenant farmer to remove a hedgerow on condition that equivalent planting takes place elsewhere on the holding. Many SSSIs are to be found on Crown Estate land, and a number of nature reserves agreements have been negotiated with the NCC and local authorities. The foreshore estates include some bird sanctuaries. An initiative of some importance in 1981 was the purchase of the Laxton estate in Nottinghamshire from the MAFF in order to preserve the system of medieval strip farming which continues there to be practised. The Great Park at Windsor is open for public recreation, and a very large number of persons use this area for walking, riding, jogging, flying model planes and other activities. Good progress is being made establishing a deer herd in the park, starting in 1979 with a nucleus of stock brought from Balmoral.

MISCELLANEOUS AREAS

We may make brief mention, finally, of a few particularly well-known areas which are governed by special legal rules. Perhaps the most unusual legal regime is to be found in respect of the 3,000 acres of the Malvern hills. These hills are under the general management of the Malvern Hills Conservators, a body corporate established under a series of statutes dating from 1884. The Conservators are partly

---

[1] For "common land" and "rights of common" see, below, Chapter 5.
[2] See, above, p. 94.

elected by local ratepayers and partly nominated by local councils and the Church Commissioners. By statute they have a general duty to prevent encroachment or building on the hills and to preserve their natural beauty for the benefit of the public. They own 2,500 acres of the hills, the remainder being in the safe hands of the National Trust. To meet their expenses they levy an annual precept on the local district council.

The royal forests of Dean and the New Forest are generally open to the public, subject to the rights of the commoners. In the case of the Forest of Dean these are the "free miners" and the "ship badgers" (sheep grazers). In the New Forest there is a special body of Verderers. These are appointed by the Crown and have duties which include the preservation of the rights of commoners and the administration of the annual pony sales.

CHAPTER 5

COMMONS

INTRODUCTION

In this Chapter we shall outline the law relating to commons; land described by a Royal Commission in 1958 as "the last reserve of uncommitted land in England and Wales", and embracing a very wide variety of landscape and habitat types. "They range from the huge heather uplands of Dartmoor and the North Pennines, to the crags of Snowdonia and the Lake District; from the Chiltern hilltops and ancient woodlands like Epping, Ashdown and the New Forest to alluvial meadows near Oxford and on the Cambridgeshire Ouse. The coast of Norfolk, the sandy heaths of Surrey and Suffolk, and the suburban lungs like Wimbledon and Clapham in London and the Strays of York are all commons"[1].

Our principal concern will be with the modern law and with proposals for its reform, designed to increase the recreational value of these areas. However, in explaining the modern law a little of the history of commons will be summarised. Quite apart from helping us to understand the present rules of law, this history is of some contemporary significance because a number of the legal developments of centuries past have left, as we shall see, enduring features on the landscape.

HISTORY

It is important to appreciate from the outset that the word "common" is used in two different, though related, senses.

---

[1] *Our Common Right – the story of common land* (Open Spaces Society).

We speak of land as being "common land"; and we also refer to "rights of common" or "commoners' rights" which are possessed in respect of common land by certain owners of property, though not the public generally.

Medieval Agriculture

The ideas of "common land" and "rights of common" date back many centuries and were part and parcel of the medieval system of agriculture. At exactly what time the system to be described came into being is not clear; in any case it would have developed only gradually into a system, rather than have "come into being" at any particular moment. However, the pattern of rural organisation outlined below was certainly widespread in England and Wales throughout the centuries between the Norman Conquest and the eighteenth century, when significant changes occurred. Indeed, the fundamentals of the system most likely date back to Saxon times.

What, then, was this typical pattern of agriculture? Some differences existed between earlier and later periods in these centuries. At any rate from the Norman period our attention must focus on the manor as the principal social, economic and agricultural unit. Lands would be owned by the lord of the manor, and these lands would be worked by many of the local villagers. Some of the land was worked solely for the benefit of the manorial lord and this was known as his "demesne" land. In return for their services the lord would allow the villagers to work other strips of land within the large open fields around the village for their own benefit. Disputes within the manor concerning these matters of agricultural organisation were determined by the manorial court; and this "court" also met periodically to deal generally with matters of local agricultural administration. In each case decisions were reached in accordance with the custom of the manor, and in due course entitlements under manorial custom became recognised also by the King's Courts as "copyhold tenure", and hence part of the common law itself. In time, therefore, it became appropriate to think of villagers as "owners" of their particular strips of land. In many parts of the countryside it is still possible to discern the old open-field patterns of ploughing, with the modern field divisions superimposed. In one village, Laxton in Nottinghamshire, the original system of open-field agriculture continues to this day.

However, not all land was suitable for, or needed for, arable open-field cultivation. Land not suitable for such use was "manorial waste" and villagers generally acquired, by custom, certain rights in respect of such "waste". Except perhaps as far back as the Saxon period such land was not considered to be collectively owned. It was owned, at least from Norman times, by the lord of the manor but his ownership became subject to rights in respect of that land of the tenants of the manor. Moreover, such rights of common developed also in respect of arable land when not in cultivation; for example, when left fallow or after crops had been harvested the tenants might have rights to graze their animals. However, our main concern is with the manorial waste. The kinds of land not suited to cultivation were of a variety of types: uplands, woodlands, lowland heath and scrub, undrained marshes and peat bogs. As such the term "common land" does not denote land of any particular physical description, apart from its nature of not having been readily cultivatable. As one writer has explained, "common land is found where mountain sheep range the fells, in fertile lowland valleys, rimming the coasts and on sandy heaths, along the verges of roadsides, in dingle and copse and fast in the grey grip of the great metropolis. Some are wide-flung, five-figured acreages of open country, others are tiny allotments tucked away among village gardens[1]. Just as the kinds of land which formed manorial waste were of a number of types, so the customary rights of the commoners took a variety of forms. Examples include the right to pasture animals, to cut peat or turf, and to take bracken. The common feature of these entitlements was that they involved the right to take advantage of the natural products, or "fruits", of the land in question. These common rights

---

[1] J. Wager, unpublished University of Cambridge thesis (1966), quoted in *Our Common Right*, see above p. 156.

were of very considerable importance to villagers; they should not be thought of simply as rather quaint local customs. Villagers depended on these rights to gain fuel for their homes, fodder for their animals, and even to supplement their own diets. These rights of common were a very significant part of the rural economy. Commons may not have been cultivatable but they certainly were fruitful.

Enclosures

This quite sophisticated system of self-sufficient local agricultural organisation continued, without fundamental change, until the middle of the eighteenth century. At around that time there began to be introduced certain advances in agricultural practice, such as the periodic shift between arable and pasture husbandry, which were not well-suited to the open-field medieval system. Accordingly, landowners began to petition Parliament for permission, given by enactment of a specific Act of Parliament in each case, to enclose land with hedges, fences or walls, thereby excluding the commoners from the exercise of their rights. When this was to be done special Enclosure Commissioners were appointed to survey the land and assign particular parcels of land to all former owners of open-field strips. Such parcels were then enclosed, and it is from this period that many of our hedgerows date. To provide access to and from landholdings new rights of way were also created by the surveyors around the edges of the new fields.[1] These changes had a marked effect on the look of the landscape, but were not, it seems, particularly harmful to the village economy. Such harm came a little later, when from around 1800 there began the enclosure, not only of the former open fields but also, of the common land itself. Changes in agricultural techniques were making some of this land cultivatable whereas earlier it had not been, and the high price obtainable for produce resulting from the Napoleonic Wars prompted lords of manors to make full use of all available land. The result was that many villagers who had previously been able to provide for their needs by a combination of

---

[1] See, above, p. 62.

working their small fields and exercising their commoners' rights ceased to be able to continue to do so. The choice facing these people was then a stark one: leave the countryside and go to the mushrooming industrial cities, or become a hired farm labourer. The magnitude of the changes can be seen from the estimate that whereas in 1790 some four-fifths of the population lived in the countryside, this proportion had dropped to one half by 1840.

Nineteenth Century Reaction

Enclosures continued through the first half of the nineteenth century, some four thousand local private Acts of Parliament being passed in the hundred years up to 1836, resulting in the enclosure of millions of acres. In that year a general Enclosure Act was passed which simplified enclosure by avoiding the need for the full legislative procedures in respect of each separate enclosure, laying down a less onerous procedure to be followed instead, and establishing a permanent enclosure commission. This Act was soon replaced by the Inclosure Act 1845, which was to similar effect; but by this time a reaction against enclosure had already begun to be felt. The extent to which common land was being lost began to give rise to concern. In the late seventeenth century it was estimated that about half the area of England and Wales was common or waste land. By the mid-nineteenth century this area had reduced to around 2½ million acres. The incidence of enclosure varied much, however, from region to region, reflecting differences in agricultural activity. Areas such as the East Midlands suffered much enclosure. Northamptonshire has only thirty six commons, of which thirty two are smaller than one acre. By way of contrast, Cumbria possesses, still, vast tracts of common land (a fifth of the total national area), as also does, for example, Powys and North Yorkshire. Following growing concern in the mid nineteenth century, in 1865 the Commons Preservation Society was established.[1] This body,

---

[1] The society is now called the Open Spaces Society, and continues to do much useful work. It has published a very valuable account of the law of commons, to which the authors are much indebted: see P. Clayden: *Our Common Land* (4th ed, 1985).

which was supported by a number of influential public figures, campaigned against enclosure of commons both by taking action in the courts to challenge unlawful fencing, and also by more direct action. An early example of action of the latter kind was the breaking down, in the hours before dawn one morning in 1866 of two miles of fences enclosing some 400 acres of Berkhamstead Common in Hertfordshire, which the owner Earl Brownlow had erected to convert that area to his own exclusive use. Similar direct action occurred in relation to enclosure of Epping Forest in the same year, this time resulting in successful legal proceedings being brought by the Society. The general change in attitude can be seen also from legislation dating from this period. Since the Metropolitan Commons Act 1866 and the Commons Act 1876 the legislation has been more concerned with the preservation of commons than with easing the process of enclosure. The reasons for the shift of approach are not difficult to appreciate. From this period till the present day the desire to preserve commons has been motivated more by the wish to retain areas of open land where town residents may take air and exercise, than simply to protect the historical rights of commoners. In some areas, it is true, such rights are still of considerable economic importance. This is the case, for example, in relation to the right to graze sheep on commons in upland areas, on which the viability of much hill farming depends. However, in most areas the modern importance of common land is seen in its recreational potential, together with the value of many such areas as habitats for animals, birds and plants. The law has, as we shall see, failed fully to adjust to this change. It still remains the case that most commons are privately owned areas over which commoners may have certain rights but over which the public generally have none. Moreover, with the decline in the regular exercise of commoners' rights the proper management of commons has been a matter of some concern. Many commons having changed from being very efficiently "cropped" areas to becoming increasingly like areas of wilderness, disappearing under bracken and scrub. The law's deficiencies are, however, to some degree mitigated by the fact that the National Trust owns over 200 commons, and the Crown Estate owns extensive tracts of common land in Wales.

RIGHTS OF COMMON

A considerable number of different rights of common may exist at the present day for the benefit of those owning land formerly part of the manor; and which ones apply in relation to any individual common depends on the history and practice in respect of that common. However, there are six general categories which encompass most rights, and of these the common of pasture is the most widespread and important. The six categories may be described as follows:

Common of Pasture: This is the right to graze a defined number of animals on common land. The right will be to graze particular kinds of animals, which may be, for example, horses, oxen, cattle, sheep, goats or geese. As mentioned earlier, these rights are still of very considerable economic importance in areas of hill farming.

Estovers: This includes rights to take small branches of trees for certain purposes, such as for fuel, for fencing or for building; and to take bracken or furze for bedding and litter for animals. The practices of "coppicing" and "pollarding" trees ensured that woodlands provided a high but sustainable yield of small branches. These practices involved cutting trees low to the ground (coppicing), or above the height at which animals could chew new shoots (pollarding), so that they produced a large number of small vertical branches instead of a single trunk. The right in some areas to take larger pieces of timber for building is that of "housebote".

Turbary: This right involves entitlement to cut turf or peat for fuel for the commoner's home.

Pannage: The right to take pigs to a woodland common and to allow them to feed on the acorns and beech-mast which have fallen to the ground.

Piscary: The right to take fish in reasonable numbers,

for the commoner's own consumption, from waters on the common.

Common of Soil: This somewhat rare right involves the taking of stone, sand, gravel, or other matter from the common for use on the commoner's own land.

THE COMMONS REGISTRATION ACT 1965

The cumulative effect of this history, and the many statutes, meant that over the years a good deal of uncertainty developed as to precisely who had what rights over which land; and even where the **rights** were well established and well known, it often might not be clear who **owned** the common land. A Royal Commission was therefore appointed to consider the matter of common land, and one of its recommendations, in its Report in 1958, was for the establishment of a definitive register of both common land and of rights of common.[1]

This recommendation was implemented by the Commons Registration Act 1965. This required that there should be registered, in registers maintained by county councils, all land claimed to be common land and all claims to rights of common. Certain areas have been exempted from this requirement: the New Forest, the Forest of Dean and other areas specified under the Act by the Secretary of State (*eg.* the Stray, at Harrogate).[2] Outside these exempted areas registrations had to take place by 1970 and were initially only "provisional", thus allowing objections to be made to the registrations before they became "final". Objections had to be lodged within time periods prescribed by regulations, and at the latest by mid 1972. If no objection was lodged to a provisional registration the registration became final. The Act provides that the consequence of final registration is that the registration is conclusive evidence of the matters registered as at the date of registration. Moreover, the converse also applies. Any rights which formerly existed, or

---

[1] Cmnd. 462. Other recommendations are referred to later in this chapter.
[2] 1965 Act s. 11.

any former common land, ceased to exist, or be such, if not registered by 1970.[1] Registers are publicly available documents, kept by county councils, metropolitan districts and London Boroughs. It was obviously of importance to secure as complete registration of land and rights as possible. Accordingly, the Act provided that local authorities (districts, parishes, communities) could take the initiative to make provisional registrations as well as private individuals.

Although the aims of this legislation were no doubt laudable, its detailed provisions have caused some difficulties. For example, in the short time provided for registration not all commons were in fact registered, and those not registered accordingly lost that status. Also, as no obligation existed to notify owners of land of a registration in respect of that land, some land has been registered incorrectly owing to absence of timely objection. A particular problem has arisen in respect of incorrectly registered commons (or village greens) on which a dwelling house is situated (or beside which such a dwelling is situated, and where the common or green is a part of the dwelling's garden (or "ancillary" land). Such properties have often proven difficult to sell, at any rate at full market value. To alleviate such problems, Parliament intervened in 1989 to provide, in the Common Land (Rectification of Registers) Act, that objections to inclusion of any such land on the register may be made up until July 1992. Such objections are to be referred to the Commons Commissioners (see below) who will inquire into the matter, and if satisfied that the registration was incorrect, and also that the dwelling house has been present since 1945, will authorise the registration authority to cancel the registration.

Disputed Registrations: Commons Commissioners

The 1965 Act established a procedure to deal with disputed initial registrations. Where an objection was lodged in good time the registration authority has been obliged to refer

---

[1] Note the curious result in *Corpus Christi College, Cambridge v Gloucestershire C. C.* [1982] 3 All ER 995. The land was conclusively common land, but common land over which there were no conclusively registered rights of common!

the matter to a Commons Commissioner for determination. Commissioners are persons appointed by the Lord Chancellor, chosen from barristers or solicitors of at least seven years' standing. The Commissioner decides the dispute following the holding of a local public hearing into the matter. At the hearing witnesses may be called by both the person seeking registration and the objector, and documentary evidence may be put before the Commissioner. Local councils also have a right to be heard at such hearings. After the hearing the Commissioner issues his written determination as to the validity or otherwise of the disputed registration.[1] On this matter the decision of the Commissioner is final, subject only to a right of appeal to the High Court on a point of law. Many disputes were referred to Commissioners during the 1970s and, indeed, their work continues to this day. In addition to resolving disputes as to registrations, they also resolve disputes as to the **ownership** of commons and investigate the ownership of unclaimed common land.

The 1965 Act also makes provision for deregistration in circumstances where a common has been registered but no rights of common registered, or where registered rights of common have ceased to exist (for example, by them having been purchased by the owner of the land). On deregistration the land may very likely increase in value as it becomes more capable of development. One kind of land, land which was manorial waste, is capable of remaining common land even though no rights of common attach. However, even in respect of land of this nature the owners were able until recently to exploit a loop-hole in the 1965 Act so as to realise the development potential of the land. According to a court decision reported in 1980, where the common was land which had been "waste of the manor" (as was some 1800 of the 8675 commons in England and Wales), that land would cease to be common land and so could be deregistered if the owner sold the manorial land to which the waste land had attached. This decision, which had put under threat

---

[1] See *Re West Anstey Common* [1985] 1 All ER 618: Commissioner should determine the validity of the registration and not simply consider the substance of the **particular** objection raised.

some eighty per cent of commons in southern England, was overruled by a decision of the House of Lords in 1990. Their Lordships held that although the wording of the Act might be ambiguous, the clear intention of the legislature was that land which was indeed "waste of the manor" at the date of registration remained common land notwithstanding subsequent separation of ownership between that land and the manor itself[1].

Proof of Rights

Where registration has been sought for rights of common and the rights are disputed it has been necessary for the would-be commoner to prove his rights. This may be done in various ways. In some cases there may be in existence an express grant of rights of common by deed executed by the owner of land, or there may be an Act of Parliament which as part of a scheme of enclosure granted rights of common over certain of the land. More usually, however, no such express grant or statutory right can be shown and reliance is placed on the doctrine of "prescription". This is a doctrine by which a practice which can be shown to have been carried on "as of right" and "without interruption" over a period of years may thereby become a matter of legal right or entitlement. At common law a claim to prescriptive right could be defeated by showing that the practice had commenced later than the year 1189 (the so-called limit of legal memory).[2] This often made claims difficult to prove and so the Prescription Act 1832 was passed to make proof of prescriptive titles a little easier. The position under this Act is that if the claimant can show 30 years exercise of the asserted right of common prior to the objection being raised, the claimant will not lose simply because it can be shown that the exercise of the right commenced after 1189. The objector must show that the exercise commenced not "as of right" but by permission of the owner of the land; and if

---

[1] *Hampshire CC v Milburn* [1990] 2 All ER 257.

[2] Medieval statutes had revised periodically the period of "living memory", but this practice ceased when the date arrived at 1189. In time, therefore, the idea of proof of practice "beyond living memory" or from "time immemorial" became proof beyond "**legal** memory".

the alleged "right" has been exercised for **60** years, such permission of the owner must be proven by production of written evidence.

Loss of Rights

An objection to a provisionally registered right of common may in some cases be founded, not on an assertion that no right of common has ever existed, but, instead, on the plea that although such a right may once have existed it now no longer exists. How, then may a right of common be lost? There are a number of possible ways. It will happen if the common land and the property of the commoner have come into single ownership; and this is so even if the two parcels of land are later sold or passed to different owners. Equally, a commoner may give up his rights by deed—the owner of the common may seek to "buy out" the commoners of their rights. In respect of some rights of common the permanent exhaustion of the product of the land may terminate commoners' rights. Thus, when all the peat is dug the common of turbary will end. Temporary exhaustion does not, however, do more than suspend rights. Another way is by the operation of statute; for example, by inclosure legislation, or where common land is purchased compulsorily by a public authority under the procedure of the Acquisition of Land Act 1981 (or its predecessors) or the Commons Act 1899. A degree of special protection is, however, afforded to commons against compulsory acquisition by public authorities. Typically, the legislation requires either that equally advantageous "exchange land" be given in its place, or that the compulsory purchase order be subjected to the scrutiny and approval of Parliament and not just the Secretary of State as is ordinarily the case. A final way in which rights of common may be lost is by abandonment. However, mere non-use is not the same as abandonment. The courts, or the Commissioners, will look for evidence of an intention to abandon a right of common. Thus, if a cottage is demolished and not replaced, this will be construed as abandonment of, for example, any right to cut peat for fuel to warm that cottage; but if the cottage is demolished in order to build another, the right will continue for the benefit of the new building. The mere non-exercise of a right of common does not, of itself, amount to abandonment; though, if non-use continues for a long enough period, it may be strong evidence of such.[1] Exactly what period of non-use may lead to such an inference of abandonment is impossible to state. Certainly the degree of exercise of a right which is needed to **maintain the right in existence** may be far less than that necessary to **establish** or create such a right under the doctrine of prescription.

PUBLIC ACCESS

So far we have been concerned principally with the relationship between the owners of common land and those property owners who have rights of common in respect of that common land. It is now time to broaden the discussion to consider rights of the public generally.

Members of the public do not have, and never have had, at common law any rights to wander at will over, or even simply to walk across, common land. Commons are not "commonly owned", and rights of common extend only to the local commoners (not even all local residents) allowing them certain rights over that land. Beyond this, the owner of a common has the normal rights of an owner of land, including the right to evict trespassers from the land. However, he may not exclude the public by fencing the land as this will interfere with the exercise by commoners of their rights,[2] Also, as with any other land, it may be that public or private rights of way exist over the property.[3]

Lawful access to commons by members of the public is generally dependant, therefore, on certain statutory provisions, or on the consent of the landowner being obtained. The statutory provisions are to be found in a variety of Acts

---

[1] See, for example, *Scrutton v Stone* (1893) 9 TLR 478 *per* Charles J.: "In the present case the non-user has been so long that I think I am bound to infer an intention to renounce the right".

[2] Law of Property Act 1925 s. 194 (See below p. 170).

[3] See, above, Chapter 3.

of Parliament, though even collectively it is estimated that they only authorise public access to about a fifth of the 1.37 million acres (the combined size of Surrey, Berkshire and Oxfordshire) of common land which today remain. The earliest legislation, understandably, concerned those commons nearest to, and within, the densely-populated London area. The Metropolitan Commons Act 1866 accordingly provides for rights of access to commons in that area, such as Wimbledon and Tooting Bec. The Act, as also later Acts to be considered, provides for the making of bye-laws to regulate the public's use of the commons, and also makes provision for the proper management of the commons. Outside the metropolis similar provision was soon made for a few commons under the Commons Act 1876. The procedure for applying this Act to a common is, however, complicated and onerous. A 'provisional order' has to be made by the appropriate minister and this has to be confirmed by Act of Parliament. Accordingly, not very many commons have been made the subject of this procedure, although the Clent Hills in Hereford and Worcester do provide a well known example.

The 1876 Act was supplemented by the rather simpler procedures of the Commons Act 1899. This empowers district councils to make schemes for commons within their areas providing for public access. Something like two hundred schemes have been made under this Act.

Where commons have been acquired by the National Trust the land is required, by the terms of the National Trust Act 1907, to be kept as an open space for the recreation and enjoyment of the public. Also, some special local statutes make similar provision in relation to particular areas, such as, for example, the Malvern Hills Act 1884.

The most important provision, however, is to be found in the Law of Property Act 1925 s. 193. Under this section members of the public have rights of access for "air and exercise" on any of the commons falling within the following categories:

(a) metropolitan commons (*ie* ones within the approximate area of the former Greater London Council);

(b) commons wholly or partly situated in an area which before the reorganisation of local government in 1974 was a borough or an urban district.

This section also applies to "rural" commons to which the Act has been extended by deed made by the lord of the manor or other person owning the land. The section also regulates conduct on such commons. It is made an offence, amongst other things, to drive vehicles[1], light fires or camp on any common to which the section applies

PROTECTION AND MANAGEMENT OF COMMONS

The most important statutory provision for the protection of commons is section 194 of the Law of Property Act 1925. Unlike section 193, considered immediately above, this applies to virtually all commons. It prohibits a number of actions in respect of commons unless the prior consent of the Secretary of State has been obtained. The actions in question consist of the erection of any building or fence, or the construction of any other work which prevents or impedes access to the land. In addition to the more usual acts of enclosure this also includes such matters as constructing car parks,[2] sports pavilions, and public conveniences. The Secretary of State is required, in reaching his decision, to advertise the application for public objection, and to have regard to the respective interests of the owner of the land and the inhabitants of the neighbourhood. In relation to constructions principally for the public's benefit, such as those mentioned above, the consent of the Secretary of State would normally be granted. Fencing may often be permitted to constrain livestock so long as adequate stiles are provided.

Each of the various statutes, which we have considered, providing for public access to commons also contains pro-

---

[1] See also, Road Traffic Act 1972 s. 36.

[2] *A-G v Southampton Corporation* (1969) 68 LGR 288.

visions as to the management of commons to which it applies. Accordingly, arrangements will differ depending on whether the Metropolitan Commons Act 1866, the Commons Act 1876, the Commons Act 1899, section 193 of the Law of Property Act 1925, or some other localised special legislation applies.[1] In some cases responsibilities are given to special bodies of Conservators (consisting of a mixture of interest groups); more commonly bye-law making powers have been given to district councils. It may also be noted that the Open Spaces Act 1906 permits county, district and parish councils to purchase any open space for the purpose of public recreation. They can then make bye-laws regulating public use of the land. Such bye-laws may also be made, with consent of the owner of the land, even in respect of open spaces not owned by the local authority.

VILLAGE AND TOWN GREENS

These areas, which may or may not be commons,[2] are nevertheless also subject to the registration requirements of the 1965 Act. Separate registers are kept for commons and greens, and in the case of greens it is only the green and not the rights over it, asserted by the local inhabitants of a defined locality, which are the subject of registration. The expression "village or town green" is defined as meaning:

"land which has been allotted under any Act for the exercise or recreation of the inhabitants of any locality **or** on which the inhabitants of any locality have a customary right to indulge in lawful sports and pastimes **or** on which the inhabitants of any locality have indulged in such sports or pastimes as of right for not less than twenty years."

These are often areas of land amounting to only a few acres. The need for the 1965 Act's provisions to apply was because, as with commons, much uncertainty existed as to ownership and rights over such areas.

---

[1] See, for example, the Dartmoor Act 1985.

[2] The 1965 Act states that village and town greens are not to be considered as commons, but this is simply to allow a distinction to be drawn between "commons" and "greens" so as to allow separate registers to be created.

The rights which local inhabitants may claim over a green must be reasonably precise; for example, to play specified games or to dance around may-poles or to practice archery. As with common land, and any other land, such rights cannot include the right simply to wander at will.[1] The rights arise out of local custom from time immemorial, and the proof of any such rights will require an investigation of the local history. A colourful example of this came in the case of *New Windsor Corporation v Mellor*.[2] in which the status as a green of an area of land in Windsor called Bachelors' Acre was investigated. The land had belonged to the borough for many centuries (since "time immemorial") and for at least 300 years local inhabitants could be shown to have practised archery, and later when the long bow went out of use, practised firing their muskets. At times this use fell into abeyance but even during such periods evidence could be found to the effect that such customary rights were acknowledged to exist. In particular, in the early nineteenth century, a group calling themselves the Bachelors of Windsor had formed to assert the customary rights of inhabitants against any acts done to the land which would prejudice such continued use. The court held that the evidence produced demonstrated that there was sufficient evidence for the Commons Commissioners to have found that the land was indeed "land on which the inhabitants . . . have a customary right to indulge in lawful sports and pastimes", and so was properly registered as a green.

Greens, whether in a village or a town, may in some cases still be in private ownership, subject to these various rights of the local inhabitants; but more usually nowadays such areas are owned by parish or community councils, or in urban areas by district councils.[3] In cases where a Commons Commissioner is unable to discover in whom the ownership of a registered green is vested, it is provided that the green

---

[1] *A-G. v Antrobus* [1905] 2 Ch. 188.

[2] [1975] 3 All ER 44.

[3] Local Government Act 1894. Management powers may be exercised under the Open Spaces Act 1906.

shall vest in the parish or community council (or the district council in an urban area).[1]

REFORM

The Royal Commission which reported in 1958 made three principal recommendations concerning common land. The first, dealing with registration of commons and rights of common, has already been considered. The other two recommendations were that rights of public access should extend generally to all commons, and that there should be proper schemes for the management of all commons. This was of importance to preserve and make valuable recreational use of "this last reserve of uncommitted land". On these latter two matters no implementing legislation has been passed, the official view having been, it seems, that such reform should await the completion of the registration process. The legal rules as to public access and management remain, therefore, at one and the same time both over-complex and inadequate. Over-complex because they are contained in so many differing pieces of legislation; and inadequate because they do not apply to all commons.

Some hope for the future arose, however, out of the report of the Common Land Forum. This informal body was established by the Countryside Commission in 1983 to consider what proposals the Commission should recommend to government for new legislation on commons. The Forum consisted of a wide variety of different interest groups— farmers and landowners, walkers, local authorities and others. It agreed a report which was submitted to the Countryside Commission in May 1986. Of the twenty-two disparate organisations represented on the forum only the Welsh Farmers' Union failed to agree to the report. The Countryside Commission promptly announced its acceptance of the report in full. The most significant recommendations, of a total of 102, relate to general public access and the management of commons.

---

[1] 1965 Act s. 5.

The Forum recommended that legislation should be passed to provide that, within a five year period, the owners, commoners and local authorities should, in respect of each and every common, form a management association and agree a suitable management scheme. Such schemes should take into account, and balance, the needs of agriculture, public access, nature conservation, landscape and other relevant interests. Two basic "models" would be promulgated – one for recreational commons, the other for grazing commons. Each model could then be tailored by management associations to their own particular circumstances and needs.

At the end of the designated five year period all commons would become open to public access for quiet enjoyment on foot. Certain restrictions would apply in the interests of public safety, the preservation of sites of special scientific importance (SSSIs) and sites of historic interest, the protection of young trees or lambing ewes, or to protect land from erosion from over use. Although the right of access would be on foot only, the Forum recommended that in cases where informal horse riding was already taking place, this should be allowed to continue. In other instances it should be at the discretion of the management association to decide whether to permit horse riding on a particular common. As regards dogs, the Forum recommended that these "natural accompaniments" of walkers should be kept on leads on grazing commons, and should generally be required to be prevented from disturbing birds and animals.

Initial indications from the Government were that implementation in legislation of the Forum's recommendations would ensue. Such a promise formed a part of the Conservative 1987 election manifesto. However, the combination of a heavy legislative programme in the early years of the administration elected in 1987, and the vocal opposition of groups opposed to the reforms has resulted in there having been no legislative action; and, indeed, there has been a significant retreat from earlier statements of full support for the Forum's report. The main opposition has come from a relatively small group of owners of grouse moors. These, acting under the aegis of the Moorland Association, oppose public freedom to roam over this heather moorland commons (a third of the total area). Instead, they seek that public access be restricted to designated footpaths. Not only would this involve not implementing a recommendation for open access which had been agreed by the very broad-based Forum; it would, it has been argued, amount in reality to a restriction of actual freedom of access. In areas such as the North York Moors walkers have habitually, albeit without legal right, wandered the hills. If legislation were to emphasise this absence of right and provide instead for footpath designation, it would provide encouragement to landowners to exercise their rights in respect of those that wander at will, and would severely limit public access in these wild open places to just a limited number of narrow corridors. A Government statement, in July 1990, has given support to these ideas; ideas far different from the forum's access proposals. Under those proposals the general right of access would only not apply if a management association sought and obtained approval from the Secretary of State to depart from the model scheme; and, prior to such approval, the matter would be fully aired at a public inquiry. The Government's new proposals seem to avoid such public and ministerial involvement; leaving landowners, commoners and local authorities to decide the issue themselves.

THE SIGNIFICANCE OF ACCESS

We have in this chapter, and those immediately before it, described numerous different legal categories of land. In some situations we have noted that members of the public may have rights of access to such land notwithstanding that the land always remains in the ownership of some particular person or body, and no land is owned by the public in general. It may be helpful if we now summarise some of the basic principles which regulate what the public may do, or may not do, in the exercise of their rights of access.

The first point to stress is that the answer will depend on

the nature of the particular right of access in question. Is it, for example, a right to use a public right of way, or to navigate a river, or to have access to open country under an agreement or order, or to enter a country park, or to go onto common land? In each of the above cases what is permitted and what is forbidden in the enjoyment of the rights of access depends on the particular rules conferring those rights. Thus, it may be recalled, those exercising rights over a public right of way may "pass and repass" and also do things reasonably incidental to such passage. This would normally include stopping to admire a view or to rest awhile. It is unlikely that it includes a right to enjoy a picnic and certainly would not extend to a right to camp overnight. To picnic or camp without the consent of the landowner would involve a civil wrong (trespass) but not, without more, any criminal liability. By contrast the rights of the public may be more extensive over areas which are covered by access orders or agreements, areas which are country parks, and over some commons. Here, by contrast with rights of way, the public may wander at will, picnic, play games and so forth. However, even here limits to permitted activities exist in the form of the particular wordings of the statutory grants of access (*e.g.* for "recreation and exercise" in the case of commons) and also because there will commonly exist bye-laws imposing criminal penalties in relation to activities such as camping, lighting fires, or the use of motor vehicles. The law can therefore not be stated simply, in a form applicable to all situations. In each case the following questions need to be considered:

(i) is there any right to be on the land in question? In this connection it should be remembered that a number of the designations of land which we have considered (*e.g.* National Parks, AONBs) confer no special rights of access.

(ii) If no such rights exist will entry constitute a crime (e.g. in relation to defence lands) or, as, is more usually the case, simply the civil wrong of trespass?

(iii) If a right of access does exist what conduct is

allowed? If a particular activity is not permitted is this simply because to do so without the landowner's permission will amount to a trespass, or is it a breach of the criminal law as laid down in a bye-law or an Act of Parliament?

CHAPTER 6

PROTECTION OF BIRDS, ANIMALS AND PLANTS

INTRODUCTION

The importance of a rich and varied flora and fauna to our enjoyment of the countryside need hardly be stressed. Moreover, it is an enjoyment which may be shared both by those knowledgeable about the natural world and those less aware. The pleasure to be gained from scenic countryside is, for all of us, much enhanced by bluebell woods, clusters of cowslips and primroses, wild flowers of all colours and forms growing in profusion along way-side verges, poppy fields, bird-song in woodlands, the fluttering of butterflies and the scampering of rabbits and other small animals which flee for cover as footsteps approach. This list could be continued almost endlessly, but the examples are sufficient to show that protection of flora and fauna is an important matter for all who gain pleasure from the countryside. It is not a matter of significance only to the trained botanist or zoologist: one can enjoy bird-song without being able to identify the caller (or even spot where it is singing from), and one can appreciate a diverse and plentiful array of wild flowers although able to name but few. The importance today of protection of flora and fauna is all the greater because, during the decades since the second world war, much has been lost both in terms of variety and density. The "simple pleasures" with which we began would have constituted such common features of the countryside for them to have been taken for granted only two generations ago. But things have very rapidly changed. The combination of numerous factors, such as the removal of hedgerows and small woodlands, the drainage of wetlands and ploughing of pasture for arable farming, the increased use of pesticides

[178]

and herbicides, and the proliferation of coniferous wood-land, has had very marked consequences; and this quite apart from the activities of builders and developers. Cow-slips and primroses are nowadays more easily seen in sub-urban gardens than in the wild, the poppy field is a sight rarely seen, and "living" broadleaved woodlands are now less common than dark, and eerily quiet, plantations of conifers. And if flora and fauna which were commonplace so little time ago are becoming more difficult to find, the harm done to rarer species can easily be imagined.

What measures are necessary to provide satisfactory pro-tection for our birds, animals and plants? How may we seek to prevent further losses and try to restore depleted populations? In broad terms any policy for species protec-tion must operate on two fronts. It must seek to ensure that the wide range of habitats essential to the continued existance of a diverse flora and fauna are maintained, paying particular regard to the kinds of habitat under greatest threat; and, also, it is necessary that there be adequate laws, sufficiently enforced, directly protecting individual species of birds, animals and plants from the harmful actions of hunters, collectors and others. The rarer the species, the more prized the quarry, and the more significant each loss.

We have already considered much of the law relating to habitat protection. Such laws, in some shape or form, may be traced back many years. For example the original idea of a "forest" was a medieval legal concept: an area of woodland and open land within which the forest laws would apply. These laws protected game within the forest by pre-serving the forest habitat and by outlawing poaching. In modern times we think of habitat protection in order to preserve wildlife for its own sake, rather than to ensure good sport; and the areas of law most relevant are those we have considered relating to SSSIs,[1] Nature Reserves,[2] Marine Nature Reserves,[3] and Environmentally Sensitive

---

[1] See, above, p. 127.
[2] See, above, p. 121.
[3] See, above, p. 125.

Areas,[1] together with the general conservation obligations of bodies such as the Forestry Commission,[2] the Water Companies and the National Rivers Authority,[3] and the MAFF[4] itself. Nor, of course, should the activities of bodies such as the National Trust, the RSPB or the numerous County Trusts for Nature Conservation be overlooked.

In this chapter our concern will be with the laws which protect particular species of birds, animals and plants from harm. Much of this law is contained in Part I of the Wildlife and Countryside Act 1981, though there are also, as we shall see, some important provisions contained in other Acts; for example, those which deal separately with badgers and deer. We shall not in general, however, be concerned with the laws which protect birds and animals from acts of cruelty[5] as distinct from acts which may endanger the species.

PROTECTION OF WILD BIRDS

Wild birds, their nests and their eggs, receive a degree of protection by virtue of a number of criminal offences contained in the Wildlife and Countryside Act 1981. The provisions are quite complex, owing to the need to differentiate between species as regards extent of protection, and to provide for circumstances in which actions which are generally prohibited may be permitted. A matter of some controversy in relation to this last matter is the extent to which the protection laws should restrict actions by owners and occupiers on their own land. Obviously the cause of conservation requires exemptions afforded to owners and occupiers to be closely drawn and carefully monitored. The issue is controversial because where such exemptions do not apply the legislation takes away the traditional common law right of an owner or occupier of land to capture or kill (and thereby bring into his private ownership) any wild bird or

---

[1] See, above, p. 135.
[2] See, above, p. 143.
[3] See, above, p. 10.
[4] See, above, p. 8.
[5] For a full account see G. Sandys-Winsch, *Animal Law* Shaw and Sons, Ltd.

animal on his land, and to act as he wishes in respect of wild plants growing there.

Basic Offences

The basic protection for birds is afforded by the creation of the following criminal offences. These relate to wild birds; and "wild bird" is defined[1] as "any bird of a kind which is ordinarily resident in or is a visitor to Great Britain in a wild state", not being one that has been bred in captivity, and not including "poultry"[2] nor, generally, any "game bird".[3] The provision about "bird in captivity" can give rise to difficult problems of proof, though developments in genetic "fingerprinting" may assist determining the ancestry of a particular bird.

It is an offence intentionally[4]:
  (i) to kill, injure or take any wild bird;
  (ii) to take, damage or destroy the nest of any wild bird while that nest is in use or is being built; or
  (iii) to take or destroy an egg of any wild bird; the term "destroy" including doing anything calculated to prevent an egg from hatching.[5]

Furthermore, an offence is committed if any person has in his possession or control:

  (i) any live or dead wild bird, or any part of or anything derived from such a bird; or
  (ii) an egg of a wild bird, or any part of such an egg.[6]

---

[1] 1981 Act s. 27(1).

[2] Domestic fowls, geese, ducks, guinea-fowls, pigeons, quails and turkeys: 1981 Act s. 27(1).

[3] Pheasants, partridges, grouse (or moor game), black (or heath) game and ptarmigan: 1981 Act s. 27(1). Close seasons nevertheless apply under the Game Acts. Pheasants may be shot between 1 October and 1 February; partridges, between 1 September and 1 February; grouse, between 12 August and 10 December; black game, between 20 August and 10 December; ptarmigon, between 12 August and 10 December (Scotland only).

[4] It is the **acts** discribed which must be intentional. It is no defence that the defendant was unaware that the bird was "wild": *Kirkland v Robinson* (1987) Crim LR. 643.

[5] 1981 Act s. 1(1).

[6] 1981 Act s. 1(2).

The scope of these "possession and control" offences is, however, qualified so that no offence is committed where the person in possession or control can show that the bird or egg had not been killed or taken in contravention of the provisions of the 1981 Act, or of earlier legislation.[1] It is also a defence for the defendant to show that the bird or egg was sold (to him or any other person) otherwise than in contravention of the legislation.

Enhanced Protection: Schedule 1

The provisions described above are designed to protect the 500 or more species of wild birds in Britain generally. Certain species are, however, afforded a somewhat higher degree of protection. Schedule 1 to the 1981 Act lists a number of species, and in relation to these any person convicted of any of the offences described above is liable to a higher maximum penalty[2] than in respect of other birds; and, furthermore, certain additional offences exist in relation to these scheduled birds only. Thus, it is an offence intentionally:

(i) to disturb any wild bird included in Schedule I while it is building a nest or is in, on, or near, a nest containing eggs or young; or

(ii) to disturb dependent young of such a bird.[3]

The provisions of Schedule 1 are set out immediately below. We have set out the common, rather than the latin, scientific, names. The list of species is in two Parts. Part I lists kinds of bird subject to this special protection throughout the year; Part II, the birds which are specially protected during their close season only: which is, for these birds, the period between the start of February and the end of August.

---

[1] Protection of Birds Acts 1954 to 1967.
[2] 1981 Act, s. 1(4) and 21(1).
[3] 1981 Act s. 1(5).

SCHEDULE 1

BIRDS WHICH ARE PROTECTED BY SPECIAL PENALTIES

PART I

AT ALL TIMES

Avocet
Bee-eater
Bittern
Bittern, Little
Bluethroat
Brambling
Bunting, Cirl
Bunting, Lapland
Bunting, Snow
Buzzard, Honey
Chough
Corncrake
Crake, Spotted
Crossbills (all species)
Curlew, Stone
Divers (all species)
Dotterel
Duck, Long-tailed
Eagle, Golden
Eagle, White-tailed
Falcon, Gyr
Fieldfare
Firecrest
Garganey
Godwit, Black-tailed
Goshawk
Grebe, Black-necked
Grebe, Slavonian
Greenshank
Gull, Little
Gull, Mediterranean
Harriers (all species)
Heron, Purple
Hobby
Hoopoe
Kingfisher

Kite, Red
Merlin
Oriole, Golden
Osprey
Owl, Barn
Owl, Snowy
Peregrine
Petrel, Leach's
Phalarope, Red-necked
Plover, Kentish
Plover, Little Ringed
Quail, Common
Redstart, Black
Redwing
Rosefinch, Scarlet
Ruff
Sandpiper, Green
Sandpiper, Purple
Sandpiper, Wood
Scaup
Scoter, Common
Scoter, Velvet
Serin
Shorelark
Shrike, Red-backed
Spoonbill
Stilt, Black-winged
Stint, Temminck's
Swan, Bewick's
Swan, Whooper
Tern, Black
Tern, Little
Tern, Roseate
Tit, Bearded
Tit, Crested
Treecreeper, Short-toed

Warbler, Cetti's   Whimbrel
Warbler, Dartford   Woodlark
Warbler, Marsh   Wryneck
Warbler, Savi's

PART II
DURING THE CLOSE SEASON

Goldeneye
Goose, Greylag (in Outer Hebrides, Caithness, Sutherland and
Wester Ross only)
Pintail

Game or "Sporting" Birds and Pests: Schedule 2

In addition to the birds in Schedule I which receive **special**
protection, there is also a list of birds which receive **less**
than the ordinary protection described at the outset. This
list is in Schedule 2, set out below. In relation to any of the
birds listed in **Part I** of Schedule 2 no offence under the
1981 Act is committed by killing or taking (or injuring in
attempt to kill) so long as the actions take place outside the
close season.[1] This list comprises game and "sporting" birds.
Part II of Schedule 2 lists certain birds widely regarded by
landowners as pests in respect of which "authorised persons" may do, with impunity, certain things which would
otherwise be criminal offences. "Authorised persons" is
defined[2] to mean variously the owner or occupier of land
on which the actions take place (and persons acting with
their authority), persons authorised in writing by the county
or district council for the area on which the actions take
place, and persons authorised in writing by the Nature Conservancy Council (or, in Wales, the Countryside Council)
or the National Rivers Authority, a water company or a
sewerage company. Any such "authorised persons" will not
be guilty of any of the offences listed at the start of this
section by reason only of their having:

---

[1] 1981 Act s. 2(1). Generally the close season is from 1 February to 31 August.
For the capercaillie and woodcock it extends to 30 September. For the snipe it
ends with 11 August. For wild ducks and geese below high water mark the period
begins on 21 February.
[2] 1981 Act s. 27(1).

(i) killed or taken a bird listed within Part II of Schedule 2, or injured such a bird in the course of attempting to kill it;

(ii) taken, damaged or destroyed the nest of such a bird; or

(iii) taken or destroyed an egg of such a bird.

It may be noted that birds within **Part II** of Schedule 2 can be "killed" at any time of the year but only by "authorised persons". Birds within **Part I** may be "killed" by any persons but only outside their close seasons.

SCHEDULE 2

BIRDS WHICH MAY BE KILLED OR TAKEN

PART I

OUTSIDE THE CLOSE SEASON

Capercaillie	Mallard
Coot	Moorhen
Duck, Tufted	Pintail
Gadwall	Plover, Golden
Goldeneye	Pochard
Goose, Canada	Shoveler
Goose, Greylag	Snipe, Common
Goose, Pink-footed	Teal
Goose, White-fronted	Wigeon
(in England and Wales only)	Woodcock

PART II

BY AUTHORISED PERSONS AT ALL TIMES

Crow	Magpie
Dove, Collared	Pigeon, Feral
Gull, Great Black-backed	Rook
Gull, Lesser Black-backed	Sparrow, House
Gull, Herring	Starling
Jackdaw	Woodpigeon
Jay	

During 1990 the Government announced that in order to

comply with obligations under the EC Birds Directive it intended to amend the 1981 Act so that owners and occupiers would need to seek permission by licence prior to taking action to kill the pest birds listed in Schedule 2 Part II. Although the Government stressed that the change was only to be one of form, and that such permission would be readily forthcoming in appropriate cases, the proposal was condemned by farmers as being unduly burdensome and bureaucratic. In the light of this response the Government has agreed to review the position.

Areas of Special Protection

In addition to the general offences, and the rules giving greater or lesser protection to listed species, which we have considered, there is also provision for the creation, by the Secretary of State, of Areas of Special Protection.[1] The designation of such an Area requires the consent of all the owners and occupiers of the land, though such consent may be assumed if no such persons have raised objection within three months of notice having been given to them of the Secretary of State's intentions. If to give such notice to all owners and occupiers in the area in question is impracticable the Secretary of State may advertise his proposals in a newspaper circulating in the area instead; and the three months period then runs from the date of advertisement. If within three months of actual notice or such advertisement any owner or occupier has objected, the Secretary of State shall not make the order designating the area as one of special protection unless, or until, any such objection has been withdrawn.

What is the consequence of such designation? The special protection arises from the fact that the Order can create additional offences applicable to all or part of the area. To begin with, the offences of **disturbing** a bird building a nest or which is in, on, or near a nest containing eggs or young, and of **disturbing dependent young** can be made to apply to any wild birds to which the designation order applies rather than just to those listed in Schedule I. The designation order

---

[1] 1981 Act s. 3.

may apply to all wild birds or to particular species, at the discretion of the Secretary of State making the Order. Secondly, it can be made an offence for any person to **enter into the area**, or any specified part of it, at any time or during any specified period. It is not, however, an offence to enter if this is done in accordance with provisions in the Order.

Such designation is not particularly common (some 37 areas have been designated) but may be useful when it is felt necessary to keep people well away from a particular location, such as one where a rare species may nest. A limitation on the powers of designation is the requirement that there be no objection from the owners and occupiers of the land in question. Perhaps to encourage such persons not to object, the Act contains a widely drafted provision which states that "the making of any order . . . with respect to any area shall not affect the exercise by any person of any right vested in him, whether as owner, lessee or occupier of any land in that area or by virtue of a licence or agreement". This would clearly prevent any order from effectively forbidding an owner or occupier from entering onto a part of his own land, or authorising others to do so. Beyond this the extent of the immunity given is not clear. What about an owner or occupier who wishes to organise a gymkhana beside the nest of a bird to which the order applies? If this is the exercise of a right vested in him as owner or occupier, and if those who attend are exercising rights arising from agreement with the owner or occupier that they may enter onto the land for this purpose, then no offence is committed notwithstanding the degree of disturbance that may be caused to the nesting bird or its dependent young. The aim of the Act seems to be to subject to criminal penalties those who trespass on the land without the approval of the owner or occupier; it does not seem greatly to restrict the activities of the owner, the occupier or those whom they have invited onto the land.

G

General Exceptions to Liability

So far we have outlined a number of criminal offences designed to protect wild birds. However in addition to these various provisions there are listed in the 1981 Act a number of **exceptions** to criminal liability which are applicable generally to the offences we have considered.[1] Thus, nothing done by instruction of the Minister of Agriculture, Fisheries and Food under the Agriculture Act 1947 section 98 will constitute an offence; nor anything done under, or in pursuance of, an order made under the Animal Health Act 1981 sections 21 or 22. These provisions allow various sorts of action to be taken to prevent and control plant and animal disease. The second general exception applies to the killing of a bird which has been so seriously disabled, otherwise than by the defendant's own unlawful act, that there is no reasonable chance of it recovering, and also the taking of a disabled bird solely for the purpose of tending it and releasing it when no longer disabled. In this connection it should be noted that it is not a good practice to release such a bird directly into the wild. The bird should be given to a licensed rehabilitation keeper, who may be contacted through the RSPB. A third general exception is of special importance because of its potentially wide scope. It provides that a person shall not be guilty of an offence if he shows that the act which would otherwise constitute an offence was "the incidental result of a lawful operation and could not reasonably have been avoided". The point to note is that the Act does not require the court to ask whether it would have been reasonable to have avoided doing the "lawful operation" in the circumstances; it simply requires consideration of whether, in performing that lawful operation, the consequence was or was not one which could reasonably have been avoided. Thus, if to destroy a nest is the incidental, and not reasonably avoidable, result of removing a hedgerow (the "lawful operation") the defence applies. The defence would not, however, seem to extend to the situation where the purpose of removing the hedge was to destroy the nest: in such a case the destruction would not be the

---

[1] 1981 Act s. 4.

"incidental result" of the lawful operation. Other "lawful operations" which may have harmful incidental consequences and yet be lawfully performed in full knowledge of those consequences include the drainage of wetlands, and the destruction of nests of field-nesting birds by ploughing and harvesting. Lastly, the general exceptions to liability permit "authorised persons", as defined above, to do things which would otherwise constitute offences where they can show that such action was necessary in order to preserve public health, or public or air safety; to prevent the spread of disease; or to prevent serious damage to livestock, foostuffs for livestock, crops, vegetables, fruit, growing timber or fisheries. These last "authorised person" exceptions do not, however, apply to acts done in relation to birds listed for special protection in Schedule I.[1]

Methods of Killing and Taking Birds

Although it is not our purpose in this chapter to deal with laws concerned with cruelty, as distinct from those concerned more directly with species protection, it is appropriate to mention that the Wildlife and Countryside Act 1981 also contains provisions which prohibit, except under licence, certain **methods** of killing or taking wild birds; which prohibit, except under licence, the sale or offer for sale of certain live or dead wild birds or their eggs; and which provide for the registration of captive birds and lay down certain rules for their protection in captivity. Moreover, certain of these provisions are as much the consequence of a desire for species protection as with the prevention of pain and suffering. Thus, a number of methods of killing or taking birds are outlawed on the grounds, it would seem, that they are indiscriminate as between species or simply that they are likely to be too effective in terms of numbers of birds. Accordingly, the setting in position of traps and snares calculated to cause bodily injury to any wild bird coming into contact with them is unlawful; as is the setting in position of any poisonous, poisoned or stupefying sub-

---

[1] See also, below p. 198, for the further general defence relating to actions done **under licence**. This applies to "animals" and "plants" as well as to "birds" and so will be considered towards the end of this chapter.

stance.[1] Other provisions of the 1981 Act seem designed to ensure "fair play" between hunter and hunted, and to ensure that the birds have a sporting chance! In this connection we may note, for example, the prohibition of "any device for illuminating a target or any sighting device for night shooting" and the use of sound recordings as decoys.[2]

Trade and Advertisements

The provisions prohibiting the buying and selling of live or dead wild birds or their eggs, and prohibiting advertisements showing intent to buy or sell, are designed to suppress the trade in such items.[3] These are important offences because the willingness of collectors to pay high prices for the rarer birds and their eggs poses very real threats to such species. The mere existence of the offences may hinder this trade to some extent, but to be really effective there is a clear need for a degree of zeal in relation both to the detection of offences and the prosecution of those caught. In this matter the activities of the Royal Society for the Protection of Birds are of great importance.

The 1981 Act does not, however, prohibit all trade in wild birds and eggs. It draws a distinction between live birds (and their eggs) and dead birds. The prohibition in relation to trade in the former category is almost total, the only exceptions being birds, ringed and bred in captivity, which are of species listed in Part I of Schedule 3. As regards dead birds, the provisions prohibit trade except in relation to those of species listed in Parts II and III of Schedule 3. Part II lists species in which trade of dead birds is allowed at any time of year; Part III lists dead birds which may be traded, but only between September 1st and February 28th. Wider powers to trade in dead birds may, however, be acquired by becoming registered under regulations made by the Secretary of State.

---

[1] 1981 Act s. 5(1)(a)—exceptions are provided in s. 5(4) and (5).

[2] 1981 Act s. 5(1)(c) and (d).

[3] 1981 Act s. 6.

SCHEDULE 3

BIRDS WHICH MAY BE SOLD

PART I

ALIVE AT ALL TIMES IF RINGED AND BRED IN CAPTIVITY

Blackbird	Linnet
Brambling	Magpie
Bullfinch	Owl, Barn
Bunting, Reed	Redpoll
Chaffinch	Siskin
Dunnock	Starling
Goldfinch	Thrush, Song
Greenfinch	Twite
Jackdaw	Yellowhammer
Jay	

PART II

DEAD AT ALL TIMES

Pigeon, Feral	Woodpigeon

PART III

DEAD FROM 1ST SEPTEMBER TO 28TH FEBRUARY

Capercaillie	Pochard
Coot	Shoveler
Duck, Tufted	Snipe, Common
Mallard	Teal
Pintail	Wigeon
Plover, Golden	Woodcock

PROTECTION OF WILD ANIMALS

Basic Offences

The offences contained in the Wildlife and Countryside Act 1981 relating to the protection of wild animals in many ways parallel those described above in respect of birds. Thus, the basic offences are:

(i)   intentionally to kill, injure or take any wild animal included in Schedule 5; and

(ii) to have in one's possession or control any live or dead wild animal included in Schedule 5, or any part of, or anything derived from, such an animal.[1]

The animals within Schedule 5 are listed at the end of this section. In relation to the "possession and control" offence there is a proviso that the offence is not committed if the defendant can show that the animal had not been killed or taken in contravention of the provisions of the 1981 Act, or earlier legislation[2]; or that the animal had been sold to him or to any other person otherwise than in contravention of the legislation.

There are also parallels to the "nesting" offences which we noted earlier in relation to birds. Thus, it is an offence intentionally:

(i) to damage or destroy, or obstruct access to, any structure or place which any wild animal included in Schedule 5 uses for shelter or protection; or

(ii) to disturb any such animal while it is occupying a structure or place which it uses for that purpose.[3]

It should be noted, however, that this offence is not committed by anything done within a dwelling-house[4]

Exceptions to Liability

As in relation to birds, a number of general exceptions to criminal liability apply.[5] Thus, actions done under the powers in the Agriculture Act 1947 and the Animal Health Act 1981 to prevent and control disease will not be unlawful; and there are "mercy" clauses, like those described in relation to birds, permitting the killing of animals which have been seriously disabled and which have no reasonable chance of recovering, and the taking of an animal which has been disabled in order to tend it and then release it. The

---

[1] 1918 Act s. 9(1) and (2). For protection under other Acts of bats, badgers, deer and certain other animals, see, below, pp. 198–207.
[2] The Conservation of Wild Creatures and Wild Plants Act 1975.
[3] 1981 Act s. 9(4).
[4] But, see further, below p. 202 on "bats".
[5] 1981 Act s. 10.

principle, noted before, which exempts from liability actions which are the "incidental result of a lawful operation and not reasonably avoidable" also operates; and the Act permits an "authorised person" to kill or injure a Schedule 5 wild animal if he can show his action was necessary to prevent serious damage to "livestock, crops, vegetables, fruit, growing timber or any other form of property or to fisheries". However, this last defence cannot be relied on except where a licence from the Minister of Agriculture, Fisheries and Food has been applied for, and only then until a decision on such a licence is taken. Such licences are considered, further, later in this chapter.[1]

SCHEDULE 5

ANIMALS WHICH ARE PROTECTED[2]

Adder
Anemone, Ivell's Sea
Anemone, Startlet Sea
Apus
Atlantic Stream crayfish
(certain offences only)
Bats, Horseshoe (all species)
Bats, Typical (all species)
Beetle, Rainbow Leaf
Beetle, Violet Click
Burbot
Butterflies:
    Northern Brown Angus
    Adonis Blue
    Chalkhill Blue
    Large Blue
    Silver-studded Blue
    Small Blue
    Large Copper
    Purple Emperor
    Duke of Burgundy Fritillary
    Heath Fritillary

Glanville Fritillary
High Brown Fritillary
Black Hairstreak
Large Heath
Mountain Ringlet
Chequered Skipper
Lulworth Skipper
Silver Spotted Skipper
Swallowtail
Large Tortoiseshell
Wood White
Cat, Wild
Cicada, New Forest
Cricket, Field
Cricket, Mole
Dormouse
Dolphins (all)
Dragonfly, Norfolk Aeshna
Frog, Common*
Grasshopper, Wart-biter
Leech, Medicinal
Lizard, Sand

---

[1] See. below p. 198.
[2] Asterisks denote protection by certain offences only (Trade Offences—s9(5) 1981 Act).

Lizard, Viviparous*
Martin, Pine
Mat, Trembling Sea
Moth, Barberry Carpet
Moth, Black-veined
Moth, Essex Emerald
Moth, New Forest Burnet
Moth, Reddish Buff
Moth, Viper's Buglon
Mussel Freshwater Pearl
Newt, Great Crested
(otherwise known as Warty
newt)
Newt, Palmate*
Newt, Smooth*
Otter, Common
Porpoises (all)
Sandworm, Lagoon

Shad, Allis
Shrimp, Fairy
Shrimp, Lagoon Sand
Slow-worm*
Snail, Glutinous
Snail, Sandbowl
Snake, Grass*
Snake, Smooth
Spider, Fen Raft
Spider, Ladybird
Squirrel, Red
Toad, Common*
Toad, Natterjack
Turtles, Marine (all species)
Vendace
Walrus
Whale (all species)
Whitefish

Methods of Killing or Taking Animals

The 1981 Act also prohibits certain **methods** of killing or taking wild animals. Some methods are prohibited in respect of **all** animals. For example, the use of any live mammal or bird as a decoy for the purpose of killing or taking any animal; also, the use of any self-locking snare which is of "such a nature and is so placed as to be calculated to cause bodily injury to any wild animal" coming into contact with it. Other methods are prohibited when their use kills, takes or endangers **certain species**. Thus, actions are prohibited which involve the use of certain items (such as traps, snares, poisons) to take or kill any animal listed within Schedule 6: or when they involve the setting in position of such items where they are "so placed and of such a nature as to be calculated to cause bodily injury" to an animal listed within Schedule 6. In relation to **other** species the use of non self-locking snares is permitted so long as they are inspected at least once every day. A principal reason behind these prohibitions would seem to be the indiscriminate nature of these methods. The Act also protects species within Schedule 6 from methods which are over-effective or unsporting. Thus, as with wild birds, the use of such methods as sound decoys, sighting devices for night-shooting, automatic or semi-automatic weapons and dazzling lights are prohibited.

SCHEDULE 6

ANIMALS WHICH MAY NOT BE KILLED OR TAKEN BY CERTAIN METHODS

Badger
Bats, Horseshoe (all species)
Bats, Typical (all species)
Cat, Wild
Dolphin, Bottle-nosed
Dolphin, Common
Dormice (all species)
Hedgehog

Marten, Pine
Otter, Common
Polecat
Porpoise, Harbour (otherwise known as Common porpoise)
Shrews (all species)
Squirrel, Red

PROTECTION OF WILD PLANTS

Basic Offences

The provisions of the Wildlife and Countryside Act 1981 concerned with the protection of wild plants are considerably less complex than those relating to birds and animals. Again, there are clear parallels between the basic offences. Thus, it is an offence intentionally:

(i) to pick, uproot or destroy any wild plant included in Schedule 8; or

(ii) uproot any wild plant not included in that Schedule, unless one is an "authorised person".[1]

The term "pick" is defined to include the gathering or plucking of any part of a plant without uprooting it. This would, therefore, include seed collection.

The plants contained in Schedule 8 are listed at the end of this section. Neither of the above offences are, however, committed when such acts are "an incidental result of a lawful operation and could not reasonably have been avoided."

---

[1] 1981 Act s. 13.

The effect of the two offences, referred to above, is that owners and occupiers (*ie* "authorised persons") of land may on that land uproot any plant **not** within Schedule 8, but may not even pick, let alone uproot or destroy any plant within Schedule 8. Persons who are not owners or occupiers of the land in question commit an offence in uprooting, without the owner's consent, any plants at all and may only pick plants not within Schedule 8.

In addition there is an offence of having in one's possession any live or dead wild plant included in Schedule 8, or any part of or anything derived from such a plant. Furthermore, trade in such items is forbidden, as also is advertisement of willingness to trade.

SCHEDULE 8

PLANTS WHICH ARE PROTECTED

Adder's Tongue, Least
Alison, Small
Broomrape, Bedstraw
Broomrape, Oxtongue
Broomrape, Thistle
Cabbage, Lundy
Calamint, Wood
Catchfly, Alpine
Cinquefoil, Rock
Club-rush, Triangular
Coltsfoot, Purple
Cotoneaster, Wild
Cottongrass, Slender
Cow-wheat, Field
Crocus, Sand
Cudweed, Jersey
Cudweed, Red-tipped
Diapensia
Eryngo, Field
Fern, Dickie's Bladder
Fern, Killarney
Fleabane, Alpine
Fleabane, Small
Galingale, Brown

Gentian, Alpine
Gentian, Fringed
Gentian, Spring
Germander, Cut-leaved
Germander, Water
Gladiolus, Wild
Goosefoot, Stinking
Grass-poly
Hare's-ear, Sickle-leaved
Hare's-ear, Small
Hawksbeard, Stinking
Heath, Blue
Helleborine, Red
Helleborine, Youngs
Horsetail, Branched
Hound's tongue, Green
Knawel, Perennial
Knotgrass, Sea
Lady's-slipper
Lavender, Sea
Leek, Round-headed
Lettuce, Least
Lily, Snowdon
Marsh-mallow, Rough

Marshwort, Creeping
Milkparsley, Cambridge
Naiad, Holly-leaved
Orchid, Early Spider
Orchid, Fen
Orchid, Ghost
Orchid, Late Spider
Orchid, Lizard
Orchid, Military
Orchid, Monkey
Pear, Plymouth
Pennyroyal
Pigmyweed
Pink, Cheddar
Pink, Childling
Ragwort, Fen
Ramping-fumitory, Martin's
Restharrow, Small
Rockcress, Alpine
Rockcress, Bristol
Sandwort, Norwegian
Sandwort, Teesdale

Saxifrage, Drooping
Saxifrage, Tufted
Solomon's-seal, Whorled
Sow-thistle, Alpine
Spearwort, Adder's-tongue
Speedwell, Fingered
Speedwell, Spiked
Spurge, Purple
Starfruit
Star of Bethlehem, Early
Stonewort, Foxtail
Strapwort
Violet, Fen
Viper's-grass
Water-plantain, Ribbon leaved
Wood-sedge, Starved
Woodsia, Alpine
Woodsia, Oblong
Wormwood, Field
Woundwort, Downy
Woundwort, Limestone
Yellow-rattle, Greater

GENERAL PROVISIONS OF PART I OF THE 1981 ACT

In addition to the separate rules, summarised above, applicable to birds, animals, and plants, there are a number of provisions in the 1981 Act which apply generally to all three categories.

Acts Done Under Licence

To begin with, most of the offences we have considered will not be committed if the acts in question have been done under or in accordance with the terms of a licence granted by the "appropriate authority".[1] The "appropriate authority" may be, depending on context, the Secretary of State for the Environment, the MAFF or the Nature Conservancy Council (or in Wales, the Countryside Council). Such licensing power may be useful, for example, when action is neces-

---

[1] 1981 Act s. 16.

sary to prevent one species becoming so numerous as to endanger others in a particular area.

Proceedings and Penalties

Proceedings in respect of offences committed under the 1981 Act may be taken either by the police, or by a local authority[1] or by any private individual or body, such as the RSPB or the RSPCA Wardens employed by local authorities may be of significance in this connection and some police forces have officers who as part of their duties act as "Wildlife Liaison Officers". Where a person is convicted for an offence the court is required, in addition to imposing a fine, to order the forfeiture of any bird, nest, egg, animal or plant in respect of which the offence was committed; and it **may** order the forfeiture of any vehicle, animal, weapon or other thing used to commit the offence.[2] The level of the maximum fine which can be imposed depends on the particular offence charged, but a provision worthy of note is that where a charge relates to more than one bird, nest, egg, animal or plant the maximum fine for that particular offence may be imposed in relation to each bird, nest, etc.[3]

BADGERS

These delightful creatures have a whole Act of Parliament to themselves, in addition to the protection already noted, by being listed within Schedule 6 to the Wildlife and Countryside Act 1981 (prohibiting certain **methods** of killing or taking). The reason for the additional legislation was to deal with the menace of badger hunting and the practice of badger baiting. These animals, who do little harm to anyone, have been subjected to the "country pursuit" of being prised from their underground setts with badger tongs, and being baited by dogs (often after having had limbs broken) before finally being killed for their coats and bristles. This practice, sadly, still continues, a Nature Conservancy Council survey in the late 1980s suggesting some 10,000

---

[1] 1981 Act s. 25(2).
[2] 1981 Act s. 21(6).
[3] 1981 Act s. 21(5).

badgers being killed each year by baiters; but at least now there are charges which may be brought as and when offenders are caught. The Badgers Act 1973 makes it an offence wilfully to kill, injure or take any badger, or to attempt to do any of those things.[1] It is also an offence to dig for a badger. For some years prosecutors encountered difficulties when proceeding against persons who had been apprehended whilst digging, and without having actually taken or injured a badger, because such persons would claim to have been digging, quite lawfully, for a fox. The prosecution would fail unless it could be proved beyond reasonable doubt that this was untrue, and that those apprehended were in fact hunting for a badger. The law was, therefore, altered by the Wildlife and Countryside (Amendment) Act 1985 to make successful prosecution less difficult on the "digging", and also the "attempt" charges. Thus, it is now provided that if in such a case there is evidence from which it could reasonably be concluded that the accused was attempting to kill, injure or take a badger, or was digging for a badger, he will be presumed to have been doing so unless the contrary is shown.[2] This means that the prosecution no longer needs to prove those things beyond reasonable doubt. So long as there is evidence from which the appropriate conclusion could reasonably be drawn, the onus shifts to the defence to disprove the statutory presumption. This does not, however, require the accused to prove beyond reasonable doubt that he was not after a badger; he must simply satisfy the court that it is more likely than not that he was not acting with that purpose. However, the fact that foxes may often seek sanctuary in badger setts makes this contention not always implausible, and so successful prosecution remains a difficult matter.[3]

It is also an offence for any person to have in his possession or under his control any dead badger, or any part of or anything derived from a dead badger; though a person is not guilty if he can show that the badger had not been

---

[1] Note the increased penalties contained in Criminal Justice Bill 1991.

[2] 1973 Act s. 1(1A) and s. 2(2); each subsection added by the 1985 Act.

[3] Note the private member's Bill before Parliament (1990–91) to outlaw damage to badger setts.

killed in contravention of the Act, or that the badger or other thing in his possession had been sold by the original offender to a purchaser who had no reason to believe the badger had been unlawfully killed.[1] Possession or control of a live badger is, subject to limited exceptions, also an offence under the Act; as also is the offer for sale of live badgers[2].

The prohibitions apply equally to owners and occupiers of the land in question as well as to others, an "authorised person" exemption in the 1973 Act having being removed by the Wildlife and Countryside Act 1981. However, a number of general exceptions to the operation of the offences apply. These are in very much the same form as the ones considered in respect of protection of animals under the 1981 Act. Thus, one may take a badger in order to tend it when it has been disabled, or kill it if it has been so seriously disabled that to kill it would be an act of mercy. Equally no offence is committed when the killing or injury is the unavoidable incidental result of a lawful action. Badgers may also be killed if the person doing so can show that it was necessary to prevent serious damage to land, crops, poultry or any other form of property. However, such action is only permissible provided that an application has been made for a Ministry licence (to authorise such actions), and the action is necessary pending a decision upon such application. Such licences, like the ones under the 1981 Act, may be issued to allow, otherwise unlawful, actions for a variety of purposes. Such purposes include conservation of badgers, the ringing and marking of badgers, the prevention of serious damage to land, crops, etc, and to prevent the spread of disease. In this connection a controversial matter has been the licensing by the Ministry of Agriculture, Fisheries and Food of the killing of thousands of badgers by gassing, in order to prevent the spread of bovine tuberculosis amongst cattle. Some doubt has been expressed as to whether badgers are indeed guilty of causing this harm. Indeed some would argue that the spread of the disease is

---

[1] 1973 Act s. 1(2) and (3), as substituted by WCA 1981 Schedule 7, para 8.
[2] 1973 Act s. 3.

actually the other way around; the cows certainly infect the badgers, but evidence is lacking of the badgers returning the disease to uninfected cattle. In any case the problem is largely a localised one in the South-West of England and should not have been used, as it appears to have been, as an excuse for more widespread unlawful killing of badgers.

DEER

Although there is legislation dealing specifically with deer, this is designed principally to protect these animals from acts of cruelty and to preserve numbers of animals as a species of game, rather than to promote conservation as an end in itself. Nevertheless, since the provisions do provide some degree of species protection it is appropriate to consider them, albeit briefly, here.

The Deer Act 1963 makes it an offence to take or wilfully kill deer of any species listed in Schedule 1 to the Act during the close season for that species.[1] Schedule 1 lists four species, Red, Fallow, Roe and Sika Deer, and specifies the start and end of the close season for each sex of each species. It is also an offence to take or wilfully kill any deer, of whatever species, at night time; and this is regardless of whether it is the close season or not.[2]

As with the other legislation we have considered, the Act provides a number of general exceptions to the scope of these offences. In particular, an authorised person (*eg* the occupier of the land) may take or kill any deer, other than at night, which is on any cultivated land, pasture or enclosed woodland if damage is being done to crops, vegetables, or growing timber and the action taken is necessary to prevent serious further damage.

Deer are further protected by the Deer Act 1980. The 1963 Act, as we saw, is concerned to protect certain categories of deer, at certain times of year, from actions done by any persons; even by the owner of the land upon which the

---

[1] Deer Act 1963 s. 1(1).
[2] 1963 Act s. 2.

deer are to be found. The 1980 Act, in contrast, is concerned to protect all deer at all times from the activities of poachers: that is, persons who enter onto land without the consent of the owner or occupier in search or pursuit of any deer and with the intention of taking, killing or injuring such deer.[1] Even if entry onto the land is by consent it is nevertheless still an offence, without the consent of the owner of the land, to take, kill, or injure any deer, to search for or pursue any deer for that purpose, or to remove any deer carcase. The Act also restricts lawful trade in venison to licensed game dealers,[2] who must keep detailed records of the venison which comes into their possession and also of the persons from whom the venison was obtained.[3]

BATS

The Wildlife and Countryside Act 1981 affords a degree of protection to bats additional to that which is provided by the fact that all kinds of bats are listed within Schedule 5. As was noted earlier, the 1981 Act provides that its prohibition on intentionally damaging, destroying, or obstructing access to any structure or place which such a listed animal uses for shelter or protection, or disturbing such an animal occupying the structure or place, does not make unlawful anything done within a dwelling-house.[4] In the case of bats, however, this exception to the scope of the offence only applies fully to actions done within the **living area** of the dwelling-house. As regards other areas (*eg* the loft) the exception to liability cannot be relied on unless the defendant has notified the Nature Conservancy Council of his proposed actions, and allowed the Council reasonable time to "advise him" as to whether the actions should be carried out, and, if so, by what method.[5] This provision, it should be noted, does not require compliance with the NCC's advice; it simply requires that the NCC have the opportunity

---

[1] Deer Act 1980 s. 1(1).
[2] Licensed under the Game Act 1831 and the Game Licences Act 1860.
[3] Deer Act 1980 s. 3 and Schedule I.
[4] 1981 Act s. 10(2). See, above. p. 191.
[5] 1981 Act s. 10(5).

to give that advice before action can lawfully take place. This requirement to notify, and be advised by, the NCC also applies to the operation in relation to bats of the "incidental and not reasonably avoidable result of a lawful action" defence.[1] But, again, there is no requirement to comply with the advice given. The operation of these provisions was shown in a case before the Magistrates at Bedale, in Yorkshire, in February 1986. A timber merchant was convicted of intentionally killing a colony of Brandt Bats when he had sprayed the roof space of a cottage in order to destroy woodworm, the spray also killing the bats. He was fined £500 and ordered to pay £200 costs. He would have avoided criminal liability if he had notified the N.C.C. and given them reasonable time to give him advice.

If, however, such advice need not be complied with, what value is there in these provisions? Much is likely to depend on the sort of advice that is given. In this connection it is worth noting that bats do no harm within a roof-space. A high proportion of the declining bat population now live in the roof-spaces of modern houses. They have moved from their belfries to more modern homes. The decline of the bat population, which commenced in the 1940s, is thought to be a result of land drainage and pesticides reducing their insect food supply. If the bat population which remains is to survive it is, perhaps, necessary for us to be willing to share part of our homes with these animals.

FISH

The common law has for centuries treated fish as a special form of property. Thus, fish in private waters or in non-tidal rivers or streams can be taken only by, or with the consent of, the owner of those waters (the owner or owners of the banks at either side), or by persons who have been granted or have acquired by long use a right to take the fish (a right of "piscary"). By contrast, anyone may take fish in tidal waters or from the sea, subject only to bye-laws made by the statutory authorities which normally require purchase

---

[1] 1981 Act s. 10(3)(c). See. above. p. 193.

of a licence. Sea fishing is also controlled by legislation which specifies the sizes of mesh which may be used in nets.

Sturgeon, much prized in former times as a source of caviar and isinglass, is a royal fish when found in coastal or estuarine waters, and as such may be taken only under licence from the Crown. The same principle applies to whales, which also have been regarded for centuries as the prerogative of the Sovereign. Wild Swans also belong to the Crown, but swans on private waters and tamed swans duly marked may belong to private owners. The right to mark swans may be acquired by long use or by grant from the Crown. In addition to the common law, the Salmon and Freshwater Fisheries Act 1975 prohibits the taking or killing of salmon, trout or other freshwater fish (not including eels) by methods such as firearms, spears or lights.

These common law and statutory provisions are not concerned primarily with the conservation of fish life, but they have acted as a limitation on the wholesale taking or slaughter of fish stocks. The voluntary regulation by anglers through their regular competitions has had much the same effect, although the widespread use of lead pellets as sinkers for their lines has been the cause of many swan deaths on our rivers. Legislation to outlaw the import and supply of lead pellets came into force at the beginning of 1987. Critics argue, however, that the law needs to go further and prohibit also the *use* of lead pellets.

IMPORTED SPECIES

Lessons from the past demonstrate the harm which can sometimes result, for existing fauna and flora, from the introduction of new species from overseas. Of course, such importation is not always to be discouraged. After all, a good deal of the diversity of our existing flora and fauna is the result of introduction of plants and animals within historical times. Nevertheless, in some instances the results of importing new species have been unfortunate. Familiar examples include the release of mink and coypus into the wild. This action by breeders, disappointed at the unprofitability of keeping these species captive for their fur, has led to extensive populations in East Anglia; and the effect on levels of fish in rivers and on small animals has been quite serious. Another well-known illustration of the danger of importation of a new species is the damage that would result to potato crops if the Colorado Beetle became widespread. This danger is taken so seriously that the law imposes a positive duty on any person who spots such a beetle to take it to the police![1] The rapidity with which a species can become established, if the conditions suit, is shown by the fact that that common weed of disturbed soil, the rosebay willowherb, is not native to England but arrived when its seeds were imported with bales of wool from the Antipodes.

The law, therefore, takes a cautious stance towards the introduction of new species. The Wildlife and Countryside Act 1981 prohibits any person from releasing or allowing to escape into the wild any animal which:

(i) is of a kind which is not ordinarily resident in, or is not a regular visitor to Great Britain in a wild state; or

(ii) is included in Part I of Schedule 9 (animals already in the wild but whose further release is undesirable).

It is also an offence for any person to plant, or otherwise cause to grow in the wild, any plant which is included in Part II of Schedule 9.

---

[1] See. below. p. 250.

SCHEDULE 9

PART I

ANIMALS WHICH ARE ESTABLISHED IN THE WILD

Bass, Large-mouthed Black
Bass, Rock
Bitterling
Budgerigar
Capercaillie
Coypu
Dormouse, Fat
Duck, Carolina Wood
Duck, Mandarin
Duck, Ruddy
Eagle, White-tailed
Frog, Edible
Frog, European Tree
(otherwise known as Common
tree frog)
Frog, Marsh
Gerbil, Mongolian
Goose, Canada
Goose, Egyptian
Heron, Night
Lizard, Common Wall
Marmot, Prairie (otherwise
known as Prairie dog)
Mink, American

Newt, Alpine
Parakeet, Ring-necked
Partridge, Chukar
Partridge, Rock
Pheasant, Golden
Pheasant, Lady Amherst's
Pheasant, Reeves'
Pheasant, Silver
Porcupine, Crested
Porcupine, Himalayan
Pumpkinseed (otherwise
known as Sun-fish or Pond-
perch)
Quail, Bobwhite
Rat, Black
Squirrel, Grey
Terrapin, European Pond
Toad, African Clawed
Toad, Midwife
Toad, Yellow-bellied
Wallaby, Red-necked
Wels (otherwise known as
European catfish)
Zander

PART II

PLANTS

Hogweed, Giant
Kelp, Giant

Knotweed, Japanese
Seaweed, Japanese

ENDANGERED SPECIES

Brief mention may be made of the controls which exist
under the Endangered Species (Import and Export) Act
1976.[1] This chapter has been principally concerned with the

---

[1] As amended by the WCA 1981 Schedule 10.

protection of the flora and fauna of England and Wales, whereas the 1976 Act is designed to restrict international trade in animals and plants which are endangered in the world as a whole.

The 1976 Act creates a number of offences including making it an offence to export or import any mammal, bird, reptile, amphibian, fish, mollusc (whether dead or alive) listed in Schedule I or any dead or alive plant listed in Schedule 2. There is a similar prohibition on the import and export of things derived from endangered species, such as elephant tusks and certain furs, listed in Schedule 3.

The Secretary of State may vary the lists in the Schedules, and may also issue licences for the import or export of particular animals or plants, when he is so advised by some relevant scientific authority.

CHAPTER 7

POLLUTION

INTRODUCTION

In this chapter we shall be concerned with the law's response to the threats to the countryside which arise from a variety of different kinds of pollution. To begin with we shall examine the way in which the common law developed principles to protect landowners from the harmful or offensive activities of "unneighbourly" neighbours. These rules, principally the law of nuisance, still apply, and may be of value to the individuals especially affected by the activities in question. However, it was evident from a fairly early time that the common law alone was inadequate to regulate and control what we would now call acts of pollution. It would not be sufficient to rely on affected individuals to bring civil actions, at their own expense, in the courts; moreover, others, interested in the protection of the environment but not themselves landowners affected by the pollution, would likely not have standing in the courts to bring such actions. What was necessary was legislation which would impose statutory duties, the breach of which would constitute criminal offences; together with the conferment of detection and enforcement obligations on public agencies. It is with the modern legislation of this kind that the bulk of this chapter will be concerned; the most significant legislation being the Control of Pollution Act 1974, the Water Act 1989, and the Environmental Protection Act 1990. In considering the legislation we shall examine the controls exerted over a number of different forms of pollution. These will be considered under the following broad headings—atmospheric pollution, pollution of land, pollution of inland waters and the sea, and pollution by noise. As a final matter it will be appropriate to discuss controls over pests and pesticides.

THE COMMON LAW

Private Nuisance

The common law, being from early times much concerned with the protection of property rights, developed long ago the action of **nuisance** in order to protect owners and occupiers of land from the harmful or anti-social activities of others. The remedies which may be granted to a successful plaintiff are an award of damages to compensate him for the nuisance suffered, and, in an appropriate case, an injunction forbidding continuation of the acts or activities constituting the nuisance. If an injunction has been obtained and the person to whom it is addressed fails to comply with its terms, proceedings for contempt of court may be brought. In such proceedings the court may impose penalties of imprisonment or a fine, or may do both. In addition to these court remedies there is the remedy of self-help. A person against whom a nuisance is being committed may, in certain circumstances, take action to abate the nuisance—that is, to stop the nuisance. This is, however, a limited power. It may, for example, authorise the taking of action to prevent fire spreading to one's land, or to stop water flooding onto one's property: but it would not permit physical force against the owner of neighbouring property to prevent continuance of his deliberate actions.

In what circumstances will the law regard a person's actions as constituting a nuisance? A number of general points may be made, and examples from decided cases provide illustrations. In the first place a distinction needs to be drawn between actions which harm the plaintiff's land itself, and actions which simply spoil the plaintiff's enjoyment of his land. Both kinds of action may constitute nuisance, but it is rather easier to show actionable nuisance in the former type of case than in the latter. Examples of the former kind have included: the percolation of noxious chemicals onto the plaintiff's land from that of the defendant[1]; damage to the plaintiff's trees and shrubs resulting from the emission of noxious vapours[2]; damage to the plaintiff's market garden crops caused by fumes from creosoted wood blocks belonging to the defendant[3]; the leakage of oil from the defendant's railway trucks, causing water on the plaintiff's land to become unfit for his cattle[4]; the causing of sewage to collect on the plaintiff's land[5]; and damage to the plaintiff's house caused by vibrations from machinery operated by the defendant[6]. These are all examples of successful claims in which the actions of the defendant caused some physical harm to the plaintiff's property. It is more difficult to succeed when the nature of the claim is simply that there has been interference with the use or enjoyment which the plaintiff may wish to make of his land. Here the courts have long recognised that they should be careful not to pander to the susceptibilities of over-sensitive owners of land. A degree of "give and take" and of tolerance between neighbours is expected, and, as was said in one case, "the law does not regard trifling inconveniences; everything must be looked at from a reasonable point of view"[7]. In short, the courts will decide whether the plaintiff is being unreasonable in complaining, or whether he is being subjected to interferences by the defendant which it is not reasonable that he should have to suffer. In deciding this issue, account is taken of a variety of relevant circumstances. Thus, for example, the neighbourhood where the events take place may be important. Noise which might not constitute a nuisance in an urban area may be regarded as such in the countryside; and pollution of the air by smoke or smells may be differently judged as between such areas. However, it would be wrong to suggest that any particular activity is more likely to be adjudged a nuisance in the countryside than in a town. This might be the case in respect of industrial or commercial

---

[1] *Maberley v. Peabody and Co.* [1946] 2 All E.R. 192.

[2] *Tipping v. St. Helen's Smelting Co,* (1863) 4 B&S 608.

[3] *West v. Bristol Tramways* [1908] 2 KB 14.

[4] *Smith v. Great Western Rail Co.* (1926) 42 TLR 391.

[5] *Jones v. Llanrwst UDC* [1911] 1 Ch. 393.

[6] *Menx's Brewery Co v. City of London Electric Lighting Co.* [1895] 1 Ch. 287.

[7] *Tipping v. St. Helen's Smelting Co.* (1863) 4 B&S 608 at 616.

activities; but smells from heaps of manure, the crowing of cockerels and other similar everyday country matters are less likely to be considered nuisances in the country than if transported to an urban setting. In addition to taking account of the neighbourhood where events occur, the times at which activities occur may be critical; as also the duration and frequency of alleged acts of nuisance. Noise made regularly at night[1] might be a nuisance, even though similar noise occurring only occasionally and always during the day-time might not be so regarded. In recent years a problem for some who live in the countryside has been the practice of some farmers of harvesting by night as well as day, and of illuminating their fields with powerful lights in order to do so. It is perhaps only the seasonal nature of such nocturnal activity which might prevent a sleep-starved neighbour from claiming nuisance.

A particular example of the "over-sensitive plaintiff" is the plaintiff whose complaint is simply that he cannot use his land for especially sensitive activities because of the actions of the defendant. A fairly recent example of this was a case where a plaintiff failed to show nuisance when the defendant Electricity Board's power lines interfered with his use of his land to relay television signals.[2] The stance of the law here is clearly that it is unreasonable to require defendants to act with such a degree of restraint that no harm is done to such especially sensitive operations; and that it is those who wish to so protect themselves who should either move to reliably "safe" areas or make appropriate agreements with their neighbours, probably involving compensation for their neighbours' agreement to restrict the use they make of their land. If the public interest genuinely requires protection for the activity in question this may be achieved by a local planning authority in its operation of planning controls. That is, by refusing planning permission for activities which would have detrimental effects. Jodrell

---

[1] See eg. *Rushmer v. Polsue and Alfieri Ltd*, [1906] 1 Ch. 234.
[2] *Bridlington Relay Ltd. v. Yorkshire Electricity Board* [1965] Ch 436. See also, *Hollywood Silver Fox Farm Ltd. v. Emmett* [1936] 2 KB 468.

Bank telescope, in Cheshire, has been protected in this way.[1]

Given the significance of the various kinds of factors described above in determining whether in any particular case an actionable nuisance has been committed, it is not possible to state in categorical terms what actions affecting another person's enjoyment of his property will or will not be a nuisance. What may be indicated, however, is that in appropriate circumstances any of a wide variety of kinds of activity may so affect a plaintiff's use and enjoyment of his land as to give him an action. Thus, smoke from bonfires may or may not constitute a nuisance depending on such matters as regularity of lighting, direction of wind, amount of smoke and times of day; and noise from model power boats which is excessive in volume, regularity and duration, may well be a nuisance in a relatively quiet area.[2]

Enough has now been said to have given a general idea of the requirements for a successful action for nuisance. However, a number of further points should be noted. First of all, if the actions of the defendant are such as to constitute a nuisance it is no defence for him to assert that the plaintiff "came to the nuisance": in other words, that the defendant was acting in the manner complained of even **prior** to the plaintiff buying or coming into occupation of his land.[3] An exception to this, however, is that it is possible to acquire a right commit a nuisance by prescription. Thus, if for twenty years a defendant has so conducted himself openly and without objection from former owners or occupiers of the plaintiff's land, the plaintiff will be unable to sue. Secondly, in some circumstances a body acting in accordance with statutory powers or duties may be able to raise the defence that it has "statutory authority" to cause the harm or interference in question. This may arise in various ways. Some statutes expressly exempt a public body from liability in nuisance in respect of the exercise of its statutory functions, though this is unusual; others expressly state that the

---

[1] See *Stringer v. Minister of Housing and Local Government* [1970] 1 WLR 1281.
[2] See *eg. Kennaway v. Thompson* [1980] 3 WLR 361.
[3] See *eg. Fanshaw v. London and Provincial Dairy Co. Ltd.* (1888) 4 TLR 694.

statute shall **not** affect nuisance liability. Often no express mention of nuisance liability is made, and then the approach of the courts is to hold that the statute gives immunity only in respect of actions which are the inevitable consequence of the exercise of the statutory power or duty. So, for example, a statute which expressly authorised the **building** of an oil refinery in a particular area was interpreted as implicitly authorising the **operation** of that refinery, and as giving to the operators immunity from action in nuisance in respect of any harm or inconvenience to neighbouring residents which was the inevitable consequence of building and operating such a refinery. Any harm or inconvenience which could reasonably have been avoided (such as that arising from careless operation) would, however, be actionable.[1]

The rules so far considered, though inevitably imprecise, are nevertheless of some value in laying down standards of neighbourly behaviour. Actual recourse to the courts may be unusual except in the more extreme cases, and is certainly to be avoided wherever possible between persons who must continue to live in close proximity to each other. The real importance of the rules is in the advice that lawyers may give in the early stages of a dispute about allegedly detrimental behaviour. In a genuine case a solicitor's letter may well suffice to restrain the wrongdoer; in a case where the complainant is simply being over-sensitive to the everyday hazards of close-proximity communal living, the solicitor should so advise his client.

Public Nuisance and Statutory Nuisances

The civil wrong of nuisance could not be adequate on its own to secure protection of the environment from smoke, vapours, chemicals, noise and other menaces. What was needed were laws imposing **criminal** penalties rather than just **civil** liability, and for enforcement to be put into the hands of public sector agencies rather than be left to the private initiative of the individual affected. To a limited extent the common law itself achieved each of these things. This is in the law of **public nuisance**, as distinct from that

---

[1] *Allen v. Gulf Oil Refining Ltd*. [1981] AC 1001.

of **private nuisance** which we have considered. Public nuisance is a crime at common law, though it also gives a right to damages to persons especially affected (*i.e.* over and above the harm suffered by members of the public generally); and in addition to proceedings in the criminal courts an action may be brought by the Attorney-General or by a local authority[1] to obtain an injunction to prevent continuance or repetition.

For a nuisance to be **public** rather than just **private** it must be of such a nature as to "materially affect the reasonable comfort and convenience of life of a class of Her Majesty's subjects".[2] By a "class of subjects" is meant a representative cross-section of a neighbourhood. Thus, if one's activities affect only one or a few individuals one may be committing a private nuisance; if they affect local residents more generally one may also be committing a public nuisance. In the latter case criminal sanctions and public authority action may ensue. However, although the common law of private and public nuisance remains of value in appropriate cases, the considerable **imprecision** of the common law of nuisance was a serious inadequacy. The concept of **statutory nuisance** has met this problem in some contexts. The Environmental Protection Act 1990 has, in Part III, consolidated miscellaneous earlier pieces of legislation, and there now exists a single statutory list of the main activities which are declared to constitute statutory nuisances. This list, subject to certain exceptions and limitations, includes:

–smoke, fumes, gases or noise emitted from premises so as to be prejudicial to health or a nuisance;

–dust, steam, smell or other effluvia arising on industrial, trade, or business premises and being prejudicial to health or a nuisance;

–any accumulation or deposit which is prejudicial to health or a nuisance;

---

[1] Local Government Act 1972 s. 222.
[2] *A.G. v. P.Y.A. Quarries Ltd. ex rel. Glamorgan County Council* [1957] 2 QB 169.

–any animal kept in such a place or manner as to be prejudicial to health or a nuisance.

It is the duty of every district council (and London borough) to inspect its area from time to time to detect any statutory nuisances which ought to be dealt with under the prescribed procedures. Where a complaint of a statutory nuisance is made to an authority by a person living within its area, the authority must take such steps as are reasonably practicable to investigate the complaint.

Where such a council is satisfied that a statutory nuisance exists, or is likely to occur, it is required to serve an "abatement notice". This notice may require the abatement of the nuisance, may forbid the occurrence of an anticipated nuisance, and may also forbid any recurrence of such nuisance. It may also require the execution of works, or the taking of necessary steps, to achieve these ends. The notice is served on the person responsible for the nuisance; or if he cannot be found, on the owner of the land in question. The person served may appeal against the notice to the magistrates' court. Failure to comply with the terms of a notice served is a criminal offence, unless reasonable excuse can be shown. In some situations it may be a defence to show that the "best practicable means" were used to prevent, or to counteract the effects of, the nuisance. Until recently the maximum fine which could be imposed following conviction was generally regarded as too low, at any rate in cases where the offence had been committed by an industrial, trade or business concern. The 1990 Act has now increased the maximum penalty in such cases to a fine of £20,000; in other cases the maximum is £2,000. Where offences continue even after conviction, further fines may be imposed in excess of this maximum. Where an abatement notice has not been complied with the local authority may, whether or not it also commences a prosecution, take action itself to abate the nuisance and to execute the notice. Its expenses in so doing can then be recovered from the person responsible for the nuisance. In particularly serious cases the local authority may take proceedings for contravention or non-compliance in the High Court rather than before the magistrates.

The 1990 Act has also extended the operation of a procedure which should be of value to individuals aggrieved by the existence of a statutory nuisance. Such individuals may themselves apply directly to the magistrates for an "abatement order", without involving the local authority. Prior to so doing the individual must give to the alleged "nuisance" written notice of his intention to bring such proceedings; and the notice must specify the matter complained of. Where the magistrates are satisfied that the alleged nuisance exists, or is likely to occur, they may issue an abatement order. In an appropriate case they may also impose an immediate fine. Non-compliance with any order issued is itself a criminal offence, subject to the sort of defences described earlier in respect of local authority abatement notices. Following a conviction the magistrates may order the district council to take appropriate action to do any thing which the convicted person had been obliged to do under the terms of the order. In cases where the individual complainant successfully shows a statutory nuisance existing at the time of his complaint, the magistrates are required to order the defendant to pay to the complainant such expenses as that person has properly incurred.

These various provisions, in their particular contexts, are of much value; however, they were not adequate to deal with the more serious problems of environmental pollution. What was necessary was legislation which would impose more or less precise standards and controls in relation to each of the more important categories of environmental pollution. It is to this legislation that we may now turn our attention.

ATMOSPHERIC POLLUTION

In this section we shall consider pollution by smoke and by chemical vapours, and will also examine the problems raised by "acid rain", motor vehicle exhausts and straw stubble burning.

Smoke

Smoke consists of carbonaceous particles emitted in the process of combustion. It is this form of atmospheric pollution to which the Clean Air Acts of 1956 and 1968 were addressed, and in respect of which their provisions have proved a considerable success. The quantity of smoke emitted into the atmosphere is now much less than a few decades ago, with very beneficial consequences in terms of the health of residents of formerly dark and grimy industrial cities.

Dark Smoke

The Clean Air Act 1956 imposed a prohibition on the emission of dark smoke from any chimney (industrial or domestic);[1] and this was extended by the Clean Air Act 1968 to cover emissions of dark smoke from any industrial or trade premises even though not from a chimney.[2] The 1968 Act accordingly prohibits the emission of dark smoke from fires on open sites so long as they are used for industrial or trade purposes. Therefore, to produce dark smoke from a fire on a demolition site would constitute an offence under this legislation.[3] Certain exceptions to this criminal liability are provided for. So, for example, there are defences which recognise that emission of dark smoke may be unavoidable during the lighting up of a cold furnace; that furnaces may produce dark smoke owing to some malfunction which was not reasonably foreseeable or avoidable; or that unsuitable fuel may have to be used in circumstances where suitable fuel is unavailable.[4] Also, no offence is committed if the emission of dark smoke lasts no longer than such periods as are specified in regulations made by the Secretary of State.[5]

Given the generality of this prohibition on "dark smoke" it is important that this term be understood. Fortunately the matter is very simple. The 1956 Act states that dark smoke

---

[1] Clean Air Act 1956 s. 1.

[2] Clean Air Act 1968 s. 1.

[3] *Sheffield City Council v. A.D.H. Demolition Ltd.* (1983) *Times* 18th June.

[4] 1956 Act s. 1(3).

[5] See eg. the Dark Smoke (Permitted Periods) Regulations 1958 (1958 S.I. No 498).

means smoke which, if compared in the appropriate manner with a chart known as a Ringelmann Chart, would appear to be as dark as or darker than Shade 2 on that chart.[1] Ringelmann charts are pieces of card which when viewed at an appropriate distance appear to show a variety of shades from black to white.

The regulation of dark smoke alone would not, however, have been sufficient to have dealt with the problems of smoke pollution. Accordingly the 1956 Act provided that henceforth new furnaces of any considerable size which are installed should, so far as practicable, be smokeless; and also that such new furnaces be provided with "arrestment plant" to prevent grit and dust particles from being emitted.[2] In each case the requirements of the Act are satisfied provided that the furnace installed complies with plans submitted to, and approved by, the local authority. Moreover, the height of new chimneys is subject to special controls designed to prevent the emissions from the chimney being a nuisance or being prejudicial to health in the neighbourhood.[3] The control here is that of local authority approval of the height of a proposed chimney, together with the requirement of using the chimney in accordance with any conditions imposed. There is a right of appeal to the Minister, against refusal or conditions.

Smoke Control Areas.

As regards **domestic** premises, the most important provisions of the legislation have been those relating to "smoke control areas", or in more common parlance "smokeless zones." The 1956 Act provides that a local authority may make an order declaring all or any of its area to be such.[4] At one time such orders needed ministerial confirmation, but this is no longer the case.[5] Nor, now, is there required to be a local inquiry into objections to a proposed order, though the obligations to advertise proposals and to consider

---

[1] 1956 Act s. 34(2).
[2] 1956 Act ss. 3 and 6; 1968 Act s. 3.
[3] 1968 Act s. 6.
[4] 1956 Act s. 11.
[5] Local Government, Planning and Land Act 1980 Sched. 2.

any objections lodged remain.[1] A smoke control area order comes into effect six months after it has been made. It then becomes an offence to emit smoke from the chimney of any building within the smoke control area, subject to it being a defence to show that the emission of smoke was caused only by the use of "authorised fuel". "Authorised fuels" are those declared to be such by ministerial regulations. These regulations list particular brands of solid fuel produced by particular manufacturers and also gas. Smoke control orders may exempt specified buildings or classes of buildings from their controls, and may exempt specified fireplaces or classes of fireplace. There is also a power given to the Secretary of State to exempt generally any particular kinds of fireplace which are capable of burning unauthorised fuel without producing a substantial quantity of smoke.[2] Numerous such exempting orders have been made.

It may be noted that domestic bonfires are not prohibited in smokeless zones. Any such prohibition will be a matter for local authority bye-laws made under the Local Government Act 1972.

Certain provisions reinforce these smoke control rules. Thus, local authority grants are available to assist with the cost of adapting domestic fireplaces to enable them to burn authorised fuels. This subsidy has been of very great importance to the success of smoke control zones. The cost does not fall entirely on local authorities; they themselves are subsidised in this expense by the central exchequer.[3] Another provision of some importance is that it is an offence to sell by retail any fuel other than authorised fuel for delivery to a building in a smoke control area.[4] Given that dealers in fuel should know the boundaries of smoke control areas and should know what fuels are authorised, this provides a degree of protection to the unwitting householder. A problem has arisen in recent years of the sale of non-

---

[1] 1956 Act Sched. 1, as amended by the Local Government, Planning and Land Act 1980.
[2] 1956 Act s. 12(4).
[3] 1956 Act s. 13.
[4] 1968 Act s. 9.

H

smokeless coal from local shops and garages. The Environmental Protection Act 1990 contains a provision which would permit the Secretary of State to make regulations banning such sales in smoke control areas. This should help further prevent the unwitting use of "illegal" fuel by members of the public.

Chemical Vapours and Gaseous Emissions

Whereas control over smoke pollution is generally a matter for the environmental health officers of local authorities, the functions in relation to the increasing quantities of, often less visible, chemical vapours and gases emitted are conferred on H.M. Inspectorate of Pollution. This body was created in 1987 by an amalgamation of the former industrial Air Pollution Inspectorate, the Hazardous Waste Inspectorate, and the Radioactive Substances Inspectorate. The new inspectorate was established as a body under the superintendence of the Department of the Environment. It is expected shortly to be afforded independent "agency" status.

The principal legislation on chemical vapours was for long the Alkali, etc. Works Regulation Act 1906, supplemented by the Health and Safety at Work etc. Act 1974. There was under these Acts a long list of "scheduled works" and "scheduled processes". Such works and processes were required to be registered annually with the Inspectorate, and were subject to inspection by that body. It was an offence for the owner or person having control over such a work or process to fail to use the "best practicable means" for preventing the emission into the atmosphere from the premises of noxious or offensive gases or substances.[1]

These air pollution control arrangements are to be superseded and strengthened by important new provisions of the Environmental Protection Act 1990. This Act follows the earlier approach of concentrating attention on those industries and processes which have the potential to cause most harm to man and the environment, but goes beyond the

---

[1] 1906 Act s. 2; Health and Safety at Work etc. Act 1974 ss. 5 and 33.

former legislation by introducing a system of Integrated Pollution Control. Under this new approach it will no longer be the case that, in respect of these particular processes, separate laws and controls will apply to their emissions to the air, to land, and into water. Though of value, the former approach suffered a disadvantage that controls which had been exercised to protect one environmental medium had, on occasion, resulted in an increase of harm to another medium, and an increase in the harm to the environment overall. For example, technology has been developed which now enables industry to reduce or make harmless many of its emissions to the atmosphere. A by-product of the technology may, however, be an additional quantity of solid or liquid waste for disposal, usually either by landfill or by discharge into water. It can be the case that the disposal of the by-product of pollution control technology is more problematic than were the originally intended discharges to the atmosphere. What gradually became apparent from this deficiency in the former system of control was the need for an approach to pollution control which sought not only to regulate the production processes of an industry so as to minimise the quantity of harmful solid and liquid waste and gaseous emissions which had to be disposed of; but which also took an overall view of the best way of disposing of such waste.

The 1990 Act is intended to achieve these aims. It should impose the most advanced pollution minimisation and control technology on the industrial processes to which it applies, and is intended to permit the imposition of a control "strategy" in respect of such pollutants as remain in order to achieve disposal in the way which causes least overall damage to the environment (the Best Practicable Environmental Option – BPEO).

To pave the way towards the achievement of these objectives an important step was taken, back in 1987, by the formation of HMIP, bringing together several, formerly separate, inspectorates so as to facilitate, institutionally, the proposed cross-media approach to control. Under the 1990 Act, the Secretary of State has prescribed which particular processes fall within the Integrated Pollution Control (IPC) system. The listed industrial processes cover some 5,000 industrial installations and the system of IPC is to be phased in over a period of time. Starting in April 1991, IPC will have been brought into operation in respect of existing large combustion plants, and also in respect of newly established installations to be covered by IPC. As well as "new" installations and processes, IPC will also operate from this date in respect of substantial modifications to existing plants. Other existing plants which are to be subject to IPC will become so in accordance with a published programme, beginning in April 1992 and being completed in November 1995. This timetable, extending over several years has been necessary in view of the very considerable volume of work which the introduction of IPC has given to the, rather understaffed, Pollution Inspectorate.

From the specified date each installation subject to IPC must have been granted an authorisation from HMIP; and its operations must then be carried on in accordance with the various conditions which will be contained in the particular authorisation. It is in these conditions that lies the heart of pollution control under IPC. Of particular importance is a provision in the Act that in every authorisation there shall, in addition to any express conditions, be implied a condition that the Best Available Techniques Not Entailing Excessive Cost (BATNEEC) be adopted in order to prevent releases into the environment, to minimise such releases as cannot be prevented, and to seek to render harmless such releases. Guidance is being issued by HMIP in relation to a large number of different kinds of process in order to make clear, and to standardise, the extent of the obligation this imposes. The guidance is being worked out in consultation with the industries concerned, although HMIP has been at pains to stress that this should not lead observers to believe that demanding standards will not be set.

The BATNEEC concept incorporates the principle that as control technology develops, so should standards required of industry become more stringent. Such rises in standards will effect new authorizations as the guidance notes are from time to time updated. In relation to existing authorisations there is an obligation on HMIP to keep the conditions under periodic review, with a minimum obligation of a review of each authorisation every five years.

In addition to the express or implied BATNEEC conditions, the Act also provides that conditions can be imposed to ensure compliance locally with any environmental quality objectives (*e.g.* as to the quality locally of water or air), and to allow the UK to ensure compliance with any international environmental obligations. In other words, taken as a whole, the conditions should require "state of the art" technology to minimise harmful emissions from the controlled process, permit a "critical loads" approach to be adopted so as to ensure that the overall level of emissions into a particular environmental medium in a particular area does not exceed that with which the local environment can cope, and allows the central government to require the imposition of emission limits in order to ensure overall UK compliance with internationally agreed obligations (*e.g.* in relation to discharge of CFC's or "greenhouse gases). Taken together with the further obligation in the Act that HMIP should impose conditions which seek to secure the least environmentally damaging means of discharge as between the various environmental media, this new system would seem to establish a satisfactory framework for the exercise of pollution control over the most potentially harmful of industry's activities.

Whether or not the new legislation proves successful in its actual operation will depend on a number of factors. In particular, concern has been expressed as to the adequacy of the resources of HMIP to handle the large amount of work involved in introducing this new system, and thereafter to monitor and take enforcement action against those who fail to comply with obligations. In the past the various inspectorates have sought to foster a good working relationship with industry, taking the view that more can be achieved by education and persuasion than by a vigorous prosecution policy. There are indications that a stricter and more rigorous monitoring and enforcement policy is now intended by HMIP, but this objective may not be achieved unless adequate manpower and other resources are provided. Another matter which may hinder the effective implementation of IPC is the institutional division between HMIP and the body responsible for water pollution matters, the National Rivers Authority. The 1990 Act contains important provisions which permit the NRA to veto any authorisation which may lead to a failure by the NRA to achieve a statutory water quality objective in an area; and the NRA may also require that an authorisation should contain any condition which it considers to be appropriate. These powers of the NRA will require there to be very close consultation and liaison between that body and HMIP. It remains to be seen whether the "water" aspects of IPC will in this way be adequately taken into account. It may be that in due course some amalgamation of HMIP and the NRA will be necessary.

In addition to IPC in relation to the prescribed processes, described above, the 1990 Act also provides for the listing by the Secretary of State of a further range of processes which, in accordance with a phased programme of introduction between April 1991 and April 1992, will become subject to substantially similar authorisation and condition procedures to be exercised, not by HMIP but, by local authorities. The processes so prescribed are ones which it is important should be subject to proper control, but which are not so potentially harmful to the environment as those in the full IPC category. In relation to this second list of processes local authorities have powers of control over discharges to the atmosphere only. In other words, in this context local authority air pollution powers have been extended beyond the "smoke" powers considered earlier in this chapter, and extend to control over gaseous emissions. The nature of the controls are the same as those described above in connection with IPC (involving BATNEEC obligations etc), except that no issues can arise for local authority determination as regards the best practical environmental option for emissions to the various environmental media: in this context, it will be remembered, the powers relate only to the regulation of atmospheric emissions.

Acid Rain

A pollution problem which has come to prominence in recent years is that of "acid rain". Whereas the imposition of obligations to emit gases from tall chimneys has been reasonably successful in alleviating pollution problems for the immediate surrounding population and landscape, it has become apparent that the gases emitted from the chimneys can be carried long distances on the prevailing winds, and can produce adverse environmental effects not only far away within a single country, but can produce a situation where activities in one country may result in environmental harm in another.

The gases which contribute most to the phenomenon called acid rain are sulphur dioxide (SO_2 – produced when coal or oil is burnt) and oxides of nitrogen (NO_x – produced when a wide variety of materials are burnt). The principal sources of emission of these gases to the atmosphere are the burning of fossil fuels at power stations and other large combustion plants, and from motor vehicle exhausts. The emissions travel through the atmosphere eventually being deposited in dry or liquid sulphuric or nitric acid form.

The effects of acid rain may be various. It may result in an increase in the acidity of rivers and lakes, thereby causing harm to fish and other aquatic life. Such effects were first observed in Scandinavia but the problem is now known to be quite widespread, occuring also closer to home in the mountains of Wales and in Scotland. Acidic gases seem also to have adverse effects on the growth and health of trees, they cause corrosive deterioration in the stonework of buildings and in stained-glass windows, they may cause toxic releases from soils resulting in adjacent water pollution, and can have other significant ecological effects by bringing about an increase in plant nutrient levels.

The very nature of this particular pollution problem has required there to have been some concerted international action. From Britain's point of view this has been principally organised through the EC, but in order to seek to bring under control emissions from Eastern Europe (which have caused much damage in W. Germany and Scandinavia) a Convention on Transboundary Air Pollution has also been negotiated through the UN Commission for Europe.

The most significant EC measure on this matter has been an EC Directive of 1988 on emissions from large combustion plants (which produce some 85% of UK SO_2 emissions). This directive requires emission levels of SO_2 to be reduced in Britain by 20% by 1993, 40% in 1998 and 60% in 2003, in each case in comparison with levels in 1980. The achievement of these obligations is to be by a mixture of advanced pollution control technology (in particular by fitting Flue Gas Desulphurisation equipment at power stations), by energy production from sources which do not produce SO_2 (*e.g.* gas), and by promoting the cause of energy efficiency so as to minimise the power requirement within the economy. Difficulties abound nevertheless: the FGD process is costly, especially to retrofit to existing plant; it also requires large quantities of limestone, putting the landscape of some of our most scenic areas at risk, and the process produces large amounts of gypsum which gives rise to further problems of disposal.

The level of NO_x emission is also subject to concerted international action. The UK, along with many other countries of Europe and N. America has undertaken to freeze overall levels of such emissions, from 1994, at 1987 levels. Further, the EC Directive of 1988 requires large combustion plant emissions of NO_x to be reduced progressively, to achieve a 30% reduction by 1998. In addition, in the EC context the problem of NO_x from vehicle emissions has begun to be tackled. Directives require emission levels from new passenger cars to be reduced, from 1993, to a level only achievable by the fitting of catalytic converters. The catalytic converter solution is not, for fuel economy reasons, appropriate to deal with the important NO_x pollution problems of diesel vehicles. It is expected, however, that EC rules will impose increasingly strict emission standards on such vehicles, so to stimulate the development of engine technology to achieve significant emission reductions.

Stubble Burning

The practice of burning stubble on fields following the harvesting of crops, particularly cereals, became widespread in the 1980's and gave rise to a good deal of public concern. This centred on a variety of matters, such as the pollution of the atmosphere resulting from the large quantities of smoke, the danger to drivers of motor vehicles on nearby roads as visibility became reduced, the damage to hedgerows and trees when fires got out of control, and the harm done to flora and fauna. Moreover, objection was also raised to the practice in terms of good husbandry; the argument here being that the traditional practice of ploughing stubble into the soil was preferable in terms of maintaining soil condition and nutrients. The justification generally put forward in favour of burning stubble has been an economic one. It is cheaper in terms of labour costs to burn stubble, and then add artificial fertilisers, than to plough stubble into the soil.

The response of government was, initially, to resist pleas that stubble burning be prohibited, and instead to seek to **regulate** the practice. A set of model bye-laws was published in 1984, and local authorities have been encouraged to make bye-laws in this form.[1] Although there is no obligation on local authorities to make any bye-laws a very large number have done so. The bye-laws do not have to be in accordance with the "model" but, since bye-laws require ministerial approval before they can come into effect, good reasons need to exist to justify any departure.

The model bye-laws apply in terms only to straw and stubble burning after the harvesting of cereal crops. Thus, the bye-laws would not seem to regulate the practice in relation to other crops, such as oil seed rape. When they do apply they impose quite stringent conditions on the practice. They restrict stubble burning to the day time and to week-

---

[1] For the model bye-laws see Home Office Circular 24/84.

days (not Bank Holidays). There must be gaps of at least 150 metres between areas being simultaneously burnt, and there are limits to the size of any individual fires (10 hectares/25 acres). There should also be a firebreak of at least 5 metres width around any area being burnt, and the firebreak should be at least 25 metres wide to protect such things as buildings, hedgerows, trees, haystacks and telegraph poles. Such firebreaks are created by removing straw and ploughing or cultivating the strip. Prior notice of intention to commence burning should be given to the local authority and also to the local fire brigade, and during the whole period that burning is taking place there should be present two responsible persons, at least one of whom is experienced in the burning of straw or stubble. There must also be on hand a specified minimum quantity of water in mobile containers and also at least five implements for use as firebeaters. Finally, ash from the fire must be incorporated into the soil within 36 hours. Heavy rainfall may itself achieve this result; otherwise ploughing or other cultivation will be necessary. The model bye-laws impose criminal penalties for failure to comply with any of the various obligations.

In addition to the existence in many areas of bye-laws in this, or similar, form, the Highways (Amendment) Act 1986 has imposed general criminal liability where the lighting of a fire causes the user of any highway consisting of or comprising a carriageway to be injured, interrupted or endangered by the smoke from the fire (or any fire caused by that fire). It is a defence to such a prosecution for the defendant to show that at the time the fire was lit he was satisfied on reasonable grounds that any such consequence was unlikely, and also that before and after the fire was lit he had done all that he reasonably could to prevent any such consequences.

This policy of regulating rather than prohibiting the practice of stubble burning is likely, however, soon to be superseded by the exercise of stronger controls under the Environmental Protection Act 1990. Under this Act the Minister of Agriculture, Fisheries and Food or the Secretary of State for the Environment may make regulations prohibiting or restricting the burning of crop residues by farmers on agricultural land. It will be noted that the 1990 Act refers to "crop residues", and this term serves to extend controls beyond the ambit of the model byelaws, discussed above, which have been applicable only to straw or stubble burning. Any regulations made under the 1990 Act may also contain exemptions from their general terms; and these exemptions may apply nationally or just to particular areas, may apply to all crop residues or to just certain specified ones, and may apply in all circumstances or just in certain specified situations. Where regulations restrict rather than prohibit activity, the regulations may impose requirements to be complied with both before and after the burning takes place. Where appropriate, in the light of any such regulations, the Minister may repeal any local authority byelaws previously governing the matter.

It is as yet too early to know exactly what use will be made of these wide powers. The White Paper on the Environment, published in the autumn of 1990, has, however, indicated the government's intention to make regulations which will generally prohibit this practice as from 1993.

NOISE POLLUTION

Noise pollution is more a problem of the cities than it is the countryside. Nevertheless, where noise is experienced in rural areas it may be especially offensive, spoiling the tranquility normally to be expected. The main general legislation is Part III of the Control of Pollution Act 1974, though other Acts deal with specific problems.

Noise Nuisances

Reference was made earlier in this chapter to the concept of statutory nuisance, and the procedures associated with the tackling of such nuisances. In this context it should be remembered that "noise" may qualify as a statutory nuisance. Local authorities are therefore under a statutory obligation to inspect their areas from time to time to detect anything which ought to be dealt with as a noise nuisance.

Where such a nuisance is discovered (or, more likely, has been reported to the authority) the procedure involves the service of a noise abatement notice on the person responsible for the nuisance. This notice will prohibit or restrict the noise in question. The person served may appeal against the notice to the Magistrates' Court. In the absence of a successful appeal it is an offence to fail to comply with the notice and proceedings may be taken, by the local authority, in the Magistrates' Court. It is, however, a defence if it can be shown by the defendant that he had used the best practicable means to prevent, or counteract the effect of, the noise.[1] As mentioned in other contexts, this imports a rather uncertain standard into the statutory obligation. Some guidance may, however, be gained from Codes of Practice issued by the Secretary of State and to which the magistrates are required to have regard.[2] Such Codes have been issued in relation to a number of matters, such as ice-cream van chimes, model aircraft noise, noise from open construction sites and from audible intruder alarms.

The 1974 Act also permits proceedings before the magistrates in respect of noise nuisances to be taken by individual aggrieved occupiers.[3] The procedure here is for the magistrates to make an order, any failure to comply with which renders the person to whom it is directed guilty of an offence.

The Environmental Protection Act 1990 has strengthened these provisions by providing that where a noise nuisance emanates from an industrial or commerical source the maximum criminal penalty shall be raised from £2,000 to £20,000. It is expected that central government guidance will be issued to local authorities in order to seek to produce greater consistency between authorities as to what constitutes a nuisance and what action to take.

---

[1] 1974 Act s. 58(5).
[2] 1974 Act s. 72(6).
[3] 1974 Act s. 59.

Noise Abatement Zones

There has, since the 1974 Act, also been power in district councils to create "noise abatement zones";[1] a power not, in fact, very commonly used. An order creating such a zone will specify whether it applies to the whole area of the local authority or just part of it, and will specify to which buildings or class of buildings it applies. If objections are lodged to a council's proposed order, these objections must be considered by the authority prior to finally deciding whether or not to make the order.

What is the consequence of the making of an order establishing a noise abatement zone? The answer is that once such an order has come into effect it becomes an offence for the level of noise from any building to which the order applies to increase unless the written consent of the local authority has been obtained.[2] Once the order has been made the local authority is required to measure the levels of noise emanating from such buildings and to record this information in a "noise level register".[3] Although there is no right of appeal against the making of a noise abatement zone order, there is a right of appeal to the Secretary of State against any entry in the noise level register. There is also a right of appeal to the Secretary of State against a refusal of permission to exceed the registered noise level, or against conditions contained in a consent given.

The creation of a noise abatement zone also gives to the district council power to serve a "noise reduction notice".[4] This may be done where it appears to the local authority that the level of noise emanating from any building to which the noise abatement order applies is not acceptable, and that reduction in that level of noise is practicable at reasonable cost and would afford a public benefit. The notice will be served on the person responsible for the noise and will indicate to what level the noise must be reduced, any steps necessary to achieve that result, and the time by which the

---

[1] 1974 Act s. 63(1).
[2] 1974 Act s. 65.
[3] 1974 Act s. 64.
[4] 1974 Act s. 66.

result must be achieved. This power, therefore, permits local authorities to order reductions in noise level to below that recorded in the noise level register. There is a right of appeal against a noise reduction notice, this time to the magistrates. To contravene such an order without reasonable excuse is an offence, though in proceedings for such an offence it is a defence to show that the "best practicable means" has been used to prevent, or to counteract the effect of, the noise.

The Environment White Paper of 1990 has announced government plans to simplify procedures for the establishment of noise control zones in the hope of encouraging a wider use of these powers.

POLLUTION OF LAND

The defilement of the countryside by the deposit of litter and the disposal of waste materials is a matter with which it is important that the law should deal adequately. There are a variety of culprits. Picnickers discard paper and empty bottles, motorists throw cigarette packets and toffee papers from car windows, farmers leave empty containers and broken machinery in their fields, and industrialists deposit unwanted by-products in unsightly heaps.

Litter

Provisions of the Environmental Protection Act 1990 have recently extended legal controls over the problem of litter. To begin with, the Act extends the scope of the offence of "leaving litter". Under earlier legislation this offence only applied to the leaving of litter on land in the open air and to which the public had free access. The expression "open air" did however extend to covered places which were open to the air on at least one side. The 1990 Act provides that the offence may be committed in such places, but also prohibits the leaving of litter on certain land owned by local authorities, by designated statutory undertakers, by designated educational institutions, by the Crown, and on land within a "litter control area". The substance of the offence consists of the throwing down, or dropping, and then leaving any thing whatever in such circumstances as to cause, or contribute to, the defacement by litter of any such land. No offence is committed in circumstances where the deposit and leaving of the thing in question was authorised by law, or was done with the consent of the owner or occupier of the land.

In relation to this offence the 1990 Act has introduced a new "fixed penalty" system under which authorised local authority officers who have reason to believe the offence has been committed may give to the suspect a notice offering that person the opportunity to discharge any liability to conviction for that offence by payment instead of a penalty. The penalty is £10, but this figure can be raised by the Secretary of State.

In addition to this litter offence the 1990 Act imposes **duties** on various bodies to take steps to keep their property and to keep highways clear of litter, so far at least as is reasonably practicable. The bodies under this obligation are district councils in respect of highways (or the Secretary of State in respect of trunk roads), local authorities generally in respect of their own land, the Crown and certain statutory undertakers and educational institutions in respect of their land, and occupiers of property in litter control areas. In complying with these obligations the body in question is required to have regard to the terms of a Code of Practice issued by the Secretary of State.

Mention has been made above of "litter control areas". The 1990 Act provides that such areas may be designated by district councils in respect of land falling within descriptions prescribed by the Secretary of State. Such orders may only be made in circumstances where the council considers that unless it makes the order the presence of litter is likely to be such as to be prejudicial to the amenity of the area. Once designated the land becomes land in respect of which the basic litter offence will apply, becomes land which the occupier must keep reasonably clear of litter, and also becomes land in respect of which two further new procedures will apply. These are the "litter abatement notice" and the "street litter control notice". The former is a notice served on the owner or occupier of land to which it applies (broadly the categories of land described above in connection with the litter offence and the "clearing litter" obligations) requiring that person or body to comply with the statutory clearing obligations. Failure to comply with the terms of such a notice is an offence triable in the magistrates' court. There are also the usual default powers under which a local authority may itself take steps to clear the litter and recover its expenses from the person or body in default of the notice. "Street litter control notices" are a new device designed to deal with the problem of activities which cause litter on adjacent highways or open land. The most significant instance of this is the litter problem associated with the sale of take-away food. The notice is served by the district council on the occupier of the premises on which the activities causing the litter take place, and will state what is required to be done by the occupier to deal with the problem. The terms of the order are at the discretion of the local authority. They must, however, comply with or fall within certain requirement specified in the 1990 Act itself or in ministerial regulations.

These various provisions do much to strengthen the law in respect of defacement by litter. Their practical effect in alleviating the problem may depend much on the resources to be allocated by the public bodies in question to complying with the obligations imposed directly upon them and to enforcing the compliance of others. In times of expenditure constraint there is a clear danger that the costs involved may result in the legislation not being of great practical effect. With this danger in mind the Act contains an important provision permitting **individuals** aggrieved by the defacement by litter of any land covered by the Act to take proceedings before the magistrates. At least five days prior warning must be given to the person responsible for the land. If the magistrates find for the complainant they will make a litter abatement order and will order the individual's expenses in taking the proceedings be paid by the defendant.

This should prove a valuable procedure by which citizens may prompt performance of duties on the part of public bodies, and may enforce the obligations imposed by the Act on other persons (*e.g.* occupiers of premises in litter control areas).

Abandoned Vehicles

The Refuse Disposal (Amenity) Act 1978 imposes obligations on district councils in respect of abandoned vehicles. Where it appears to such a local authority that a motor vehicle has been abandoned without lawful authority on any land in the open air, the local authority is under a duty to remove the vehicle.[1] The cost of removing such a vehicle is recoverable from the "person responsible."[2] This term covers the person who abandoned the vehicle and also, if it is a different person, the vehicle's owner unless he can show that he was not aware of the abandonment. In addition to the duty to remove and dispose of abandoned vehicles, the 1978 Act also empowers local authorities, if they think fit, to remove other things which have been abandoned.[3]

Waste disposal

Each year industry generates some 100 million tonnes of waste for disposal on land, and a further 20 million tonnes for disposal comes from household waste. Such disposal by landfill accounts for some 90% of waste disposal. Properly managed landfill sites should involve little harm to the environment, or harm, or nuisance (smell, litter etc) to local inhabitants. The reality, however, has been a large number of poorly managed and inadequately inspected sites. The proper operation of landfill is not just a matter of tipping into a hole. It is necessary to ensure an appropriate mix of materials, to ensure that liquid effluent is contained on-site and does not leak onto surrounding land or pollute adjacent water-courses, to monitor the emission and build-up of gases from the site, to seal the site on completion of tipping and

---

[1] 1978 Act s. 3. Such abandonment is an offence under s. 2.
[2] 1978 Act s. 5.
[3] 1978 Act s. 6.

to restore the surface of the site for agricultural or other amenity use.

In the past landfill has been much the cheapest method of disposal of waste. As we shall see the Environmental Protection Act 1990 contains a number of important provisions which are expected to raise quite considerably the cost of landfill disposal. This is deliberate policy, and is intended encourage waste minimisation, waste recycling, and other disposal methods such as incineration.

In the past, local authorities have performed a wide variety of functions in relation to waste. They have been collection authorities, have operated waste disposal sites, and have exercised regulatory controls both under the planning legislation and under the site licensing provisions of the Control of Pollution Act 1974. The combination of these various functions in a single body was much criticised, and the 1990 Act now provides that although local authorities retain their regulatory functions, local authority disposal sites will be operated by new local authority waste disposal companies which will operate at arms-length from the local authority in its regulatory capacity. These new local authority companies will have to compete for disposal contracts for the disposal of waste with the private sector disposal companies, and will be subject to equally strict regulatory controls.

Planning controls, described earlier in chapter 2, apply to the establishment of extension of a waste disposal landfill site. Moreover, local planning authorities are required to produce strategic waste disposal plans estimating the nature and quantity of waste which will need to be disposed of, and the disposal facilities needed to meet this demand. Decisions on individual planning applications to establish or enlarge a site should then be taken in the light of the information in the disposal plan.

In addition to obtaining planning permission it is necessary, as a requirement of the 1990 Act and superseding the system of site licensing under the 1974 Act, for a waste management licence to be obtained. The Act provides that it shall be an offence to deposit, store or transport controlled waste (a term which covers domestic, industrial and commercial waste) in or on any land unless a waste management licence authorising such activity has been obtained and the activity is in accordance with the terms of the licence. Even where a licence has been obtained and has been complied with it is an offence to treat, keep, or dispose of controlled waste in any manner likely to cause harm to the environment or harm to human health. These offences are akin to those which existed under the Control of Pollution Act 1974. The maximum penalties for infringement have however been quite substantially increased, the maximum now being a fine of £20,000. The very significant development in the 1990 Act has been the change from "site" licensing to the licensing of the "management" of the site. This change is intended to deal with a major defect of the earlier legislation which was that site licence decisions related to the appropriateness of a site for particular kinds of waste in a particular location without also focusing on the suitability of the proposed operators to manage such a site. The result was that all too many sites were managed by persons without an adequate level of technical expertise and without an appropriate level of financial resources behind them. The 1990 Act seeks to tackle this problem by its requirement that county waste regulatory authorities should grant licences only to applicants who are "fit and proper persons". A person will fail to meet this requirement if he (or an associate) has been convicted of certain offences, if the management of the site is not to be in the hands of a technically competent person, or if the applicant is unable to arrange adequate financial support to discharge the various obligations arising from the grant of such a licence. Even where the applicant meets these criteria a licence can be refused if rejection is necessary to prevent pollution of the environment, harm to human health, or serious detriment to the amenities of the locality. In considering these last matters the local authority is obliged to consult with the National Rivers Authority.

Waste regulation authorities are required to supervise licensed activities to ensure that harm to the environment, to human health or to amenity does not occur. The authority has power to take any necessary action itself to prevent any such occurrences, and its expenses in so acting may be charged to the licence holder. The liability of the licence holder continues even after the tip is full and has been closed. In other words a duty of after-care exists. It is no longer possible, as was the case before the 1990 Act, for an operator to surrender a licence in order to evade financial responsibilities in rendering the site safe to the environment and to local inhabitants. Under the 1990 Act such responsibility remains with the licensee until such time as the local authority may grant a certificate of completion. This will only be issued when an authority is satisfied that no risk of pollution or harm remains. This is likely to be the case only some considerable time after the closure of the tip. Experience shows that tips which have appeared quite safe for a number of years may suddenly, and inexplicably, begin emitting noxious gases or liquids. The complex chemistry of reactions within landfill tips is as yet not fully understood. Once a waste authority grants a certificate of completion it takes upon itself any further financial responsibility in respect of the site.

The 1990 Act also introduces tighter controls over the handling of waste, from the point of creation through transportation and treatment to the point of its final disposal. A "duty of care" is imposed on all who handle the waste, and the duty applies not only to a persons own actions in respect of the waste but also involves an obligation to ensure that the person to whom the waste is passed is a suitable and competent person. Failure to comply with this duty is a criminal offence. The content of the duty of care is stated in general terms in the legislation and is amplified in a Code of Practice. The Act provides for criminal responsibility not just of the corporate entity involved, but also of the individuals (e.g. the responsible managers) who have been in breach of duty. The spectre of criminal liability attaching to managers of businesses in respect of the waste they produce and dispose of is, it is hoped, one which will encourage close attention to performance of obligations.

In addition to these rules governing the storage, transportation and disposal of controlled waste, further rules apply to other kinds of waste which require particularly careful handling or disposal. This applies to "special" or "hazardous" waste, and also to radio-active waste. These matters do give rise to a good deal of controversy but a full discussion is beyond the scope of this book.

POLLUTION OF INLAND WATERS

We shall consider this subject under three broad headings. First, we shall note a provision which creates a specific statutory nuisance in relation to polluted inland water. Then we shall consider the controls which exist over discharges into sewers; and then finally we shall outline the controls over discharges directly into rivers and streams and other inland waters.

Statutory Nuisances

The important provision here is section 259 of the Public Health Act 1936. We have already noted elsewhere[1] the standard procedures in respect of statutory nuisances under this Act, involving the service by district councils of abatement notices on those responsible, followed by prosecution before the magistrates in the event of failure to comply with such notices. These procedures are made applicable to polluted water by section 259, which provides for the following matters to be statutory nuisances:

-any pond, pool, ditch, gutter or watercourse which is so foul or in such a state as to be prejudicial to health or a nuisance; and

-any part of a watercourse, not being a part ordinarily navigated by vessels employed in the carriage of goods by water, which is so choked or silted up as to obstruct or impede the flow of water and thereby to cause a nuisance, or give rise to conditions prejudicial to health.

In addition to the ordinary powers of district councils to

---

[1] See, above, p. 213.

take action in respect of statutory nuisances, there is also in this context power given to parish or community councils to deal with any such filthy or stagnant water, which is likely to be prejudicial to health, by draining, cleansing, covering or taking other preventive action. In addition to taking action itself, it may contribute to the expenses of any other person in doing such things.[1]

Discharge into Sewers[2]

The law gives to every person the right to cause the drains from his premises to be connected to a public sewer.[3] Controls over the discharges that might be made from drains into sewers and thence, possibly after some degree of purification, into rivers and the sea began with statutes of the nineteenth century. The law is now contained in the Public Health Act 1936, which prohibits the passing of certain dangerous matters into public sewers. The prohibition covers:

(*a*) matter likely to injure the sewer, or to interfere with the free flow of its contents, or to affect prejudicially the treatment and disposal of its contents;

(*b*) chemical refuse, waste steam, or liquid above a certain temperature which, either alone or in combination with the other contents of the sewer, is dangerous or may cause a nuisance or be prejudicial to health;

(*c*) petroleum spirit or carbide of calcium.[4]

This necessary, but rather generally worded provision, was reinforced by legislation the following year: the Public Health (Drainage of Trade Premises) Act 1937. The scheme of the 1937 Act was that prior to discharging any trade effluent into any public sewer the person wishing to do so was required to serve a trade effluent notice on the local

---

[1] 1936 Act s. 260.

[2] See, generally, Garner *The Law of Sewers and Drains* (7th edn., 1991) Shaw and Sons.

[3] Public Health Act 1936 s. 34.

[4] 1936 Act s. 27. "Petroleum Spirit" is widely defined, including for example "any product of petroleum or mixture containing petroleum": s. 27(3).

authority and was required to comply with any conditions which that body might impose on such discharges. In addition to imposing conditions on such discharges, the authority could prohibit the discharge entirely. The 1937 Act has been amended by later legislation, as we shall see, but this basic scheme of control continues to this day.

The trade effluent notice, served now on the sewerage company, is required to state the nature and composition of the effluent, the maximum quantity which it is proposed to discharge on any one day, and the highest rate at which it is proposed to discharge effluent.[1] The conditions imposed on a consent may relate to any of these matters, and also may restrict effluent discharge to particular periods of the day, may require the elimination or diminution of any speci-fied constituent of the effluent before it enters the sewer, where otherwise its treatment would be specially difficult or expensive, and may restrict the temperature of any dis-charge or its acidity or alkalinity. In addition, consent may be conditional on the payment of additional charges, the installation of manholes or meters to ease the making of checks as to the nature, quantity and rates of effluent dis-charge, and the keeping of records and making of returns about such matters.[2] Any such conditions imposed may be varied from time to time. There is a right of appeal to the Director General of Water Services against any refusal of consent or conditions imposed.

In determining whether to grant trade effluent consent, and, if so, what conditions to impose, the sewerage company will take into account the capacity and performance of its sewage treatment works, and the obligations which it is itself required to meet as regards its own discharges from those works.

Discharges into Inland and coastal waters

We are here concerned with the protection from pollution of rivers, streams, estuaries and coastal waters, and also the

---

[1] 1937 Act s. 2(1).
[2] 1937 Act s. 2(3), as extended by the Public Health Act 1961 s. 59.

protection of underground water supplies and of reservoirs. Former legislation has been recently superseded by the Water Act 1989. More recently still, as we have seen, the Environmental Protection Act 1990 has developed controls over scheduled processes (IPC) and over landfill licensing which are to be exercised with regard being paid, amongst other things, to the protection of the aquatic environment.

An important feature of the Water Act 1989 has been the establishment of the National Rivers Authority. This body has a variety of functions, extending beyond that of water pollution control to the stategic management of water resources (an important aspect of this from an environmental point of view is the regulation under a licensing regime of abstraction of water from rivers – some rivers have suffered much in terms of habitat value because of increased levels of water extraction coinciding with recent dry years), flood defence and land drainage, salmon and freshwater fisheries, and in some areas, navigation. Its important nature conservation and recreational obligations have already been referred to in chapter one above.

The establishment of the NRA ended the former unsatisfactory situation under which the water authorities were at one and the same time both engaged in polluting activities (*e.g.* by discharging sewage into rivers and coastal waters) and were the bodies with pollution control responsibilities. These latter functions have now been transferred to the NRA, and this independent national body now monitors and regulates the activities of the new privatised water and sewerage companies as well as other industrial and agricultural concerns.

Under the Water Act 1989 the central government has acquired powers to set statutory water quality objectives in respect of coastal and inland waters, replacing the informally set objectives of the various former water authorities. The standards set will take into account the purpose or purposes for which each area of water is to be used. The NRA is under a statutory duty to exercise its various powers to ensure that these water quality standards are met.

A prime means by which the NRA may seek to comply with this obligation is by its exercise of its discharge consent powers. It is an offence, as it was under earlier legislation, to cause or knowingly permit any poisonous, noxious or polluting matter or any solid waste matter to enter any "controlled water". The expression "controlled water" covers a three mile territorial sea, estuarine waters, rivers and streams, reservoirs lakes and ponds. It also applies to underground water. The offence also applies to discharges by pipe into the sea outside the seaward limits of controlled waters. The offence may also be made applicable to certain other discharges if the NRA has served a prohibition notice in respect of such a discharge.

The very wide terms of this offence are, however, moderated by the provision in the legislation that no offence is committed where the discharge is made under and in accordance with a discharge consent. Such consents are now granted by the NRA, though former licences granted by the water authorities remain in force. The NRA has, however, power to revoke or modify the terms of consents and is for this reason carrying out a national review of discharge consents and of river and estuary water quality. From decisions taken by the NRA in relation to the grant, modification or revocation of such discharge consent a right of appeal lies to the Secretary of State.

In the past there has been much criticism that consents imposed have been insufficiently strict, and of a lack of rigorous enforcement by way of prosecution of those who are found to have breached consents. The NRA has in its brief period of existence given reason to believe that it will be, in its own words, a "tougher and more effective regulator". At the same time the NRA has stressed that it must also be "realistic in its approach and expectations". It has warned that it is pointless to set unrealistic discharge standards, that it should take into account the time and cost involved in introducing pollution control technology to a particular plant, and that prosecution of breaches is best restricted to situations where recurring breaches have occurred evidencing a disregard for the law or a failure to supervise discharges adequately, and situations where a single discharge is one which has given rise to severe pollution or is clearly attributable to culpable mismanagement or neglect.

It is principally by these means that the NRA may seek to ensure that the standards set either nationally or by the EC in relation to water quality are met. Such standards have been much in the news in the last few years, in particular the standards relating to drinking water and to bathing waters. As regards the former, a particular concern in Britain has been the level of nitrates in our drinking water. In some areas the levels have exceeded the maximum permitted levels under the EC Drinking Water Directive. A principal source of the nitrates in water is the leaching of the chemical from agricultural land, and this has been attributed to the increased use of artificial nitrogenous fertilisers in post-war years. In order to try to tackle this problem the Water Act 1989 makes provision for the designation of Nitrate Sensitive Areas in which certain agricultural operations, such as the use of fertilisers, can be brought under control. In such areas farmers can qualify for annual payments if, for example, they switch from arable to low-intensity grassland cultivation. Ten areas were so designated in 1990, and in a further nine areas special arrangements have been made to ensure that farmers can obtain free advice on how to reduce nitrate leaching from their land. The Water Act provides that the Nitrate Sensitive Areas policy may be operated either on a "voluntary" basis under which farmers in an area are simply encouraged by financial inducements voluntarily to enter into binding management agreements about their use or non-use of their land; alternatively, the Act gives the government powers to impose obligations generally on farmers in a designated area, and such obligations may be imposed with or without payment of compensation. Understandably the policy at present is to try to secure an appropriate reduction in nitrate leaching without recourse to the compulsory powers.

POLLUTION OF THE SEA

Only a rather brief summary of this topic is justified in a book on the law of the countryside. However, some discussion is needed because even if the quality of the sea and ocean environment is a little beyond our scope, we **are** concerned with the state of beaches and estuaries, and what is deposited in the sea all too often becomes washed up on land.

The legislation on this matter is largely the implementation into United Kingdom domestic law of obligations which we have agreed to in multilateral treaties with other States; and the importance of concerted international action in this matter need hardly be stressed. In addition to the discussion which follows it may be remembered that we have already considered certain provisions now to be found in the Water Act 1989 which apply to discharges into coastal waters, and by pipeline into the sea beyond the three mile limit.[1]

Oil Pollution

A number of Acts of Parliament seek to deal with the problem of oil pollution. The Prevention of Oil Pollution Act 1971[2] creates certain criminal offences and authorises certain executive action to be taken to deal with oil pollution emergencies. Most important for our purposes is that it is an offence for any oil, or mixture containing oil, to be discharged from land or a vessel into the territorial waters of the United Kingdom or its inland waters which are navigable by sea-going ships.[3] The 1971 Act also makes it an offence to discharge oil, or any mixture containing oil, into any part of the sea (high seas and territorial waters) from a pipeline, or as a result of sea-bed exploration or exploitation operations.[4] It may be noticed that the 1971 Act does not apply to oil pollution from ships beyond the territorial sea limit. Such pollution from ships is controlled by the Mer-

---

[1] See, above, p. 243.
[2] Consolidating earlier legislation dating from 1955.
[3] Prevention of Oil Pollution Act 1971 s. 2.
[4] 1971 Act s. 3.

chant Shipping (Prevention of Oil Pollution) Regulations 1983.[1] In addition to containing rules about oil discharge, these regulations require ships to be surveyed periodically and their construction to conform to certain requirements.

The 1971 Act confers emergency powers on the executive to deal with large scale oil pollution to the coast or territorial waters of the United Kingdom resulting from a shipping accident.[2] The powers are available when the Secretary of State considers them to be "urgently needed", and consist of authority to give directions to persons such as the owner, master or salvor. Such directions might, for example, be that a ship be towed away from a coast before being sunk. Such directions must be complied with, on pain of criminal penalty.[3] If giving directions is likely to prove inadequate the Secretary of State can order the taking of such governmental action as is necessary. Persons suffering damage or expense as a result of such directions or action may in certain situations claim for compensation from the Secretary of State. This is when the directions or action were not reasonably necessary in the circumstances to prevent or reduce oil pollution, or were such that the good done was likely to be disproportionate compared with the damage suffered or loss incurred.[4]

In order that prompt action may be taken to deal with oil spillages a Marine Pollution Control Unit was established in 1979. This has available to it a number of aircraft at very short notice, stocks of dispersant located at some twenty places around the coast of Great Britain, and other special equipment.

In addition to these criminal offences relating to oil pollution there is also legislation designed to ensure that compensation is available to those who suffer damage through oil pollution. Primary liability to compensate is imposed on the shipowner but in appropriate circumstances claims may also be made against the International Oil Pollution Com-

---

[1] S.I. 1983 No 1398. See especially regulations 12 and 13.
[2] 1971 Act s. 12.
[3] 1971 Act s. 14.
[4] 1971 Act s. 13.

pensation Fund, a sort of insurance fund established from contributions from those who import oil. These provisions are contained in the Merchant Shipping (Oil Pollution) Act 1971, and the Merchant Shipping Acts of 1974, 1979 and 1988.

Dumping

So far we have considered the discharge of oil into the sea. The deposit of other substances is governed now by Part II of the Food and Environment Protection Act 1985.[1] This subjects to licensing controls the dumping from vessels of any substances and articles into the sea or under the sea-bed.[2] The provisions apply to British vessels anywhere in the world, and to foreign vessels within the three mile territorial waters. The term "substances and articles" is not further elaborated in the Act and is clearly of broad scope. This has made necessary a long list of operations, involving deposit of substances or articles into the sea, which are exempt from licensing control. These include the deposit by dredgers of water overflow, and the launching of vessels into the sea! The most common activities in respect of which licences are sought include disposal of solid waste dredgings, sewage sludge, liquid industrial waste and sludge, colliery waste and fly ash from power stations. The licensing authority is generally the MAFF. In determining applications for licences regard must be paid to such matters as the "need to protect the marine environment, the living resources it supports and human health", the need to "prevent interference with legitimate uses of the sea", the "practical availability of alternative methods" of dealing with such substances or articles, as well as other matters considered by the licensing authority to be relevant.[3] Licences may be granted subject to such conditions as the licensing authority considers appropriate. Such conditions might, for example, require initial dilution of a substance prior to discharge, or discharge into the wake of the dumping ship to ensure more rapid dispersal, or require the dumping ship to be moving

---

[1] Repealing and replacing the Dumping at Sea Act 1974.
[2] 1985 Act s. 5.
[3] 1985 Act s. 8.

at a minimum speed whilst dumping. In relation to the most toxic kinds of material it may be appropriate to refuse licences for dumping at sea. The disposal of nuclear waste at sea is covered by these licensing requirements, though this practice was discontinued, even as respects low level waste, in 1983 following a trade union ban on handling such materials (Transport and General Workers Union and National Union of Seamen). The dumping of high level nuclear waste at sea was banned by international agreement in 1972.

Against conditions imposed, or against outright refusal of a licence, there is no right of appeal as such; instead the Act provides a right to make representation to an independent committee,[1] though in practice matters are resolved more informally than by this procedure.

Dumping at sea without a licence, and failure to comply with conditions imposed on a licence, are criminal offences.[2] Remedial action may be taken by government to protect the marine environment, the living resources it supports and human health from harm which is threatened as a consequence of dumping either without licence, or otherwise than in accordance with licence conditions. Expenses reasonably incurred in this matter may be recovered from any person convicted of such illegal dumping.[3]

Particular concern exists about the water quality of the North Sea, a more or less enclosed area of water bounded by numerous industrial countries many of which have traditionally regarded the ocean as a cheap and expedient place in which to dump industrial waste products and sewage waste. Awareness that the North Sea is not inexhaustible in its capacity to absorb such products without harmful environmental efffects to marine life, and thence through the food chain possibly to humans, has led to several conferences of North Sea states in order to try to secure a concerted programme of control.

---

[1] 1985 Act s. 8 and Sched 3.
[2] 1985 Act s. 9.
[3] 1985 Act s. 10.

In 1987, the second such conference agreed that steps should be taken to reduce the input of certain particularly dangerous "red list" substances into rivers and estuaries feeding into the North Sea. A reduction of some 50% in such discharges between 1985 and 1995 was agreed. In Great Britain this reduction is to be assisted by the operation of Integrated Pollution Control to the discharges and manufacturing processes of the most potentially dangerous industrial plants, and by the review by the NRA of all discharge consents for discharges to rivers and estuaries.

Further steps were taken at the third conference in 1990. Land-based alternatives are to be found to replace the dumping of industrial waste and sewage sludge at sea. The former is to be stopped by the UK by 1993; the latter by 1999. In addition steps have been taken to discontinue the practice of waste incineration from incinerator vessels in the North Sea, and research is being conducted into how best to reduce the volume of toxic substances which enter the North Sea not by dumping, or from rivers or estuaries, but instead arrive from the atmosphere. In addition stricter controls than over other "red list" substances are to apply to polychlorinated biphenyls (PCBs).

Further discussion of measures to protect the North Sea environment is beyond the scope of a book on "countryside" law. However, it is appropriate to end by noting that these various steps to be taken in relation to the North Sea may themselves cause disposal problems which may have an effect on the countryside. Alternative land-based methods of disposal will have to be found for these bulky or highly toxic substances. This will involve confronting controversial and technically difficult issues of method, location and cost.

PESTS AND PESTICIDES

Laws relating to pests and pesticides need to achieve two principal objectives. They need to ensure that necessary action can be taken to prevent infestations of harmful pests, whilst at the same time regulating the more dangerous methods by which such action may be taken.

Pests

As regards the former matter there are certain rules which are designed to prevent damaging pest populations developing. In appropriate circumstances the owner or occupier who fails to take care to control pests on his land might be liable in nuisance for harm caused to his neighbours.[1] Where the evil is the build-up of certain weed populations action may be taken by the MAFF under the Weeds Act 1959. The weeds subject to this control are spear thistle, creeping or field thistle, curled dock, broad-leaved dock and ragwort. The MAFF can order an occupier of land to take such action as is necessary to prevent the spread of these weeds. Unreasonable failure to comply with a notice served is an offence, and default action may be taken at the expense of the occupier. Similar legislative powers exist in relation to rats and mice. The local authority may serve a notice on a landowner requiring steps to be taken against these animals.[2] If such a notice is not complied with the local authority may enter on to the land and take the necessary action itself. The cost of such default action may then be recovered from the owner of the land. Likewise the Minister of Agriculture, Fisheries and Food may make a rabbit clearance order requiring that a specified area be cleared of these animals.[3] This power was introduced to try to prevent the spread of myxamitosis, but may be used now simply to deal with problems caused by excessive numbers of rabbits in an area. A further statutory provision designed to regulate pest populations is that dealing with the Colorado beetle. For many years there has been an obligation on anyone discovering such a beetle to imprison it and take it to the nearest police station. Failure to comply with these obligations constitutes a criminal offence.[4]

In this context we may also mention a development which has very recently become the subject of legislative regulation. Scientific techniques of genetic modification can now

---

[1] See, above, pp. 209–213.
[2] Prevention of Damage by Pests Act 1948.
[3] Protection of Animals Act 1954.
[4] Destructive Insects Acts 1877–1927, and S.R.&O. 1933 No. 830.

produce new strains of species much more rapidly than by former breeding methods. It is also now possible to transfer genes between non-related species. Many very beneficial developments may flow from research such as this. For example, the technology has been used for the development of valuable pharmaceutical products. It is also being used for the development of better quality plants, to control pests by biological rather than chemical means, and to breakdown waste products by biological means. The possibility of controlling oil spills biologically has even been mooted.

This new technology has, however, given rise to some concern. It is one thing to modify genes in a closed, laboratory, environment. It is another to release the new genetic material into the environment at large. Fears exist that such releases may have detrimental environmental effects. Reminders are given of the effects of the release of rabbits into Australia. Accordingly, the Environmental Protection Act 1990 has established a new system of control over such releases to the environment. The Act requires, except where exemptions apply, that those who are involved in various ways with genetically modified organisms, shall carry out an assessment of risks to the environment that may flow from their activities with that organism. Such persons must also notify the Secretary of State of their intended activities. The Secretary of State may require consent to be obtained prior to them embarking on such notified activities. This may be done either in relation to activities specified generally in regulations, or in relation to particular instances which have been notified. In any case where consent is required it is an offence to act without such consent; or where consent has been granted subject to conditions or limitations, not to comply with such. In addition the Act imposes a general duty on all those involved with GMOs to use the best available techniques not entailing excessive cost (BATNEEC) to keep the organisms under control and to prevent environmental damage. The Act also provides for the appointment of inspectors who will have powers of entry onto premises to ensure the legislation is complied with. They also are given powers to seize organisms and render them harmless in circumstances where there is reason to believe there may be imminent danger to the environment.

Pesticides

Statutory controls over the use of pesticides (and herbicides) are of surprisingly recent introduction, though the possibility of an action for damages at common law has long existed if harm is caused by another person's negligent use of chemicals.[1] For many years, instead of statutory regulation, reliance was placed on a code of Practice agreed between the MAFF and the manufacturers.[2]. These provisions have now been put on a statutory basis by Part III of the Food and Environment Protection Act 1985 and the regulations made thereunder.

The regulations[3] prohibit the advertisement, sale, supply, storage or use of any pesticide unless Ministerial **approval** has been given in relation to that pesticide and a **consent** obtained in relation to that activity. Moreover, any conditions attached to such approval and consent must be complied with.[4] The term "pesticide" is widely defined to include not only pesticides but also substances, preparations and organisms prepared or used for a number of specified purposes, such as protecting plants or wood or other plant products from harmful organisms, regulating the growth of plants, and rendering harmful creatures harmless.[5] In other words, it applies to wood preservatives, weedkillers, insecticides and fungicides. There is, however, an extensive list of kinds of pesticides and substances **not** covered by the regulations. These include substances reguiated by other legislation (such as the Medicines Act 1968 and the Food Act 1984), pesticides used in adhesive pastes, and preparations used as insect repellants by human beings. Ministerial approval of a pesticide may be of various kinds: an "experimental permit" to enable testing and development

---

[1] *Tutton v. A. D. Walker Ltd.* [1985] 3 All ER 757.

[2] The only pesticide legislation was the Farm and Garden Chemicals Act 1967, controlling the labelling of a wide range of chemicals in agricultural use.

[3] The Control of Pesticides Regulations 1986 (S.I. 1986 No. 1510).

[4] Regulation 4.

[5] Regulation 3(1).

to be undertaken in order to provide safety and other data, a "provisional permit" for a stipulated period, or a "full approval" for an unstipulated period. Any approval of a pesticide may, at any time, be revoked or suspended; and any conditions to an approval may be amended. The Government is advised on these matters by an independent committee of scientific experts: the Advisory Committee on Pesticides.

The regulations require not only that a pesticide has been approved but also that consent to its advertisement, sale, supply, storage or use in the particular manner intended has been given. Such consents indicate the "basic conditions" subject to which consent to such activities is given. Schedules to the regulations set out "model" basic conditions in relation to each activity,[1] though these need not all apply to any particular consent, nor are they the only conditions which may be specified.[2] A few examples of "model" conditions will give an idea of their contents. Thus, for example, in relation to advertising consent it may be made a requirement to state in the advertisement the active ingredient of each pesticide mentioned, and any special degree of risk to human beings, creatures, plants or the environment. In relation to sale, supply and storage, conditions may require that these things only be done by, or under the supervision of, a person with a certificate of competence in such duties. As regards the actual use of pesticides the basic conditions include requirements to "take all reasonable precautions to protect the health of human beings, creatures and plants, to safeguard the environment and in particular to avoid pollution of waters", to refrain from unapproved mixing together of approved pesticides, not to use pesticides unless competent in their use (in some cases, such as those who provide commercial pesticide services, this may require a certificate of competence), and requiring employers to give adequate instruction and guidance to those in their employment about the use of such pesticides.

The reasons for these various controls on the use of

---

[1] Schedules 1–4 of the 1986 Regulations.
[2] Regulation 6.

chemicals are several. Chemicals can leach through soils and into watercourses causing harm to river life, they can kill indiscriminately both desirable and undesirable insects, animals and plants, harm may be done to predators of animals killed as the poison is carried along the "food chain", and unless spraying of chemicals is done with care it can easily drift over an unintentionaly wide area. For these reasons the pesticide residues in food, animal feed, and wildlife is monitored by government; as are pesticide residue levels in drinking water.

Appendix A

Members of the public enjoying the countryside should remember that they have not only rights but also duties. In particular, they should always observe the terms of the Countryside Commission's Country Code:

Enjoy the countryside and respect its life and work

Guard against all risk of fire

Fasten all gates

Keep your dogs under close control

Keep to public paths across farmland

Use gates and stiles to cross fences, hedges and walls

Leave livestock, crops and machinery alone

Take your litter home

Help to keep all water clean

Protect wildlife, plants and trees

Take special care on country roads

Make no unnecessary noise.

Appendix B

ORGANISATIONS AND ADDRESSES

Governmental Organisations

BRITISH WATERWAYS BOARD, Melbury House, Melbury Terrace, London NW1 6JX, Tel: 071–725 8005

COUNTRYSIDE COMMISSION, John Dower House, Crescent Place, Cheltenham GL50 3RA, Tel: 0242 521381

CROWN ESTATE COMMISSIONERS, Crown Estate Office, 13–15 Carlton House Terrace, London SW1Y 5AH, Tel: 071–214 6000

DEPARTMENT OF THE ENVIRONMENT, 2 Marsham Street, London SW1P 3EB, Tel: 071–212 3434

ENGLISH HERITAGE, 23–25, Savile Row, London W1X 2HE, Tel: 071–734 6010

FORESTRY COMMISSION, 231 Corstophine Road, Edinburgh EH12 7AT, Tel: 031–334 0303

MINISTRY OF AGRICULTURE, FISHERIES & FOOD, Whitehall Place, London SW1A 2HH, Tel: 071–233 3000

NATIONAL RIVERS AUTHORITY, 30–34, Albert Embankment, London SE1 7TL, Tel: 071–820 0101

NATURE CONSERVANCY COUNCIL, Northminster House, Peterborough PE1 1UA, Tel: 0733 40345

WELSH OFFICE, Cathays Park, Cardiff CF1 3NQ, Tel: 0222 825111

Voluntary Organisations

BRITISH TRUST FOR CONSERVATION VOLUNTEERS, 36 St. Mary's Street, Wallingford, Oxfordshire OX10 0EU, Tel: 0491 39766

BYWAYS AND BRIDLEWAYS TRUST, The Granary, Charlcutt, Calne, Wiltshire SN11 9HL, Tel: 024 974 273

CIVIC TRUST, 17 Carlton House Terrace, London SW1Y 5AW, Tel: 071–930 0914

COUNCIL FOR NATIONAL PARKS, 45 Shelton Street, London WC2H 9HJ, Tel: 071–240 3603

COUNCIL FOR THE PROTECTION OF RURAL ENGLAND, Warwick House, 25 Buckingham Palace Road, London SW1W 0PP, Tel: 071–976 6433

COUNCIL FOR THE PROTECTION OF RURAL WALES, 14 Broad Street, Welshpool, Powys SY21 7JP, Tel: 0938 2525

COUNTRY LANDOWNERS' ASSOCIATION, 16 Belgrave Square, London SW1X 8PQ, Tel: 071–235 0511

CYCLISTS' TOURING CLUB, Cotterell House, 69 Meadrow, Godalming, Surrey GU7 3HS, Tel: 048–68 7217

FAUNA AND FLORA PRESERVATION SOCIETY, 79–83 North Street, Brighton, East Sussex BN1 1ZA, Tel: 0273 820445

FRIENDS OF THE EARTH, 26–28 Underwood Street, London N1 7JQ, Tel: 071–490 1555

GREENPEACE, 30–31 Islington Green, London N1 8XE, Tel: 071–354 5100

LANDSCAPE INSTITUTE 12 Carlton House Terrace, London SW1Y 5AH, Tel: 071–839 4044

MARINE CONSERVATION SOCIETY, 9 Gloucester Road, Ross-on-Wye, Herefordshire HR9 5BU, Tel: 0989 66017

MEN OF THE TREES, Sandy Lane, Crawley Down, Crawley, Sussex, Tel: 0342 712536

NATIONAL FARMERS UNION, Agriculture House, Knightsbridge, London SW1X 7NJ, Tel: 071–235 5077

NATIONAL TRUST FOR PLACES OF HISTORIC INTEREST OR NATURAL BEAUTY, 36 Queen Anne's Gate, London SW1H 0AS, Tel: 071–222 9251

OPEN SPACES SOCIETY, 25A Bell Street, Henley-on-Thames, Oxfordshire RG9 2BA, Tel: 0491 573535

RAMBLERS' ASSOCIATION, 1–5 Wandsworth Road, London SW8 2LJ, Tel: 071–582 6878

ROYAL SOCIETY FOR NATURE CONSERVATION, The Green, Nettleham, Lincoln LN2 2NR, Tel: 0522 752326

ROYAL SOCIETY FOR THE PREVENTION OF CRUELTY TO ANIMALS, The Causeway, Horsham, West Sussex RH12 1HG, Tel: 0403 64181

ROYAL SOCIETY FOR THE PROTECTION OF BIRDS, The Lodge, Sandy, Bedfordshire SG19 2DL, Tel: 0767 80551

WILDLIFE LINK, 45 Shelton Street, London, WC2H 9HJ, Tel: 071–240 9284

WOODLAND TRUST, Autumn Park, Dysart Road, Grantham, Lincolnshire NG31 6LL, Tel: 0476 74297

WORLD WILDLIFE FUND, Panda House, 11–13 Ockford Road, Godalming, Surrey GU7 1QU, Tel: 04868 20551

YOUTH HOSTELS ASSOCIATION, Trevelyan House, St. Stephen's Hill, St. Albans, Herts. AL1 2DY, Tel: 0727 55215

Alphabetical Index

INDEX

A

1993 Supplement

(January 1993)

This supplement seeks to explain, in, it is hoped, a readable form, the more significant developments in countryside law during 1991 and 1992. As such it brings the second edition of the main text up to date in respect of the most important matters. It does not, however, purport to be a comprehensive up-date in respect of all matters of detail.

CHAPTER 1: PROTECTION AND ENJOYMENT OF THE COUNTRYSIDE

i. In terms of changes to the principal legislation considered in the main text of the book, the most significant matter, discussed in some detail below, has been the enactment of the Planning and Compensation Act 1991; an Act which has made a number of important changes to the provisions of the consolidated planning legislation of 1990. In addition to these important new measures much legislation on matters to do with water was consolidated in 1991: provisions from a wide variety of Acts, passed over a number of years, being brought together, but without changes of substance being made, to comprise what is now the Water Industry Act 1991, the Water Resources Act 1991, the Statutory Water Companies Act 1991 and the Land Drainage Act 1991. Note also the passage during 1991 of two Acts of Parliament on the subject of badgers; necessitating, in 1992, a further, consolidating, Badgers Act (below, chapter 6). Parliament has even found time to consolidate the deer legislation in the Deer Act 1992.

ii. Developments on the international and the European Community plane look set to be of increasing significance as regards the rural environment. It remains too early to speculate on the effects on UK countryside law of the Rio Summit of May 1992: the Declaration on Sustainable Development, the framework conventions on climate change and biological diversity, the statement of principles for the sustainable management of forests. First signs of such impact may emerge when the UK produces its national plans for the containment of greenhouse gas emissions, for conserving genetic resources, and for the implementation of the forestry principles (all promised by the end of 1993).

Also on the international plane, there are glimmers at the time of writing of a GATT agreement which may result in further extensification of agricultural production and an increase in the area of set-aside agricultural land.

At EC level a broad-ranging 5th Environmental Action Programme ("Towards Sustainability") has been produced by the Commission (and approved by the EC Council), presenting the EC's programme for action on the environment in the period up until the end of the millennium. A significant feature of the programme is its focus on the need for action to go beyond the further tightening of controls over "point-source" polluters (eg factory sites with their chimneys and outlet pipes) and to look to ways of changing patterns of behaviour throughout society in the direction of sustainability. This will require an imaginative approach to the utilisation of a broad range of legislative and other instruments (eg economic and fiscal devices), as well as further implementation of the policy that environmental considerations should be integrated into all aspects of governmental policy-making.

As an example of such progress in the integration of environmental considerations into "other" EC policies, the UK Government has been keen to point to the agreement reached in May 1992 on reform of that traditional environmental villain, the EC Common Agricultural Policy; involving a commitment that all Member States should operate programmes to encourage environmentally sensitive farming. The "agri-environment action plan" requires States to draw up programmes, inter alia, to encourage reduced chemical inputs, extensification of crop and livestock production, the long-term set-aside of farmland, and the management of land for public

S2

access and recreational purposes. Such plans must be produced by mid 1993 and be approved by the Commission. Also, the revised CAP requires that support for the arable sector be linked to set-aside requirements, and that land which was permanent grassland at the end of 1991 should not be eligible for conversion to supported arable production. Set-aside conditions will involve stricter environmental conditions than hitherto.

Also at EC level the Maastricht Agreement (when ratified) may have significant implications. This wide-ranging revision of the EC constituent treaties will render as one of the EC's various principal objectives "the promotion of sustainable growth respecting the environment". It also provides for the extension of the system of qualified majority, as distinct from unanimous, voting in the Council of Ministers; although, perhaps significantly in our context, the single State veto will remain in respect of fiscal matters, town and country planning, land use measures (except for waste management matters), and measures which significantly affect a State's freedom of choice between the various energy sources. It is generally thought that the majority voting procedures, involving an inability in a single or minority of unwilling States to block measures and an increase in the significance of the pre-environment European Parliament as regards the shape and detail of legislation, will help progress to be made in the general development of EC environmental policy.

A matter which may, possibly, have an adverse affect on the development of EC policy is the attention currently focusing on the notion of "subsidiarity". Immediately following the Danish referendum "No" vote in 1992 there emerged statements from the Commission that it should restrict its attentions to those matters in respect of which it was essential to EC objectives that policy be agreed, and rules made, at EC level. It was even indicated that a trawl would be made through the vast corpus of EC legislation to see which measures could and should be undone, and that environmental law and policy might be one appropriate area for such "set-aside". This suggestion was very quickly denied by the Environment Commissioner, but it may well be that the future of EC environmental policy will, in light of strong feelings about "subsidiarity", be one in which broad targets come to be set at EC level, with Member States being afforded very considerable discretion as to the methods and means by which they seek to achieve those goals. At the same time there is reason to think that better arrangements for monitoring State compliance with EC environmental measures will be developed, and the Maastricht Treaty includes for the first time a power by virtue of which the European Court of Justice may impose a penalty on any State which has been found to be in breach of an EC obligation and has not taken appropriate steps, following such a finding, to comply.

iii. Following concern that (i) the institutional separation between the NRA and HMIP would hinder the attainment of a properly integrated approach to pollution control, and (ii) that the new Waste Regulation Authorities (mostly county councils) might have inadequate expertise and have too local a perspective appropriately to perform their functions, Government announced in July 1992 that a new Environment Agency will be created. It will bring together all the functions of the NRA, of HMIP and the waste regulation functions of local authorities. As such it will provide in a single institution for the performance of the most significance pollution control functions in respect of water, air and land. It is not, however, intended that the Agency should take over local authority air pollution control functions (under the EPA 1990 Part I or the Clean Air Acts). No date has been set for the introduction into Parliament of the necessary legislation.

iv. The Cabinet Committee concerned with the environment is, following revision of the Cabinet Committee structure in 1992, Committee EDE. Its brief is a general one, to "consider questions of environmental policy". The idea of a list of "Green Ministers", ministers within each central department with responsibility for environmental aspects of policy, has been retained. The list may be found, inter alia, as an Appendix in the annual report on progress in implementation of the policies proposed in the September 1990 White Paper: *This Common Inheritance*. Ministers generally have been instructed that papers produced for Cabinet or Cabinet Committees should, wherever appropriate, cover any significant costs or benefits to the environment.

CHAPTER 2: PLANNING

i.   The Planning and Compensation Act 1991 has introduced a number of changes. These may be summarised as follows:

a) It has introduced a statutory presumption that development control decisions "shall be in accordance with the terms of the development plan" unless material considerations indicate otherwise. This will, it is intended, enhance the significance of such plans, making it all the more important (i) that such plans are kept up to date and that local plans cover the whole of the country; and (ii) that those who may wish to develop land and those who may wish to object to future development proposals should (a) monitor proposals for changes to development plans and (b) take such opportunities as exist to comment at draft stage and, if necessary, formally object at a later stage.

b) It has imposed an obligation on district (and borough) councils to produce local plans for the whole of their areas. It is hoped by Government that this process will be substantially complete by the end of 1996. In addition, progress must be made throughout England and Wales to produce county-wide waste local plans and minerals local plans.

County councils are required, in cases where their structure plan has not covered their entire area, to produce plans which do so cover. In addition, a system of self-adoption of plans has been introduced. Plans will not have all to be individually approved by the Secretary of State. Instead, the DOE is in the process of issuing "regional" and "strategic" guidance documents which are to guide the content of structure plans; and there is a call-in power by which the Secretary of State may bring into the Department for his own decision any structure plan about which he has concern.

In preparing development plans local authorities are, by virtue of the 1991 Act, now under a clear statutory obligation to take environmental considerations into account. They must include policies on, inter alia, the conservation of the natural beauty and amenity of the land; the improvement of the physical environment; and traffic management. PPG 12 (1992) recommends that local authorities should carry out an environmental appraisal of plans as they are produced: environmental concerns should be integrated into all planning policies.

c) The 1991 Act has strengthened local authority enforcement powers in respect of breaches of planning control. The main changes are as follows:

– the four-year time limit in respect of enforcement action in respect of operational development now runs from the date at which the operations were "substantially" completed. The rule that no enforcement action might be taken, after a period of four years, in respect of a change of use of any building to use as a dwellinghouse remains. The rule that all other breaches of planning control involving unauthorised change of use could be subject to enforcement action so long as the change had occurred after 1964 has been altered, and a ten-year limitation period introduced. To assist in cases of uncertainty as to the lawfulness or otherwise of an existing use there is introduced a new Certificate of the Lawfulness of Existing Use or Development (CLEUD).

– procedures are introduced to enable planning authorities to obtain information relating to suspected breaches of planning control. The planning authority may serve a "planning contravention notice" where it appears to the authority that there has been a breach of planning control. The notice may require the recipient (owner, occupier or person carrying out operations or using the land) to give such information as may be specified about, amongst other things, any operation carried out on the land, any use of the land, and any matter relating to any conditions subject to which planning permission in respect of the land has been granted. The notice may, again inter alia, require the recipient to state whether or not the land is being used for a specified purpose, or whether any operations specified are or have been carried on on the land, or state when any use or operations began. Failure to provide such information, or the giving of false information, is an offence.

– a new procedure has been introduced for the summary enforcement of breaches of planning conditions: the "breach of condition" notice. This provides an alternative to the procedure by way of the issuance of an enforcement notice. Unlike enforcement notice procedure there is no right of appeal against such a notice to the Secretary of State. Where a breach of condition notice is not complied with a prosecution before the magistrates may follow. At this point a defence may be raised that the defendant took all reasonable steps to comply with the terms of the notice.

– provisions to clarify the circumstances in which a local planning authority may incur an obligation to compensate a person against whom it had issued a stop notice, and thereby to encourage the use of this procedure.

d) The Act provides for new arrangements to be introduced as regards requirements to give publicity to planning applications (beyond mere entry onto the planning register). Formerly this was only *required* in limited circumstances (eg "bad neighbour" development, conservation areas, applications which affected the setting of a listed building). In practice, however, it was very common for planning authorities to notify neighbours and others of planning applications. The DOE announced, in 1992, that for the future some publicity will be required in respect of all applications for planning permission. The form of publicity should, however, vary as between categories or kinds of application. Where an application is subject to Environmental Impact Assessment, involves a departure from the development plan, or affects a right of way it will be necessary for there to be a site notice posted and advertisements placed in locally circulating newspapers. Other applications are divided into major and minor categories. As regards the former the requirement will be newspaper advertisements and whichever is appropriate as between site notice and neighbour notification; for the latter the requirement will involve just neighbour notification or site notice, whichever is appropriate. The distinction between major and minor for this purpose is explained in DOE Circular 15/92.

e) The definition of "development" now specifically includes the "demolition of buildings". However, the matter is not so simple. The new Act has conferred powers on the Secretary of State to direct that the demolition of specified categories of building should *not* be development for which planning permission is required. This power was exercised in July 1992. The direction is of some complexity but has the effect that most acts of demolition not affecting a dwelling-house will not constitute development and so not require planning permission. The matter is complicated further by the fact that the General Development Order 1988 has been amended so that even in respect of buildings which may not be demolished without planning permission it will not be necessary in every case to make a formal application for such permission. Under the GDO there will be a deemed grant of such permission. The proposed demolition must, however, not occur without notification being given to the planning authority. Upon receipt of such notice the planning authority may make an "art 4" direction (which has the effect of removing the deemed permission and requiring a formal application for permission to be made), or may simply impose requirements on the demolition as regards such matters as the method of demolition or the reinstatement of the site. The planning authority has twenty-eight days in which to decide such matters.

f)   The Act has introduced new provisions to provide for and to regulate planning agreement, henceforth to be called "planning obligations". These obligations may be of a positive as well as a negative nature; and they may be entered into by agreement with the local planning authority or by a unilateral undertaking made to the Secretary of State. The latter situation is intended to provide for the situation where a local planning authority has refused planning permission (perhaps following failure to agree planning obligations with the developer) and the developer appeals to the Secretary of State. The Secretary may now allow the appeal on the basis of there being given by the appellant an undertaking which is satisfactory to him. There is no need for the agreement of the local planning authority to be obtained; although the undertaking will be enforceable by that authority should the developer fail to comply with its terms.

ii.   Controls over the siting and design of farm and forestry buildings were tightened in January 1992, as foreshadowed in the main text.

CHAPTER 4: PROTECTION OF SPECIAL AREAS

i.   The Government has announced its intention to give the New Forest the status of a National Park. A consultation paper giving details of its proposals was published in September 1992. Following the Report of the National Parks Review Body (1991) the Government has agreed that all National Park Authorities should become independent bodies; also that the objectives of the Parks should be extended to stress that "enjoyment" should be "quiet enjoyment", suggesting a bias against certain noisy or otherwise intrusive recreational activities.

ii. The Government has approved the setting up of a body (the Sussex Downs Conservation Board) as an institution to promote the active management of an AONB. This may provide a model for the proper monitoring and management of other AONBs.

iii. Planning Policy Guidance Note *The Countryside and the Rural Economy* (PPG7, 1992) restates Governmental policy as regards development in the countryside, and in particular in specially designated areas.

iv. A draft PPG on *Nature Conservation* was issued for discussion in February 1992. This, amongst other things, provides guidance as to the matters to be considered and the tests to be applied by planning authorities considering applications for development in or near protected areas, such as SSSIs. Amendments to the General Development Order 1988 have removed permitted development rights in respect of use of SSSI designated land for purposes of motorsports, clay pigeon shooting and war games; and also require that the local planning authority shall consult the relevant national nature conservation body (eg English Nature) in any case where development is likely to affect or is within two kilometres of an SSSI.

v. Revised schemes have been introduced in respect of the five original Environmentally Sensitive Areas, and the schemes for the second list of sites are under review. The revised schemes pay more regard to the need for positive measures to enhance the particular environmental characteristics of the area. Work is under way to prepare for the designation of a further six areas in England, as well as others in Scotland, Wales and Northern Ireland.

vi. There has been some extension of the Countryside Commission's Countryside Stewardship Scheme (first introduced in 1991). This is similar to the ESA scheme in that it aims to provide financial incentives for environmentally beneficial land management. It is, however, not limited by law to particular areas. It differs from the ESA scheme in that agreements are negotiated ad hoc with landowners rather than reached in accordance with the terms of a scheme set out for the ESA as a whole. In this matter of negotiation the Countryside Commission is expected to measure anticipated environmental benefits against costs. In the first year the scheme was targeted on chalk and limestone grasslands, waterside landscapes, lowland heath, the coast and uplands. In 1992 the scheme was extended to cover historic landscapes and old meadow and pasture. A common feature of agreements reached under the scheme is the opening up of the land for public access and enjoyment.

vii. In July 1992 the Countryside Commission launched the Hedgerow Incentive Scheme, providing aid for improved management of environmentally important hedges. This came in the wake of Government figures that between 1984 and 1990 there had been identified a loss of 52,000 kilometres of old hedgerows (approx 10% of total), only partly compensated for by less environmentally rich new hedgerow planting (approx 26,000 kilometres). No steps have yet been taken, however, to extend the Tree Protection Order scheme to hedgerows.

viii. In addition to the sites designated under the Ramsar Wetlands Convention (1971) and Special Protection Areas designated under the EC Wild Birds Directive (1979), a new species of designated area will arise under the EC Habitats Directive (1992). The aim of this Directive is to help conserve Europe's rarest species of flora and fauna by means of protection of habitat types. As with Ramsar and SPAs the designation and protection device used under UK law is likely principally to be the SSSI.

CHAPTER 6: PROTECTION OF BIRDS, ANIMALS AND PLANTS

i. Following the completion of the second quinquennial review of the 1981 legislation, protection has been extended to a further 14 animals and 73 species of plants (added to Schedules 5 and 8).

ii. The Badgers (Further Protection) Act 1991 has added to

the powers of the criminal court where a dog has been used in or was present at the commission of an offence of taking, injuring, killing or being cruel to a badger under the Act of 1973. Following conviction of the defendant the court may, in addition or instead of any other punishment (i) order the destruction or other disposal of the dog, and (ii) order that the offender be disqualified, for such period as the court thinks fit, from having custody of a dog. Where the dog in question is owned by someone other than the convicted defendant, the owner may appeal to the Crown Court against any disposal or destruction order made.

The Badgers Act 1991 has established certain offences in relation to the interference with badgers' setts (defined as meaning "any structure or place which displays signs indicating current use by a badger"). It becomes an offence for any person to interfere with a badger sett in any of certain defined ways. These comprise: damaging the sett or any part of it; destroying the sett; obstructing access to or any entrance of a sett; causing a dog to enter a sett; and disturbing a badger when it is occupying a sett. It is provided that the defendant must have done one of these things intentionally or reckless as to whether any of the defined consequences ensued. No offence will be committed, however, where the acts in question were the "incidental result of a lawful operation and could not reasonably have been avoided"; or occurred in the kinds of circumstances listed in the 1973 Act and referred to in the main text (eg necessary for the purpose of preventing serious damage to land, crops, poultry etc). In the context of fox-hunting it is expressly provided that a person shall not be guilty of obstructing an entrance to a sett where the act is done for the purpose of hunting foxes with hounds. The exemption only applies where the only action done in respect of the sett is the blocking of entrances and does not involve any digging into the top or the sides of the entrances; moreover the materials used must not be packed hard into the entrances. Further, the materials used for blocking the entrances must consist only of (i) "untainted straw or hay, or leaf-litter, or bracken, or loose soil", or (ii) "a bundle of sticks or faggots, or paper sacks either empty or filled with untainted straw, or hay, or leaf-litter, or bracken, or loose soil". Where materials in category (i) are used the blocking must be on the day of the hunt or after midday on the day before; where of category (ii), the blocking must be on the day of the hunt and the sett must be unblocked again on that same day. The defendant must also have the authority of both the landowner and a recognised Hunt. A further exception for the benefit of hunters is the provision that a person shall not be guilty of an offence by reason of his hounds "marking" a badger sett provided the hounds are withdrawn as soon as reasonably practicable.

It should be noted that the where development authorised by a grant of planning permission will involve disturbance of a badger sett the developer should, in addition to the planning permission, seek a licence from the appropriate Conservancy Council authorising such disturbance. It would seem that such a developer may not rely on the more general "incidental result of a lawful operation and not reasonably avoidable" defence; although the matter is not entirely clear.

The Badgers Act 1992 has now consolidated the provisions of the 1973 and the 1991 Acts.

CHAPTER 7: POLLUTION

i. An interesting example of the principle that in judging whether conduct amounts to a nuisance some regard must be had for the nature of the locality is provided by *Gillingham BC* v *Medway (Chatham) Dock Co. Ltd. (The Times* October 10, 1991). The local authority sought injunctions to restrict movement of the port operator's heavy goods vehicles at night. It was alleged that this traffic was causing a nuisance to the surrounding residential area; and the trial judge, Buckley J, accepted that the surrounding residential neighbourhood was, indeed, experiencing considerable disturbance. It was held, however, that there was in law no nuisance. The decision of the local authority, back in 1983, to grant planning permission for the former naval dockyard to be developed as a commercial port in full awareness that it would operate as such 'around the clock' had changed the character of the neighbourhood for the purpose of the application of the law of nuisance. Although, it remains the case that there can be no planning permission to commit a nuisance, nevertheless the grant of permission might be regarded as having altered the character of the area; and that character was relevant to any decision whether or not particular activity should in that area be regarded as a nuisance.

It should be noted that although in this particular case it was a grant of planning permission which served to alter the character of the area, in other instances the same result may flow from the contents of a local planning authority's development plan.

ii. Regulations were introduced in 1991 to *regulate* the burning of certain crop residues (cereals, field beans and peas harvested dry, linseed and oil seed rape). It remains MAFF policy to introduce a ban on stubble burning to take effect prior to the 1993 harvest. However, there will be crop residues exempt from the ban. These are likely to include such interesting matters as herbage seed, reeds, lavender, hop bines and potato haulms.

iii. The Government has issued directions to ten local authorities to require them to use their powers under the Clean Air Acts to reduce smoke pollution. This action has been prompted by the failure of certain cities to have complied with EC legislation on air quality. The Government also proposes by the end of 1992 to have introduced a ban on sales of unauthorised fuels in smoke control areas; as well as a ban on high sulphur solid fuel for domestic use anywhere in the United Kingdom.

iv. Progress is being made in the introduction and implementation of the various pollution control provisions of the Environmental Protection Act 1990 referred to in the main text. The system of local authority air pollution control (LAAPC) should be fully introduced for all Part B processes (new and old) by 1993; and various sectors have been brought within the system of Integrated Pollution Control.

The Duty of Care in the Management of Waste was brought into force on April 1, 1991; supplemented by a fifty-page Code of Practice offering practical guidance to those subject to the duty (those who import, produce, carry, store, treat, or dispose of waste; and waste brokers).

The new waste management licensing provisions are to be introduced as of April 1993.

v. The NRA produced statistics in December 1990 which the Government like to describe as depicting a "slight net deterioration" in river quality in the period 1985-1990; but which critics describe rather differently. The NRA has explained that the chief river pollution problems to be tackled relate now not so much to industrial pollution sources but rather to pollution from agricultural operations. These consist of diffuse pollution (eg pesticides, phosphates, nitrates) and farm accidents (eg overflow or leakage of silage effluent).

It is expected that, after much discussion, the process of introducing statutory water quality objectives will begin in 1993.

S15